ROMANTICISM IN PERSPECTIVE:
TEXTS, CULTURES, HISTORIES

General Editors:
Marilyn Gaull, *Professor of English,*
Temple University/New York University
Stephen Prickett, *Regius Professor of English Language and Literature,*
University of Glasgow

This series aims to offer a fresh assessment of Romanticism by looking at it from a wide variety of perspectives. Both comparative and interdisciplinary, it will bring together cognate themes from architecture, art history, landscape gardening, linguistics, literature, philosophy, politics, science, social and political history and theology to deal with original, contentious or as yet unexplored aspects of Romanticism as a Europe-wide phenomenon.

Titles include

Richard Cronin (*editor*)
1798: THE YEAR OF THE *LYRICAL BALLADS*

Péter Dávidházi
THE ROMANTIC CULT OF SHAKESPEARE: Literary
Reception in Anthropological Perspective

David Jasper
THE SACRED AND SECULAR CANON IN ROMANTICISM
Preserving the Sacred Truths

Malcolm Kelsall
JEFFERSON AND THE ICONOGRAPHY OF ROMANTICISM
Folk, Land, Culture and the Romantic Nation

Andrew McCann
CULTURAL POLITICS IN THE 1790s: Literature, Radicalism
and the Public Sphere

Ashton Nichols
THE REVOLUTIONARY 'I': Wordsworth and the Politics of
Self-Presentation

Jeffrey C. Robinson
RECEPTION AND POETICS IN KEATS: 'My Ended Poet'

Anya Taylor
BACCHUS IN ROMANTIC ENGLAND: Writers and Drink,
1780–1830

Michael Wiley
ROMANTIC GEOGRAPHY: Wordsworth and
Anglo-European Spaces

Eric Wilson
EMERSON'S SUBLIME SCIENCE

Romanticism in Perspective
Series Standing Order ISBN 0–333–71490–3
(*outside North America only*)

You can receive future titles in this series as they are published by placing a standing order.
Please contact your bookseller or, in case of difficulty, write to us at the address below with
your name and address, the title of the series and the ISBN quoted above.

Customer Services Department, Macmillan Distribution Ltd
Houndmills, Basingstoke, Hampshire RG21 6XS, England

Emerson's Sublime Science

Eric Wilson

Assistant Professor of English
Wake Forest University

First published in Great Britain 1999 by
MACMILLAN PRESS LTD
Houndmills, Basingstoke, Hampshire RG21 6XS and London
Companies and representatives throughout the world

A catalogue record for this book is available from the British Library.

ISBN 0–333–71892–5

 First published in the United States of America 1999 by
ST. MARTIN'S PRESS, INC.,
Scholarly and Reference Division,
175 Fifth Avenue, New York, N.Y. 10010

ISBN 0–312–21775–7

Library of Congress Cataloging-in-Publication Data
Wilson, Eric, 1967–
Emerson's sublime science / Eric Wilson.
p. cm. — (Romanticism in perspective : texts, cultures,
histories)
Includes bibliographical references and index.
ISBN 0–312–21775–7
1. Emerson, Ralph Waldo, 1803–1882—Knowledge—Science.
2. Literature and science—United States—History—19th century.
3. Sublime, The, in literature. 4. Romanticism—United States.
5. Electromagnetism. I. Title. II. Series.
PS1642.S3W55 1998
814'.3—dc21   98–28416
                                                      CIP

This book is printed on paper suitable for recycling and made from fully managed and
sustained forest sources.

10   9   8   7   6   5   4   3   2   1
08   07   06   05   04   03   02   01   00   99

Printed and bound in Great Britain by
Antony Rowe Ltd, Chippenham, Wiltshire

To Sandi Hamilton
To her may all things live, from pole to pole,
Their life the eddying of her living soul!

Contents

Acknowledgments

Many people have helped to make this project possible over the last several years. Several mentors at the Graduate Center of the City University of New York were generous in their support and helpful in their comments. Joan Richardson, the director of my dissertation, was my enthusiastic guide throughout the entire writing process, from beginning to end; her generous character and insightful advice consistently energized the manuscript. Joseph Wittreich, William Kelly, and Angus Fletcher were always there to offer encouragement, support, and expertise at crucial stages during the composing process and throughout my years as a graduate student.

Other mentors inspired the book in profound ways. My conversations with James Hans and Philip Kuberski over the years have widened and deepened my sense of poetry, language, and thought. Allen Mandelbaum, who kindly agreed to look at my manuscript, provided more helpful advice in an hour than many could in a lifetime. Likewise, I have received kind support from one of the most powerful Emerson scholars of our age, Robert D. Richardson, Jr.

I am also indebted to several friends and colleagues whose critical acumen and intellectual goodwill have buoyed me again and again. Philip Arnold, Ken Cooper, and Terry Price have been my interlocutors since I began to take literature seriously; they have influenced this study in myriad ways. Granville Ganter helped me more than he'll ever know by perceptively reading the manuscript at a critical stage. Over the last three years, I have had many fruitful talks about Emerson with Ralph Black. I am also appreciative of my former colleagues at St John's University, especially Greg Maertz, whose critical insight helped the book considerably in its final stage, and Steve Sicari, whose benevolent presence and intelligent conversation always leave me with a new, exhilarating thought.

I offer special thanks to Marilyn Gaull, the co-general editor of the Romanticism in Perspective series. She has enthusiastically encouraged me from the time that we met, giving a young scholar the opportunities and the confidence he needs to push his first book through to completion.

Special appreciation goes to my parents, Glenn and Linda Wilson, without whose support I would never have accomplished anything.

I would also like to thank Bill and Helen Hamilton for their generous help.

Most importantly, I would like to extend my utmost gratitude to Sandi Hamilton, to whom this book is dedicated. She is the light toward which my words constantly turn.

Finally, I would like to thank the scholarly journals that published early versions of chapters in this book. Parts of Chapter 6 were originally published in the *American Transcendentalist Quarterly,* vol. 10, no. 1, March 1996; it is reprinted by permission of the University of Rhode Island. The bulk of Chapter 3 was first published in the *Emerson Society Quarterly,* vol. 42, no. 2, 1996; it is reprinted by permission of the Regents of Washington State University. A substantial section of Chapter 5 originally appeared in *Style,* vol. 31, no. 1, 1997. I very much appreciate each of these journals for publishing my work.

Abbreviations

CC   Samuel Taylor Coleridge, *The Collected Works of Samuel Taylor Coleridge*, gen. ed. Kathleen Coburn, 14 vols to date (Princeton, NJ: Princeton University Press, 1969–00).

CD   Humphry Davy, *The Collected Works of Sir Humphry Davy*, ed. John Davy, 9 vols (London: Smith, 1839–40).

CEC   Ralph Waldo Emerson, *The Correspondence of Emerson and Carlyle*, ed. Joseph Slater (New York: Columbia University Press, 1964).

CW   Ralph Waldo Emerson, *The Collected Works of Ralph Waldo Emerson*, 5 vols to date, eds Robert Spiller, Joseph Slater, et al. (Cambridge, Mass. and London: Belknap Press of Harvard University Press, 1971–00).

EL   Ralph Waldo Emerson, *The Early Lectures of Ralph Waldo Emerson*, 3 vols, eds Stephen E. Whicher, Robert E. Spiller, and Wallace E. Williams (Cambridge, Mass.: Harvard University Press, 1959–72).

ER   Michael Faraday, *Experimental Researches in Electricity*, in *Great Books of the Western World*, eds Robert Maynard Hutchins et al. (Chicago: Encyclopedia Britannica, 1952).

JMN   Ralph Waldo Emerson, *The Journals and Miscellaneous Notebooks of Ralph Waldo Emerson*, 16 vols, eds William H. Gilman and Ralph H. Orth et al. (Cambridge, Mass. and London: Belknap Press of Harvard University Press, 1960–82).

L   Ralph Waldo Emerson, *The Letters of Ralph Waldo Emerson*, 6 vols, ed. Ralph Rusk (New York: Columbia University Press, 1939).

N   Ralph Waldo Emerson, *Nature: A Facsimile of the First Edition*, intro. Jaroslav Pelikan (Boston: Beacon Press, 1985).

S   Ralph Waldo Emerson, *The Complete Sermons of Ralph Waldo Emerson*, eds Albert J. Von Frank, Teresa Toulouse, Andrew Delbanco, Ronald A. Bosco, and Wesley T. Mott, 4 vols (Columbia: University of Missouri Press, 1989–92).

TN   Ralph Waldo Emerson, *The Topical Notebooks of Ralph Waldo Emerson*, chief ed. Ralph H. Orth, 3 vols (Columbia and London: University of Missouri Press, 1990).

W   Ralph Waldo Emerson, *The Complete Works of Ralph Waldo Emerson*, 12 vols, ed. Edward Waldo Emerson (Boston: Houghton Mifflin, 1903–4).

Introduction: Poetry Realized in Nature

Ralph Waldo Emerson ascended the pulpit of Boston's Second Church on 9 September 1832 to deliver his last sermon as pastor. His theme was the Lord's Supper, a rite he no longer felt compelled to administer. He explained to his congregation that he must resign his office, for he could not continue to offer an ordinance that he found not only unsanctioned by scripture but also spiritually dead. This day, this sermon, proved the turning point of Emerson's young life. On this autumn Sunday, he broke from the forms of the church. Henceforth, he was no longer the kindly parochial pastor, but the cosmopolitan minister of terrible simplicity, preaching the laws of nature, in his words dispensing nature's perpetual force.

'The Lord's Supper', the title of that day's sermon, was until recently the only Emerson sermon to find its way into print. His son Edward reports in the 1904 edition of Emerson's works that his father did not want his sermons to be published. The Emerson family, however, saw fit to print this sermon, as '[a] record of a turning-point in his life', showing 'at once his thought and his character' (W 11: 547). Indeed, in this text we find the seeds of the ideas that would blossom four years later into the exuberant landscape of *Nature*.

Emerson struggled mightily with this monumental decision to resign his pastorship. In leaving the ministry, he would not only be renouncing the profession of his father but disappointing severely his beloved Aunt Mary Moody as well as his loyal congregation. In July of 1832, he had withdrawn into the White Mountains of New Hampshire to meditate on his decision. From there he wrote his Aunt Mary that he was 'not prepared to eat or drink religiously' (L 1: 354). However, as Emerson's recent biographer Robert D. Richardson, Jr. claims, he did not leave the church merely because of his dissatisfaction with Communion. For spiritual and intellectual reasons, he had already been pondering a separation from formal religion. His break with the church, Richardson correctly observes,

1

did not betoken a loss of faith; it signified too much.[1] Emerson found the dogmas and rituals of the church narrow, suffocating; his faith was wide, expansive as the White Mountains from which he contemplated his break. The God he believed in inhabited not old buildings. He lived in the fields of nature. He was best studied not by the preacher but by the scientist. Emerson left the pulpit so he could practice true religion.

Emerson primarily objected to Communion on the ground that it was a form without life. Supernumerary to moral growth, it had become a mere habit of belief and potentially dangerous to salvation if overemphasized. While '[f]orms are as essential as bodies', Emerson warns in his sermon that 'to exalt particular forms, to adhere to one form a moment after it is outgrown, is unreasonable, and it is alien to the spirit of Christ' (W 11: 20). Obedience to such an outmoded form is self-imposed slavery: 'Freedom', Emerson proclaims, 'is the essence of this faith. It has for its object simply to make men good and wise. Its institutions should be as flexible as the wants of men. That form out of which the life and suitableness have departed should be as worthless in its eyes as dead leaves that are falling around us' (W 11: 21).

Emerson feared that Communion and by extension church dogmas bind Christians to fabricated, inflexible forms. Jesus taught not that we should carve our souls to fit the Procrustean beds of set forms but that we should 'seek our well-being in the formation of the soul' (W 11: 22). Forms that do not grow organically from the soul, that are not elastic enough to change as nature does, are mere shadows, worthless ciphers. In the 'eye of God there is no other measure of the nature of any one form than the measure of its use' (W 11: 23).

For Emerson, ecclesiastical forms correspond to Coleridge's idea of mechanical form, a rigid structure that results 'when on any given material we impress a predetermined form, not necessarily arising out of the properties of the material' (CC 5.1: 495). In contrast, the 'formation of the soul', the proper spiritual life for Emerson, is an organic form: 'it is innate, it shapes, as it developes, itself from within, and the fullness of its developement is one & the same with the perfection of its outward form, such as the life is, such is the Form' (495).

Emerson had been assiduously reading Coleridge between his marriage to Ellen Tucker in 1829 (she would tragically die in 1832) and his resignation three years later. James Marsh's popular 1829

American edition of Coleridge's *Aids to Reflection* (1825) taught Emerson that the forms of organisms are evolved from an 'invisible central Power', an 'unseen Agency' that 'weaves its magic Eddies' through plants, animals, humans, animating and metamorphosing them. It is the 'germinal Power of the Plant' that 'transmutes the fixed air and the elementary Base of Water into Grass or Leaves, and on these the Organic Principle in the Ox or Elephant exercises an Alchemy still more stupendous'. The matter we perceive is 'the translucence of invisible Energy' (CC 9: 398). These claims, Coleridge emphasizes, 'are not fancies, conjectures, or even hypotheses, but facts'. He could sanction this confidence with the electrochemistry of his friend Humphry Davy and the electromagnetism of the Danish scientist H. C. Oersted. Their experiments, as well as those of other scientists, had recently revealed 'the dynamic spirit of the physical sciences,' showing that the 'particles' that constitute the 'visibility of an organic structure are constantly in flux'. Organic forms are like 'columns of blue smoke' or a 'steadfast-seeming cloud' in a driving air current – they are evolving patterns of spirit (398).[2]

Emerson also gathered from *Aids* that the mind is comprised of two faculties, the Reason and the Understanding. (While Coleridge did not render these words, borrowed, as everyone knows, from Immanuel Kant, with capital letters in *Aids,* Emerson did persistently; therefore, I shall write the words with capitals throughout this study.) The Reason is 'the speculative or scientific power... the nous or mens of the ancients'; Understanding, its attendant power, is the discursive power, for proving and analyzing the insights of Reason (CC 9: 223–4). Coleridge stresses that 'there can be no contrariety between the revelation [of Reason] and the understanding' (395). The intuitions of the Reason, in other words, are proven by physical phenomena. The Reason comprehends the invisible spirit underlying organisms; the Understanding relates the spirit to the processes and functions of the organisms. Reason is the ground of all truth; as Marsh glosses Reason in his preface to *Aids*: 'The first principles, the ultimate grounds of [philosophy, morals, and religion] must be sought in the laws of our own being or they are not found at all'.[3] The Understanding, the empirical faculty, finds evidence for these intuited primary principles.

Coleridge's statements on form and on the nature of the mind only exacerbated Emerson's trouble with Communion and the church, arousing the young American's faith in his own intuitions.

Church forms, Emerson thought, are overly mechanical; the formation of the soul, an organic process. Likewise, Coleridge's remarks on Reason must have inspired Emerson's most emphatic objection to Communion: it did not seem suitable to him: 'It is my own objection. This mode of commemorating Christ is not suitable to me. That is reason enough why I should abandon it' (W 11: 19). This confidence comes from his faith in Reason, his trust that his ownmost thoughts are true, ready to be proven by the Understanding.

Emerson's budding interest in the forms of nature, his nascent curiosity in the powers of the individual mind: these energized his resignation from the church. Coleridge's theories of organic form and the intuitive mind offered synthesizing visions the church lacked. While the church could impose forms on the body, it could not stimulate the spirit. While it could ground dogmas on the authority of scripture, it could not generate fresh ideas on the relationship between mind and matter, human and nature.

Science, on the other hand, as described by Coleridge, was synthesis. It attended to mergings of body and spirit. It honored the visions of the Reason, but not without proving them with the evidence compiled by the Understanding. Science as Coleridge rendered it was poetic, uncovering relations between vision and logic, subject and object, mind and matter, energy and form. Coleridge's famed method, described in *The Friend* (1818) (also read by the young Emerson) could be used by scientist and poet alike, both of whom should study organisms not only for their own sake but also to find their relation to each other and to man. It is

> natural to the mind which has become accustomed to contemplate not *things* only, or for their own sake, but likewise and chiefly the *relations* of things, either their relation to each other, or to the observer, or to the state and apprehension of the hearers. To enumerate and analyze these relations, with the conditions under which they are discoverable, is to teach the science of Method.   (CC 4.1: 451).

In this science of method, Emerson discovered a way to interweave his most heart-felt concerns. He could unify revelation and nature, life and form, insight and expression. He could be both naturalist and poet, scientist and preacher. It was this method that metamorphosed him from a writer of sermons to the author of *Nature*.

Emerson followed his break with the Church in 1832 by leaving for Europe some two months later, on Christmas Day, to begin a pilgrimage to the great writers and scientists of his day, including Coleridge. This trip, almost a year in length, was decisive in his move from the quiet life of a preacher to the agitated one of an essayist. He drew poetic inspiration (not, ironically, from Coleridge, or Wordsworth) from conversations with Thomas Carlyle in Scotland and experienced the beauty of science while looking through the achromatic microscope of Giovanni Battista Amici in Florence.

Poetics and science merged powerfully for him while he strolled through the Jardin des Plantes in Paris. There he was fascinated by the cabinets of botanical and zoological specimens classified according to internal function by A. L. Jussieu and G. L. Cuvier, among others. He saw that nature was a book whose form and content are inseparable, outward form a pattern of inward energy. Like Goethe beholding in the gardens of Palermo the *Urpflanze*, the primal botanical form, Emerson stood awed before the specimens. His revelation was at hand.

> The Universe is a more amazing puzzle than ever as you glance along this bewildering series of animated forms, – the hazy butterflies, the carved shells, the birds, beasts, fishes, insects, snakes, – & the upheaving principle of life everywhere incipient in the very rock aping organized forms. Not a form so grotesque, so savage, nor so beautiful but is an expression of some property inherent in the observer, – an occult relation between the very scorpions and man. I feel the centipede in me – cayman, carp, eagle, & fox. I am moved by strange sympathies, I say continually, 'I will be a naturalist'. (JMN 4: 199–200)[4]

Emerson had been prepared for such an epiphany ever since that momentous fall Sunday in Boston. It, contextualized by Coleridge's work, was a catalyst for his sublime science, his merging of intuitive vision, empirical science, and poetry. It was the scientific revelation out of which his *Nature* grew.

This experience in the Jardin instructs readers of Emerson to take his interests in science seriously. His vow to be a naturalist was not idle. Upon his return from Europe, he immediately began to attend assiduously to the emerging sciences of his day and to lecture on scientific subjects. His attention to science, energized by his other reading in the great hermetic thinkers (Bruno, Boehme,

Swedenborg) and in Romantic writers (Goethe and Coleridge), constituted his literary apprenticeship. It became a primary inspiration for his *Nature*, which is grounded – in spite of its metaphysical tendencies – on very specific scientific information. In *Nature*, terms like 'currents', 'spirit', 'life', 'nature' are not simply adrift in a speculative realm. Rather, they are moored to the palpable by recent scientific discovery. Emerson, like Goethe and Coleridge before him, was not content to leave poetry separate from science: he wished for a universal science that married the many to one, matter to mind, fact to poetry. He wanted to be a Romantic scientist.

ARCHAEOLOGY OF ELECTRICITY

Romantics like Goethe, Coleridge, and Emerson thrilled in harvesting disparity into unity, the many into the one. Division, atomization, alienation: all were conditions of the Romantic hell, the universe of death. Shoring fragments against their ruin, the poets, philosophers, scientists of the Romantic age dreamed of a universal science that would reveal a force binding the most diffuse phenomena, gathering the specimens of the biologist, the elements of the chemist, the thinker's arguments, the tropes of the writer. Bifurcations of mind and matter, words and things, poetry and science were to the Romantic unnatural severings destined to dissolve the cosmos into its former chaos. Redemption lay in the demiurgic activity of forging chaotic energy into dynamic forms, the transformation of the facts of science into the figures of poetry.

Emerson himself memorably depicts the dangers of extreme atomization some four years after his Paris epiphany in 'The American Scholar' (1837):

The old fable covers a doctrine ever new and sublime; that there is One Man, – present to all particular men only partially, or through one faculty; and that you must take the whole society to find the whole man. Man is not a farmer, or a professor, or an engineer, but he is all. Man is priest, and scholar, and statesman, and producer, and soldier. In the *divided* or social state, these functions are parcelled out to individuals, each of whom aims to do his stint of the joint work, whilst each other performs his. The fable implies, that the individual, to possess himself, must sometimes return from his labor to embrace all other laborers. But unfortunately, this original unit, this fountain of power, has been so distributed to multitudes, has been so minutely subdivided and peddled out, that it is spilled into drops, and cannot be gathered. The state of society is one in which the members have suffered amputation from the trunk, and strut about so many walking monsters, – a good finger, a neck, a stomach, an elbow, but never a man.   (CW 1: 53)

The American Scholar works to remedy this atomization by becoming '*Man Thinking*', a student of nature, past, present, and future, whose interdisciplinary researches transform him into the ideal teacher detailed in the 'Divinity School Address' (1838), one who 'shall see the world to be a mirror of the soul; shall see the identity of the law of gravitation with the purity of the heart; and shall show that the Ought, that Duty, is one thing with Science, with Beauty, and with Joy' (CW 1: 93).

Many of Emerson's Romantic predecessors in Europe aspired to become this ideal teacher, to discover the identity of the 'law of gravitation' (a scientific issue) with the 'purity of heart' (a concern of poetry, philosophy, religion). Both Romantic poet – a Goethe, a Coleridge, a Wordsworth – and Romantic scientist – a Humboldt, an Oersted, a Davy, a Faraday – chose for their main region and haunt the laws of nature, which included not only the behaviors of stars, forces, lightning, and plants, but also the relationships between mind and matter, human and nature, words and things. Romantic poetry, with its heightened attention to detail, its passion for truth, its reliance on energy, constituted a science; Romantic science, in its efforts to find the source of life, in its translations of natural fact into moral imperative, proved poetic. Coleridge, writing of the 'charm of chemistry', offers the definitive account of this correspondence:

It is the sense of a principle of connection given by the mind, and sanctioned by the correspondency of nature. Hence the strong hold which in all ages chemistry has had on the imagination. If in SHAKESPEARE we find nature idealized into poetry, through the creative power of a profound yet observant meditation, so through the meditative observation of a DAVY, a WOLLASTON, or a HATCHETT...we find poetry, as it were, substantiated and realized in nature: yea, nature itself disclosed to us...as at once to poet and the poem.   (CC 4.1: 471)

Goethe, in his authority as a Shakespeare and Davy, perhaps the only major poet actually to contribute successfully to the history of science, forges this relationship as well: 'They [the critics of his botanical work] forgot that science arose from poetry, and did not see that when times change the two can meet again on a higher level as friends'.[5]

In conducting the invisible, ubiquitous forces of nature into texts meant to reveal the grandeur of the cosmos, Romantic poets inaugurated a revival of the universal science dreamed of by the hermetic alchemists of the Renaissance, those equally ambitious experimenters who toiled in their smoky laboratories toward a universal synthesis of science, art, and religion. The *magi*, like Giordano Bruno or Jacob Boehme, employed the science of alchemy, the chemistry of their day, to uncover the spirit coursing through matter, hoping to find in their alembic God's perfection, which they would imitate in their own souls. Hermetic thinkers moved to science for religious reasons, practicing their sacred art to clear their path toward God. The fountainheads of Romantic theory, Goethe and Coleridge, latched onto the science of their day for the same reason that the *magi* did: to find evidence for their intuitions of the one, an empirical practice for their intuited theory. Goethe actually practiced alchemy as a young man and carried alchemical concerns and imagery over to his mature scientific work on plants and optics. Coleridge thought Davy the father and founder of 'philosophic Alchemy' and accordingly placed him in a tradition of thinkers including Bruno, Boehme, Swedenborg, and the Goethe-inspired German *Naturphilosophen*. Emerson, in his scientific and religious quest for unity in nature and art, is firmly in this tradition of 'Romantic science', what might well be called a 'new hermeticism'.

During the Romantic age, many poets and philosophers were fervently interested in science; likewise, many scientists were passionate to versify or philosophize. A kind of hermeticism revived, inspiring a collective and interdisciplinary effort to reveal a holistic force with palpable arts. Polymaths abounded: Goethe, exemplar of the age, was rightfully respected as poet, botanist, anatomist, physicist, geologist, and meteorologist; Davy, discoverer of chemical affinity, pioneer in electrochemistry, wrote verse that gained the respect of Coleridge; Alexander von Humboldt chose to combine botany and travel narrative in his *Personal Narrative* (1814–25); Joseph Henry Green, the great British anatomist, wrote a book of

Coleridgean philosophy, *Spiritual Philosophy: Founded on the Teaching of the Late Samuel Taylor Coleridge* (1865). Of course, Coleridge, in incorporating the dynamic science of Davy and Oersted into his philosophy and literary theory, and Emerson, who based his theory of the sublime and poetics and rhetoric on scientific fact, avidly participate in this eclectic tradition.

Still, it is easy to see why readers have generally tended to locate in the Romantic movement the first rifts between the two cultures of science and literature. Keats, with science in mind, could ask rhetorically in 'Lamia', 'Do not all charms fly/At the mere touch of cold philosophy?' The question is quickly answered: 'Philosophy will clip an Angel's wings,/Conquer all mysteries by rule and line,/Empty the haunted air, and gnomed mine/Unweave a rainbow'.[6] Likewise, Wordsworth memorably claimed in 'The Tables Turned' that science 'murder[s] to dissect'.[7] Coleridge consistently relegated materialism, the ostensible domain of science, to the 'Vaunted Mechanico-Corpuscular philosophy' that produced a 'universe of death' (CC 9: 398).

Yet, we now know that these poets largely had in mind the Romantic version of Newton's thought. Goethe, in his *Farbenlehre* (*Color Theory*) (1810), inaugurated this anti-Newton tradition in his intense attacks on Newton's overly abstract, purely mathematical and experimental *Opticks* (1704, 1717). Coleridge became a critic of Newton as well, excoriating Newtonian notions of mechanism, atomism, and action at a distance in several places, most notably in his *Aids to Reflection*.[8] Goethe and Coleridge were most upset by Newton's cosmology, which pictured matter as comprised of impenetrable atoms held together by gravity that acted from a distance, and his equation of truth with mathematics, which reduced the fecundity of nature to number. Romantic thinkers tended to favor a more holistic view of matter, conceiving of it as inseparable from the spirit, energy, or force that animates it, that is immanent in it. Likewise, as A. N. Whitehead has observed, Romantic thinkers generally rejected mathematical explanations in favor of more concrete, empirical ones, wishing to understand nature by passionately engaging it outdoors, not abstracting from it with pencil and paper.[9] Romantic poets and philosophers valued science for its potential as a principle of *Bildung* – for its capacity to improve the self, in truth, beauty, goodness – by connecting it to primary principles of nature through intense attention and enthusiastic understanding. The poet wanted his science blooded, his truth fertile.

Keeping in mind Romantic dreams of a hermetic unified theory of science, religion, and art, we should not be surprised when we learn that the important philosophical and poetical ideas of Goethe, Coleridge, Wordsworth, and Emerson, among others, refer to very specific scientific information of their day. Perhaps readers of Romanticism should turn archaeologists, unearthing forgotten scientific subtexts. Marilyn Gaull makes such a call, rightly observing that scientific ideas may reveal forgotten dimensions to key Romantic terms, ideas, and motifs. For example, she observes that '[t]he idea of photosynthesis... with its emphasis on respiration, may tell us more about the imagery of "correspondent breezes", of Aeolian Harps, of West Winds, of inspiration than hermetic philosophy, German idealism, or political radicalism'.[10] Indeed, the Romantic period, with its craving for amalgamation of disciplines, particularly of poetry and science, is particularly fertile ground for an archaeological excavation of forgotten scientific nuances. Romantic uses of 'spirit', 'energy', 'force', 'attraction' may have specific scientific subtexts buried underneath, undercurrents that do not reduce the meaning of the words, but give them more density, more scope, literary power.

Performing a similar scientific dig on the Victorian period, Gillian Beer shows that many words in the novels of George Eliot, like 'variation' and 'dynamic', refer to the Darwinian science of her historical moment, information now largely overlooked by modern readers.[11] Just as Wordsworth may have had Joseph Priestley's work on photosynthesis resounding in his head when he wrote of plants enjoying the air they breathe, so George Eliot may have had the phrases of the Darwin's evolutionary theory echoing in hers as she recorded interactions between character and environment. Beer sees one of her critical tasks as recovering this information in order to read the literary efforts of her period within their scientific context, thus restoring forgotten densities of meaning, cultivating texts to fuller semantic fruition.[12]

Following this work on British literature, recent scientific excavations of nineteenth-century American authors have set a standard for my present study. Laura Dassow Walls has shown that Thoreau was keenly aware of scientific issues, proposing theories late in his life that parallel those of Darwin.[13] Likewise, Lee Rust Brown has revealed how Emerson's pragmatic thinking and his related compositional practices were his ingenious deployments of the scientific methods of nineteenth-century French naturalists.[14]

I wish extend Brown's work by performing such a scientific excavation on the work of the young Emerson. Emphasizing confluence
more than influence, I track the flow of several scientific currents
coursing primarily through *Nature* (1836), secondarily through journal entries and lectures between 1832 and 1836. I attend generally to
the Romantic, hermetic synthesizing tendencies that shaped his
thought, detailing the scientific information that runs underneath
Emerson's uses of such terms as 'spirit', 'energy', 'force', 'attraction',
'repulsion', 'electricity'. More specifically, I describe a primary scientific idea that powerfully impacted Emerson's early development:
the emerging science of electromagnetics, which flows through his
conception of the sublime and his correspondent theory of composition. Emerson learned from the science of electricity that things are
not discrete and static but condensations of vast systems of force – a
discovery that struck the young Emerson as sublime. It urged him to
translate this scientific insight into a sublime writing style meant
to agitate readers as nature excited him, to shock and attract them
into a recognition of the relationship between matter and spirit.
Emerson's own book of nature, his *Nature*, is not only a prophetic
treatise unveiling the connection between matter and spirit, form
and energy, but is itself a pattern of nature's force.

I am also concerned with how Emerson's engagement with the
science of electricity inspired him to revise the scientific and philosophical *speculations* of his European Romantic forebears with undeniable *facts*: in Emerson's mind, this science had *evidenced* the
synthesizing force *philosophized* by Goethe and Coleridge. It had
confirmed the existence of spirit and registered its charge. During
his famous *Wanderjahr* to Europe in 1833, Emerson simply did not
find the Romanticism in Europe sufficiently *galvanizing*. In his
descriptions of his visits to Wordsworth and Coleridge during this
visit (CW 5: 5–7, 9–12), Emerson reveals his disappointment in the
heroes of his youth, finding them narrow-minded, cranky, old,
acquiescent to the trivial and the ordinary.[15] Leaving Europe, he
sailed back to America to embark on his own quest for a holistic
force. With scientific fact as his rudder, he would search for his own
synthesis of the three grand concerns of Romanticism: energy, nature, language.

Tracking the confluence of European Romanticism and electromagnetism in the young Emerson's work reveals an Emerson who
remained unsatisfied with mere speculation about the animating
principle of life, one who wanted hard scientific proof for the ideas

of his Romantic predecessors, one who may have had very specific scientific information in mind when celebrating 'energy' in nature and language. Following this electric current in Emerson allows us to gain deeper understanding of his Romantic conflation of dynamic things and active words. He wanted his words to be not signs, but polarized intensities; his essays, not expositions, but fields of force. This electromagnetic Emerson, in his desire for the concrete, the verifiable, not only takes a backward, revisionary glance toward his European Romantic fathers, but also a forward gaze, galvanizing a renaissance in the America of his own century and perhaps sparking key literary ideas in our own. Emerson's theories and practices were influenced by the electromagnetic theory that significantly shaped the twentieth-century scientific paradigms of Einstein and Heisenberg, paradigms that in turn impacted the Modernist poetics of writers like Joyce, Stevens, Pound. Emerson, then, is not only an innovative Romantic thinker, literally electrifying organicism, but also a potential source of several currents in more recent poetics, like imagism, vorticism, the ideogram. He stands on the threshold between Romanticism and Modernism, stealing, like Prometheus, the lightning from the Romantic age, using it to mesmerize his own age, sending it vibrating through ours.

ELECTRIC EMERSON

Critics have generally overlooked the currents of science in Emerson, especially his interest in electromagnetism.[16] Emerson was especially taken with the work of Michael Faraday, whose experiments, Emerson wrote in his journal in 1833, had perhaps uncovered the 'secret mechanism of life & sensation' in the 'great long expected discovery of the identity of electricity & magnetism' (JMN 4: 94). Galvanized by Faraday's possible discovery of the secret of life, the young Emerson attuned himself to the 'wonders' in 'Magnetism and Electricity' 'opened' by Faraday and others (EL 2:38).

Ultimately, for Emerson, Faraday's discoveries, complemented by those of Faraday's scientific mentor, Humphry Davy, proposed the possibility that 'the forms of natural bodies depend upon different arrangements of the same particles of matter; that possibly the world shall be found to be composed of oxygen and hydrogen; and that even these two elements are but one matter in different states of electricity' (EL 2: 29). This idea of electrically charged particles as the essentials of reality eventually led Emerson to write in a late essay a summation of his view of Faraday: nature

> is on wheels, in transit, always passing into something else, streaming into something higher; . . . matter is not what it appears; . . . chemistry can blow it all into a gas. Faraday, the most exact of natural philosophers, taught that when we should arrive at the monads, or primordial elements . . . we should find not cubes, or prisms, or atoms, at all, but spherules of force.   (W 8: 4).

Emerson found in Faraday a modern version of the hermetic alchemist; he was a scientist who uncovered, through rigorous experimentation, the one pervading the many. This monumental discovery encouraged the young poet to become a new *magus*, to sublimate, through vigorous troping in the alembic of *Nature*, matter into the spirit pervading it. This rhetorical activity would, he hoped, consequently instill in the minds of his readers an apprehension of the sublime, an intimation of the infinite.

Faraday to be sure offered the possibility of a *scientific* sublime, suggesting a cosmology in which each element, from atom to ant to atmosphere, is an evolving pattern of vast fields of force, rightly seen, a window to the infinite. Scientific vision and the sensation of the sublime become one; in revealing a unifying spiritual force in electricity, Faraday's science suggested that the sublime vision – a vision of the relationship between matter and the spirit animating it – is an insight into scientific fact. Through his reading in science, Emerson came to understand the sublime as an objective *fact*, not only a subjective feeling, apprehended only through a proper scientific understanding of natural process.

Emerson translated this sublime science into sublime essays constructed in the prophetic, hermetic vein, unveiling in content and embodying in form the spirit flowing through matter. Wishing his essays to bear the same qualities as nature, he crafted a style that is, to quote Ezra Pound's definition of powerful writing, 'charged with a force like electricity', 'capable of radiating this energy at a very high potentiality'.[17] An electric universe called for an electric style. As Emerson often wrote, no doubt with Faraday in mind, powerful language is electric, capable of shocking and attracting readers, of overwhelming them with force, of inspiring sublime vision. While Emerson certainly learned from Goethe, Coleridge, and

Swedenborg that nature could be viewed as a book and words as things, he concretized this insight in his own writing only after he learned from nineteenth-century scientists like Faraday how the 'things' of nature actually function. He traded the symbol for the vector.

Unearthing the 'Electric Emerson' continues the recent revisions of Emerson – what Michael Lopez, following Lawrence Buell, has correctly termed the 'de-transcendentalizing' of him – that save him from the misreadings that have typified most of our century.[18] As Newton Arvin has shown, from the First World War until recently, Emerson has been dismissed by most literary critics as an overly optimistic, mystical thinker with no sense of tragedy or evil. Recently, certain critics have radically revised this trend in demonstrating Emerson's primacy as a thinker and an artist whose dynamic, polysemous writing style expresses the tensions and energies of a problematic, complex worldview that is far from mystical.[19] Uncovering the electricity coursing through Emerson's words helps to legitimize this primary Emerson, figuring him as a fact-driven poet who harvested real lightning in his tropes, deployed to shock his age into gods on earth.

In the first chapter, called 'Sublime Science', I demonstrate how Romantic thinkers merged empirical observation with sublime vision. I detail the methodology of Romantic scientists, who combined the sublime and science, intuition and observation, deduction and induction, Reason and Understanding, Plato and Bacon. I argue that the scientific and religious climate of Emerson's America did not encourage such blendings, being instead ruled by strict empiricism, a devotion to the visible. Emerson, passionate for the invisible in the visible, for an empiricism open to sublime vision, was forced to turn to Europe, especially to Coleridge, to find a framework to accommodate his more poetic science.

In Chapter 2, entitled 'The Hermetic Current', I discuss the role of hermeticism in the development of the science of electromagnetism. I demonstrate that Romanticism and the sciences of electricity that grew out of it are elements of a new hermeticism, a revival of this ancient tradition within more empirical frameworks. I follow Coleridge in locating parallels between the discoveries and activities of the hermetic thinkers, running from Bruno to Goethe, and the scientists of electricity, Oersted and Davy. These correspondences set the stage for Emerson's appropriation of Faraday for his hermetic theory and practice.

In the third chapter, 'Electric Cosmos', I describe Emerson's participation in a major shift that took place in the nineteenth century at the hands of Faraday's science of electricity: the move from a world of matter to a world of force. Faraday's work suggested that each atom condenses the electrical energy of the entire solar system – every particle, large and small, contains and reveals vast systems of force. This hermetic insight of the relationship between the part and the whole overwhelms beholders, charging them with the sublime epiphany.

I explain how Emerson grounded his poetics on Faraday's sublime cosmology in 'Electric Words', the fourth chapter. Attending to the sciences of electricity, Emerson came to believe that words should operate like electricity. Working against American theories of language, grounded on Bacon's dream of a strictly univocal scientific language, Emerson turned again to European influences, Swedenborg and Coleridge, to find a theory of ideal language that is as dynamic and multivalent as the things of nature from which it springs. Inspired by Swedenborg's and Coleridge's equation of words and things, he soon turned to Faraday's electromagnetic model of matter to electrify nature's book, coming to equate strong writing with electric force, attempting in *Nature* to channel nature's sublime forces into his charged tropes.

In Chapter 5, 'The Electric Field of *Nature*', I closely read early sections of *Nature* to point out how its central metaphors and scenes vibrate with electromagnetic complexity. His vigorous, polysemous language does not merely signify, but dissolves into intense force-fields of signification. In these passages, Emerson fashions himself as a new prophet of nature, transcending Biblical vision through revisionary allusions, presenting electromagnetic nature as a new sacred text through his surcharged tropes. These sequences, the famous 'transparent eye-ball' passage conspicuous among them, work to shock readers into an awareness of the relationship between matter and spirit.

In 'Scientific Edification', the sixth chapter, I analyze less dense elements of *Nature*, focusing on the centripetal forces balancing the centrifugal ones of the visionary sites. I suggest that the extreme compression of the surcharged passages works to alter readers' interpretive habits, making them more aware of the density of language, urging them to attend avidly even to seemingly discursive, logical parts of *Nature*. This investigation reveals that Emerson's most static-seeming passages do not, on scrutiny, provide clarity and comfort but rather cause uncertainty and insecurity, which work to stimulate readers into active, edifying thought.

Finally, in a conclusion entitled 'Innocence and Experience', I meditate on how *Nature* is far from Emerson's juvenile 'Song of Innocence' but instead inaugurates the profound tradition of his later masterpiece 'Experience,' a 'Song of Experience,' and thus joins in the strain of the great Romantic crises odes of Wordsworth and Coleridge.

1
Sublime Science

In 1841, Emerson was enraptured by power – power of nature, force of mind. He had good reason to be. For the past five years, since the publication of his first book *Nature*, he had *galvanized* the American intellectual scene. Through the conductors of his famous lectures, most notably 'The American Scholar' and the 'Divinity School Address', he had struck his country like lightning, attracting some, repulsing others. Whatever the merit of these lectures, they *electrified*. Thinking no doubt of his forceful influence on his nation, in his 1841 'Self-Reliance', he writes that '[p]ower is in nature the essential measure of right'. He continues: 'The genesis and maturation of a planet, its poise and orbit, the bended tree recovering from the strong wind, the vital resources of every animal and vegetable, are demonstrations of the self-sufficing, and therefore self-relying soul' (CW 2: 40–1). Energy courses through and sustains planet, man, limb, leaf; it is the source of life, the vigor of the soul. It is dynamic, boundless; as Emerson proclaims later in the same essay, likening power to light: 'light, unsystematic, indomitable, will break into any cabin'. Because this light is 'immortal', 'young and joyful', 'million orbed', and 'million colored', it hums with vigor, causing static, worn structures to 'crack', 'lean', 'rot and vanish' (45–6).

This diction – centered on boundless power and light – is not merely figurative; it is a literal rendering of scientific information that Emerson had learned and assimilated much earlier, in the years between his break with the church in 1832 and his publication of *Nature*. Emerson's assiduous attention to sciences of energy and force during these years likely shaped, whether consciously or unconsciously, the master terms he would deploy the rest of his literary life: 'power', 'light', 'the sublime', 'polarity', 'electricity', 'magnetism', 'attraction', 'repulsion'. The emerging sciences of electromagnetism and electrochemistry showed the young Emerson that the power pervading the cosmos could be empirically verified as electromagnetic energy; that light is a form of electricity; that the constitution of the universe is sublime – the smallest grain of water is a pattern of the electrical energy coursing through the solar system. As he recorded in his journal, the '[s]ublime is always the true' (JMN 7: 225).[1]

Emerson's version of the sublime – of boundless power and light – was grounded in science; it constituted a curious blend of Kantian transcendentalism and Baconian empiricism, intuition and induction, holistic vision and scientific attention, relying on a clear understanding of the laws of nature for an insight into the infinite. This important empirical element of Emerson's sublime has often been overlooked. Generally readers of Emerson have followed Harold Bloom's lead, considering the Emersonian sublime solely as the moment when the poet returns to the primal source of creation, losing his temporal self to become empowered by eternal energies.[2] My analysis of Emerson's sublime is motivated by this insight of Bloom and others, yet attempts to account for a major component that they overlook: the sublime moment is dependent on a proper understanding of how nature functions. Only the *scientific* visionary, attentive to the laws coursing through nature, is adept in the sublime.

Of course, Emerson's use of the empirical world for sublime vision was not unique to him; it comprised an integral part of Romantic science – the discipline of looking for the infinite one coursing through the many. Romantics like Coleridge and Wordsworth blended tough British realism with German idealism, mixing Kant and Bacon. Unifying force – something 'far more deeply interfused', inspiring the 'sense sublime' – is to be found only in organic process – round oceans, setting suns. Primarily through his reading in Coleridge, Emerson embraced this marriage of idealism and empiricism. Living in an America preoccupied almost entirely by Baconian empiricism and Scottish Common Sense philosophy, Emerson gladly turned to the synthesizing Coleridge. His British predecessor balanced Bacon with Plato, maintaining that while invisible force emerges only through visible phenomena, the invisible nonetheless is primary.

However, while Emerson borrowed the methodologies and theories of his European predecessors, he eventually revised them in light of his engagement with the work of Davy and Faraday. The science of electricity showed more conclusively than ever before that Romantic speculations concerning the one coursing through the many are correct – a unifying force can be demonstrated, registered, palpably rendered. Through the agency of historical good fortune, Emerson began his literary career at the same time that scientists were beginning to reveal and register boundless sublime power more convincingly than ever before. While Coleridge and Wordsworth were fighting the chill of old age with orthodox notions of spirit, the young Emerson was essaying to discover the real, viable force of electricity circulating through the vast spaces of the American wild.

His sublime science – his revision of Romantic organicism with Faraday's science – electrifies the most vigorous saps of Romanticism, merging Kant's theories of matter and the sublime, Coleridge's nature philosophy, Wordsworth's sense sublime into a dynamic, attractive pattern.

THEORETICAL SUBLIME, EMPIRICAL SUBLIME

While Immanuel Kant was certainly the fruit of the Enlightenment, he was also the seed of Romanticism. In at least three countries – Germany, England, America – his critical philosophy worked to inaugurate new horizons in the study of mind, matter, the sublime. Kant's epistemology proved especially important for Romantic theories of intuition and imagination, inspiring F. W. J. Schelling's dynamic syntheses of subject and object, Coleridge's distinction between Reason and Understanding, Emerson's own ennobling of the mind as the container of time and space. Indeed, Emerson himself attributes to Kant the name of the powerful movement he helped to originate in America. Detailing the history of transcendentalism, Emerson in 1841 declared the importance of Kant: Emerson's idealism and that of his American followers acquired the name of

Transcendental from the use of that term by Immanuel Kant...
who replied to the skeptical philosophy of Locke, which insisted
that there was nothing in the intellect which was not previously
in the experience of the sense, by showing that there was a very
important class of ideas or imperative forms, which did not come
by experience, but through which experience was acquired; that
these were intuitions of the mind itself; and he denominated the
Transcendental forms.   (CW 1: 206–7)

Kant's powerful influence over Romantic philosophy of mind was perhaps equaled, though, by the impact of his notions of matter and the sublime, about which Emerson likely learned through Coleridge. Indeed, Kant's speculations on matter and the sublime provided a theoretical vocabulary that emerging scientists of force could turn to empirical fact.

Kant was one of the many late eighteenth-century thinkers who had grown dissatisfied with the Newtonian theory of matter. Newton, following Robert Boyle, believed the world to be comprised of atoms in a void; 'it seems probable to me', Newton wrote in his *Opticks*, 'that God in the beginning formed matter in solid, massy, hard, impenetrable, moveable particles.' These particles are bound together by and moved 'by certain active principles, such as is that of gravity, and that which causes fermentation, and the cohesion of bodies'.[3] For Newton, then, matter is constituted by passive particles, acted on from a distance by forces like gravity, moving through the void mechanically. Matter is separate from force, inert until moved.

Kant retorted in his *Critique of Pure Reason* (1781). He claimed that one cannot perceive empty, Newtonian space because space, along with time, is one of the categories of the mind to which the external world must conform. According to Kant, empty space is philosophically and scientifically inconsequential. It probably does not exist, and even if it does, it is beyond perception and therefore not in the realm of philosophy or science. If we cannot perceive empty space, then we must perceive a plenum. But then, Kant wondered, with what is the plenum filled? Certainly not impenetrable atoms, which presuppose a void. The substance of the plenum, like empty space, is in the category of the inaccessible *Ding an sich*, or thing-in-itself. Then, Kant asked, what do we perceive, with what do philosophy and science deal? He answered: 'We know substance in space only through the forces which work in this space, either by drawing others to it (attraction) or by preventing penetration (repulsion and impenetrability).'[4] Kant, in this succinct statement, had crumbled the foundations of Newtonian physics, exploding matter and thus collapsing the distinction between matter and spirit, leaving the scientist only with forces. Kant was fully aware of the Pandora's box he had pried open, attempting to account for his new ideas five years later in his *Metaphysical Foundations of Natural Science* (1786), a text which explores fully this proposition: 'Matter fills space, not by its pure existence, but by its special active force.'[5] Matter is continuous in a plenum of force, manifesting itself by virtue of rarefaction and condensation. Underlying differences –

different forces, disparate things – is a unity of force. This theory provided an important backdrop not only for Romantic ideas of a unifying force but also, as we shall see, for the emerging sciences of electricity.

While matter is known only through its force, for Kant this material force, indeed, nature itself, is strangely *not* the source of the sublime. In his third critique, *The Critique of Judgment* (1790), Kant considers the aesthetic of the sublime, opposing it to that of the beautiful. He theorizes that the sensation of the sublime is a mix of pleasure and pain often prompted by – but not dependent on – great displays of natural force, like hurricanes, tornadoes, oceans. While a perception of the beautiful is associated with the harmony of form, an apprehension of the sublime is related to asymmetry, formlessness. While the mind can grasp beautiful forms, sublime forces overwhelm it: the mind is unable to form a coherent image in the face of vast, boundless natural scenes, for example, that inspire ideas of the infinite and totality. Undergoing the sublime sensation, the mind is overtaxed, pained at its inability to grasp fully ideas beyond its ken; at the same time, however, it feels pleasure by intuiting, not imaging, the infinite, the total. To repeat, the sublime, though often stimulated by tumultuous natural scenes, is by no means dependent upon nature. Rather, it is ultimately a mental state, associated not with the empirical faculty of the Understanding but with the intuitive one of Reason. While beauty – the bounded, the harmonious – is external to us, comprehended by the Understanding, the sublime occurs in the mind, showing the Reason, in its ability to apprehend totality or infinity, to be superior to nature.[6] While Kant could equate matter with force, he did not base his notion of the sublime on a scientific understanding of these forces. For him the sublime exists purely on the level of idea.

At about the same time Kant published his third critique, scientists were beginning to combine, however unwittingly, Kant's speculations on matter and his theory of sublime with the help of scientific observation and natural facts. Using scientific inquiry in addition to philosophical speculation, they began to find sublime forces coursing through matter, uncovering boundless power in stones as well as stars. These turn-of-the-century scientists suggested that the sublime is not merely a mental condition, a theory, but dependent on empirical observation, a practice. The sublime is not simply mental nor is it merely, as Edmund Burke, Kant's British predecessor held, simple sensation. It is dependent on discipline, a rigorous understanding of how nature functions: only the scientific adept is prepared for holistic vision.

Many natural scientists of the period that most informed British Romanticism and the American Romanticism of Emerson, from 1790 until about 1835, were indeed sounding the heights and depths of the sublime, finding *evidence* for the infinite. Two sciences that especially unlocked sublime wonders were astronomy and geology. While these late eighteenth-century scientists of the heavens and the earth did not theorize about the sublime, they nonetheless set the stage for the organic sublime of Coleridge and Wordsworth and the electromagnetic one of Emerson.

Kant again provides the theory for these scientific practices, planting seeds for a science of the sublime in his early astronomical treatise *Universal History and Theory of the Heavens* (1755). Relying on deductive reasoning (not inductive empiricism), Kant in this treatise predicts William Herschel's theory of celestial evolution (as well as the nebular hypothesis of Joseph Louis Laplace). Kant supposes that before the formation of the heavens, matter was spread throughout all space. Gravity, a power inherent in matter, eventually caused central bodies to form, which pulled adjoining matter toward them. This attracted matter, however, was averted from merging with the central bodies by repulsion, the other force immanent in matter, and sent into a vortical motion around these primal masses. For Kant, this initial rotation set the universe in motion, inaugurating the laws that control the present universe.[7] The revolutions of the plants around the sun, he hypothesizes, are results of immense and primal powers whose ancient explosions still generate the cosmos. Indeed, the evolution of the solar system continues in the present; new stars and galaxies are in the process of emerging; the cosmos is an unfinished, evolving field of energy:

> The future succession of time, by which eternity is unexhausted, will entirely animate the whole range of space to which God is present, and will gradually put it into that regular order which is conformable to the excellence of His plan.... The Creation is never finished or complete. It did indeed once have a beginning, but it will never cease.[8]

To understand astronomy is to experience huge forces, infinite duration. This Kantian suggestion was *empirically* unfolded some thirty years later by the British astronomer Herschel. In his 1789 paper 'The Construction of the Heavens', Herschel employs concrete celestial data to argue that stellar conglomerations are evolving, unfinished, the effects of an immense central force, perhaps gravity. The celestial bodies are constantly exploding into death and life, players in a vast theater of force and strife; or, to use Herschel's own metaphor, specimens in a dynamic, evolving garden: the heavens are like

> a luxuriant garden, which contains the greatest variety of productions, in different flourishing beds; and one advantage we may at least reap from it is that we can, as it were, extend the range of our experience to an immense duration. For, to continue the simile I have borrowed from the vegetable kingdom, is it not almost the same thing whether we live successively to witness the germination, blooming, foliage, fecundity, fading, withering, corruption of plant, or whether a vast number of specimens, selected from every stage through which the plant passes in the course of existence, be brought at once to our view?[9]

Geologists were likewise beginning to reveal a vigorous universe, generated by huge powers acting over seemingly infinite periods of time. Most notably, James Hutton in *Theory of the Earth* (1795) argues that the earth is far from stable; rather, it is undergoing perpetual change, altered persistently by the action of water, air, and heat. The surface of the globe is in endless revolution, transforming slowly but inexorably. The shard of quartz in the backyard bears in it millions of years of change, is the result of universe-shattering forces. Indeed, as Hutton memorably concludes his study, the time of this earth is infinite: there is 'no vestige of a beginning, no prospect of an end'.[10]

Emerson, as we shall see, was well aware of these paradigm shifts, these transitions from a static to a dynamic universe. He embraced these scientists of force for their

> sense that scientific speculation about the infinite, the awesome, huge dimensions, durations, trauma, catastrophe, power – a favorite word often substituting for electricity, gravity, subtle and imponderable fluids – had more validity than the symmetrical, picturesque, orderly, finite taste of previous generations of scientists.[11]

Indeed, Herschel and Hutton proved prophets for an emerging *Zeitgeist* that came to value energy more than matter. The visible earth, these turn-of-the-century scientists showed, is a pattern of vast, invisible, infinite forces. The smallest bit of coal and the great sun in the sky are really *force*, in varying degrees of intensity. In the laboratories of Faraday, these ideas would soon prove undeniably true; in the tropes of Emerson, they would galvanize a literary renaissance.

ROMANTIC SCIENCE AND THE SUBLIME

These scientific ideas formed the backdrop for Romantic science, which is really a theory of the empirical sublime that blends Kant's sense of infinite force with scientific observation, that marries deduction and induction. As the work of a Hutton and a Herschel suggested, acute observation of the physical inspires intuition of boundless force. Under scientific gaze, organisms become patterns of holistic force, energy, life; an insight into this relationship between part and whole becomes sublime vision, a 'sense sublime' of the 'life of things', the 'one mind within us and abroad'.

As A. N. Whitehead has shown, Romantic organicism comprised the primary vehicle of a major shift in thought, the move from matter to force, the result of which was a marriage of invisible energy and visible patterns. The key assumption behind nineteenth-century organicism was that each part – from atom to ant to Andes – is not discrete, static, acted on from a distance, but inhabited and animated by a vast holistic force. Whitehead recognizes that in the nineteenth century mass lost 'its unique pre-eminence as being the one final permanent quality' and was renamed 'a quantity of energy considered in relation to some of its dynamic effects'. As Whitehead indicates, electromagnetic fields, along with atomicity, evolution, and conservation of energy – the four novel and central ideas of nineteenth-century scientific thought – engendered a science of organicism that attends to things as 'emergences' of energy, 'events', interactions between part and whole, intrinsic and extrinsic energy.[12] It is organicism, animated by Kantian speculations and scientific facts alike, that is the framework of the electrochemistry of Davy, the electromagnetics of Faraday, and the sublime science of Emerson.

The link between Kant the philosopher and Davy the scientist, between transcendentalism and empiricism, was Coleridge, a most persistent purveyor of organic ideas. Coleridge, like his disciple Emerson, took a *Wanderjahr* to the Continent in search of forms for his intuitions, finding what he was looking for in Germany during 1798–9. In the ensuing years, he diligently studied the work of the sage of Konigsberg, who 'took possession' of him 'as with a giant's hand'. The primary insight he gained from Kant shows up in the *Biographia Literaria* (1817):

> For since impenetrability is intelligible only as a mode of resistance, its admission places the essence of *matter* in an act or power, which it possesses in common with *spirit*; and body and spirit are therefore no longer absolutely heterogeneous, but *may* without any *absurdity* be supposed to be different modes, or degrees in perfection, of a common substratum.   (CC 7.1: 129–30)

Coleridge, along with the *Naturphilosophen* Schelling and Henrik Steffens, translated this theory of matter into a cosmology, assuming that the parts of the universe are animated and inhabited by a dynamic holistic principle:

> [I]n the World we see everywhere evidences of a Unity which the component parts are so far from explaining, that they necessarily presuppose it as the cause and condition of their existing as those parts; or even of their existing at all. This antecedent Unity, or Cause and Principle of each Union, it has since the time of Bacon and Kepler been customary to call law.   (CC 9: 75)

Following Kant and Kant's disciple Schelling, Coleridge believed that this unity manifested itself in the form of polarity: 'EVERY POWER IN NATURE AND IN SPIRIT MUST *evolve an opposite as the sole means and condition of its manifestation:* AND ALL OPPOSITION IS A TENDENCY TO REUNION' (CC 4.1: 94).[13]

Coleridge's speculations constitute a nexus between Kant's theory of matter (matter is force) and the sublime (the mind is capable of grasping totality). One apprehends a holistic 'common substratum', an 'antecedent unity', by observing visible organisms. The sublime vision is an insight into this relationship between part and whole, visible and invisible, nature and mind. Spirit is no longer purely Platonic, apprehended only by the mind, but organic,

comprehended by the senses. At the same time, one cannot apprehend the whole merely through Baconian empiricism, attention
only to the physical, but must see through, with intuitive vision,
the visible to the invisible animating forces. The organic sublime –
result of Romantic science – marries Plato and Bacon, Kant and
Hutton, Reason and Understanding.[14]

Indeed, Coleridge believed that Plato and Bacon were similar in
kind, different only in degree: both begin with principles intuited by
Reason and realize them with facts gathered by Understanding;
only Plato primarily emphasizes truth at the level of idea, while
Bacon mostly studies truth at the material level:

> it will not surprise us that Plato so often calls ideas LIVING LAWS,
> in which the mind has its true being and permanence; or that
> Bacon, vice versa, names the laws of nature, *ideas*; and represents
> what we have... called the *facts* of *science* and central phaeno-
> mena, as signatures, impression, symbols of ideas.   (CC 4.1: 492)

For Bacon, according to Coleridge, an idea is an 'intuition or discovery of ideas of the divine mind, in the same way that they
disclose themselves in things by their own signature, and this (as
is proper to the dry light's Intellection) is not in sense perception'
(493). Coleridge believes that Bacon's dry light of the intellect, his
lumen siccum, is the Reason, the faculty that inspires, directs, and
interprets empirical research, providing for the experiment a 'well-
grounded purpose', a 'distinct impression of the probable results', a
'self-consistent anticipation' (489). Bacon showed that 'an idea is an
experiment proposed, an experiment is an idea realized' (489–90).[15]

Coleridge's method structured not only the efforts of Emerson but
also the poetic thinking of his friend Wordsworth, whose sublime
visions are always grounded in the empirical. Though Emerson's
relationship to Wordsworth remained ambiguous – he wrote in
1832 that he never read Wordsworth without 'chagrin' (JMN 4: 63)
though he was eager to visit him in Europe in 1833 (4: 222–6) – it is
clear that he shared an affinity with the British poet. Wordsworth's
famous 'Tintern Abbey' (1798), for example, contains a concise version of Emerson's theory of the sublime. In that poem, Wordsworth
feels the unifying 'presence', a 'sense sublime/Of something far
more deeply interfused' through attending not only to his mind
but also to the 'light of setting suns', the 'round ocean', and the
'living air'. In these phenomena one finds the *noumena*: a 'motion

and a spirit, that impels/All thinking things, all objects of all thought/And rolls through all things'.[16]

Significantly, Wordsworth some four years later meditates on the scientific vocation of the poet. While he values poetry as the 'breath and finer spirit of knowledge' and the 'countenance of science', he dreams of a day when poet and scientist will work hand in hand.

> If the labours of men of science should ever create any material revolution, direct or indirect, in our condition, and in the impressions which we habitually receive, the poet will sleep then no more than at present, but he will be ready to follow the steps of the man of science, not only in the general indirect effects, but he will be at his side, carrying sensation into the midst of the objects of science itself. The remotest discoveries of the chemist, the botanist, or mineralogist, will be as proper objects of the poet's art as any upon which it can be employed, if the time should ever come when these things shall be familiar to us, and the relations under which they are contemplated by the followers of these respected sciences shall be manifestly and palpably material to us as enjoying and suffering beings. If the time should ever come when what is now called science, thus familiarized to men, shall be ready to put on, as it were, a form of flesh and blood, the poet will lend his divine spirit to aid the transfiguration, and will welcome the being thus produced, as a dear and genuine inmate of the household of men.[17]

Wordsworth wishes for scientific truths to be available to 'sensation', to be 'palpably material' to the human condition, to wear 'flesh and blood'. He is, like Coleridge and Emerson, concerned with how the facts of nature relate to the mind, how parts connect to the whole. His own poetic method features the interplay between deduction and induction – as Whitehead observes, 'He [Wordsworth] always grasps the whole of nature as involved in the tonality of the particular instance.'[18]

This point is demonstrated by Jonathan Smith, who claims that the prefaces to the 1800 and 1802 editions of *Lyrical Ballads* propose a 'science of poetic induction'.[19] Wordsworth calls his collection an 'experiment' by which he hopes to 'ascertain, how far by fitting to metrical arrangement a selection of the real language of men in a state of vivid sensation, that sort of pleasure and that quantity of pleasure may be imparted, which a poet may rationally endeavor to impart'. His 'hypothesis' is that the actual language of men in a condition of 'vivid sensation' will impart pleasure to readers if rendered correctly by the poet. Wordsworth suggests that he will pursue this hypothesis through induction; by attending to 'incidents and situations from common life', considering 'man and the objects that surround him as acting and re-acting upon each other', he hopes to learn and select 'language really used by men'. This steady, inductive observation of common life and language will reveal, Wordsworth hopes, 'the primary laws of our nature', 'general principles drawn from the contemplation of particular facts'.[20]

Wordsworth's 'poetic induction' corresponds to Coleridge's 'science of method', in which the mind 'contemplate[s] not *things* only, or for their own sake, but likewise and chiefly the *relations* of things, either their relation to each other, or to the observer, or to the state and apprehension of the hearers', enumerating and analyzing 'these relations, with the conditions under which they are discoverable' (CC 4.1: 451). Wordsworth, following the theory laid out in his prefaces, studies in *Lyrical Ballads* particular cases of people experiencing vivid sensations – a mad mother, a female vagrant, a forsaken Indian women, the poet himself in early spring, at Tintern Abbey after an absence of five years – in hopes of understanding them separately as well as in relation to one another, to the observer, and to the readers. He, like Coleridge, wishes to evidence with induction the 'primary laws' deduced from the mind. His poems become experiments in which ideas are realized – examples of 'poetic induction'.

Poetic induction is an apt name for the Romantic scientific methodology, the synthesis of Plato and Bacon. Like scientific induction, it requires the back and forth play of deduction and induction, working from intuited hypothesis to observed fact and back again. Also, it is experimental; just as the scientist creates conditions in the laboratory to test his guesses, so the poet works to substantiate his hunches with language. His experiments are linguistic; his specimens, words. And herein lies the difference between scientific induction and poetic induction. The poet's laboratory is not a bubbling, beaker-filled room, but the structures of his poems, or, in Emerson's case, his poetic essays. Emerson, like Wordsworth, tests his intuitions as well as scientific theories of contemporaries in the beakers, piles, and pendulums of his words.

AMERICAN MATERIALISM

The young Emerson found Coleridge's method and Wordsworth's poetic induction agreeable to his constitution. Inheriting the mantle of Jonathan Edwards, who felt God throbbing in clouds, leaves, stalks, Emerson knew that a whole divorced from parts is vacuous, parts separated from a whole, fragmentary. His epiphany in the Jardin des Plantes had revealed to him the powerful union of mind and nature, a relationship he had earlier and unsuccessfully tried to discover from his Unitarian pulpit. Transformed from a divine into a naturalist, he returned from Europe in the fall of 1833 eager to put his scientific epiphany into *praxis*. It is likely, however, that he knew that his America would be no more amenable to his scientific theories than it had been to his religious ones. He returned to an un-Romantic America where science was largely construed as a tool for the glory of the religion Emerson had left behind, an instrument for finding empirical evidence for the revelations of scripture. Emerson, however, did not desire to be a naturalist merely to gather facts or prove the existence of God from design – he wished, like Coleridge and Wordsworth, to do the work of the poet, to discover connections between mind and nature and embody them in words. Upon returning from a somewhat rebellious trip to Europe, he would again, upon arriving on his native shore, have to turn against the canons of his own land. His famous antinomianism (for Anne Hutchinson is as much his American forebear as Edwards) quickly found voice in New England lyceums only months after he unshipped.[21]

The reigning epistemology in America during the first half of the nineteenth century was modeled on the Scottish Common Sense philosophy of which Emerson had learned at Harvard, where the Scottish philosophy was 'the prevailing mode of thought'.[22] Emerson (who read the Scottish thinkers assiduously during the two years after he graduated from Harvard) and American Protestants of New England found in the work of Thomas Reid and Dugald Stewart a version of Lockean empiricism that allowed them to moor theology to physical evidence, thus saving religion from dangerous speculation, and enabled them to avoid the risk of Humean skepticism, a logical outcome, many thought, of Locke's program.

Reid, chair of moral philosophy at the university at Glasgow, wished to save philosophy from ungrounded idealism on the one hand and from skeptical empiricism on the other. He observes in

Inquiry into the Human Mind on the Principles of Common Sense (1764), 'All our curious theories of the formation of the earth, of the genera- tion of animals, of the origin of natural and moral evil, so far as they go beyond a just induction from facts, are vanity and folly, no less than the vortices of Des Cartes, or the Archaeus of Paracelsus.' A 'just induction from facts', however, cannot be garnered from Lockean empiricism, which leads, Reid argues, to skepticism: in reviving the distinction between primary qualities (qualities such as motion, extension, figure, impenetrability, believed to inhere in matter) and secondary ones (characteristics that inhere not in matter but are caused by the human mind, such as heat, cold, taste, smell, and color), Locke 'made the secondary qualities mere sensations, and the primary ones resemblances of our sensations'. If secondary qualities exist only in the mind and if primary qualities cannot be perceived by the senses, then the mind does not perceive the world, but merely its own operations; thus, mind and matter are forever separate and no knowledge of the external world is possible. To avoid this unbridgeable gap between mind and matter, Reid posits the principle of 'common sense', which requires us 'to admit the existence of what we see and feel as a first principle, as well as the existence of things whereof we are conscious; and to take our notions of the qualities of bodies, from the testimony of our senses... and our notions of our sensations, from the testimony of consciousness'. Common sense must be admitted because 'every operation of the senses, in its very nature, implies judgment or belief, as well as simple apprehension'. When we feel a pain, we not only sense it, but *believe* it to exist; when we perceive a tree, we not only apprehend it, but *believe* it to be there. Inherent in the structure of sensation is belief. With seeing comes believing. This common sense is guaranteed by 'the inspiration of the Almighty', the authoritative foundation of epistemological and moral judgments.[23]

Dugald Stewart, a disciple of Reid's, was the primary spokesman for the Scottish philosophy in America, his eloquent restatements of his teacher's ideas enchanting an entire age of American thought. Stewart, professor of moral philosophy at the University of Edin- burgh, considerably influenced the young Emerson, who was well aware that Stewart was '[o]ne of the most pleasing names in Modern English Literature', and saw him as 'an excellent Scholar and a lively and elegant Essayist' (EL 1: 374). Emerson knew well Stewart's *Elements of the Philosophy of the Human Mind* (1792) and *Dissertation:*

Progress of Metaphysical, Ethical, and Political Philosophy (1821). From the former he learned the reason why Scottish thought became *the* epistemology underpinning of American science and theology in the first part of his century and why the name of Francis Bacon was invoked as a sacred talisman for any serious inquiry. Stewart gladly describes the current state of philosophy:

> As all our knowledge of the material world is derived from the information of the senses, Natural philosophers have, in modern times, wisely abandoned to Metaphysics, all speculations concerning the possibility or impossibility of its [the material world] being created; concerning the efficient causes of the changes which take place in it; and even concerning the reality of its existence, independent of that of percipient beings: and have confined themselves to the humbler province of observing the phenomena it exhibits, and of ascertaining their general laws.

Only since the time of 'Lord Bacon' has this 'experimental philosophy' been conducted 'with any degree of success', thus keeping thinkers from the 'danger of confounding with the metaphysical speculations already mentioned'.[24] In the hands of Stewart, whose admiration of Bacon was, one historian of ideas has noted, 'intense and indiscriminate', and Reid, whose enthusiasm for Bacon, Stewart himself wrote, 'may be traced in almost every page', Bacon became for Americans the father of the inductive method: 'a strenuously empiricist approach to all forms of knowledge, a declared greed for the objective facts, and a corresponding distrust of "hypothesis", of "imagination", and, indeed, of reason itself'.[25] As Edward Everett, one of Emerson's early idols, describes his age in 1823, 'At the present day, as is well known, the *Baconian* philosophy has become synonymous with the true philosophy.'[26]

Indeed, by Everett's and Emerson's time, the Scottish Philosophy and its corollary Baconism had gained a tenacious hold on the American mind. Beginning in 1769 with the presidency of the Scottish-born John Witherspoon at the Presbyterian College of New Jersey (later to be Princeton) and spreading to the Unitarian Harvard soon after the turn of the century, by the 1820s Scottish thought was so popular that Stewart's *Elements of the Philosophy of the Human Mind* had gone through as many editions in America as it had in Britain. Likewise, the name of Bacon, a synecdoche for common sensical, inductive, scientific thought, sounded euphorically on the tongue of theologian and philosopher alike. The Presbyterian Albert Barnes could happily claim in 1832 that the Baconian method of induction 'consists in a careful and patient examination of facts, or the phenomena of the universe, and deriving from the observation of those facts the principles of a just philosophy', while the amateur scientist and lawyer Samuel Tyler could exclaim in 1844 that a primary consequence of the Baconian philosophy is that 'all the great discoveries of modern science have been British and not Continental'.[27] Even Emerson participated in this apotheosis, delivering a largely panegyrical lecture called 'Lord Bacon' in 1835.

This 'Reign of Bacon', as one historian has described it,[28] resulted in at least three consequences, one for science, one for theology, and one for metaphysics, all of which affected the young Emerson. According to historians of the age, the ascension of Bacon led most American scientists to conceive of their duty as clinging fast to induction, practice, and fact while avoiding as much as possible deduction, theory, and hypothesis. Of course, it was and is impossible for any serious scientist to eschew the latter, but American scientists of the period tried very hard to limit their inquiries to description and classification of fact, consistently fearful of ungrounded hypotheses. George B. Emerson, the President of the Boston Society of Natural History, head of the New England scientific community, summed up this tendency in 1842, when he praised the botanical taxonomy of the French scientist Augustine De Candolle at the expense of the German morphologists fathered by Goethe and admired by Ralph Waldo Emerson: De Candolle's work, the president claimed, provides an excellent example of the Baconian method, moving as it does from scrupulous observation of particulars to general conclusions then back to the particulars, with a primary aim of classification of facts:

> He [De Candolle] first minutely examined all the species of a genus, and thence drew his generic characters. From a similar full examination of all the genera of an order, he drew the ordinal characters. This done he returned to the genera and the species, and rejected from the generic what had been sufficiently expressed in the ordinal, and from the specific, what had been distinctly stated in the generic characters.[29]

George B. Emerson's remarks are fully elaborated by the Baconian popularizer Samuel Tyler, who in his *Discourse on the Baconian*

Philosophy extolled the virtues of evidence at the expense of mere hypothesis.

Tyler also claimed that the Baconian philosophy 'is consistent both in its method of investigation, and its principles with Christianity', adding elsewhere that 'the more the Baconian philosophy has been cultivated, the more has natural theology advanced'.[30] Theology in the first part of the century corroborated Tyler's assessment; religious and scientific men alike worshipped at the Baconian shrine of 'evidence', refusing to proffer any theological speculation without finding scientific proof for it, eager to connect scientific facts to scripture. Theology became known as natural theology, a school of thought largely inaugurated and exemplified by the British divine William Paley, whose most influential book succinctly describes his thought in its title: *Natural Theology: or, Evidences of the Existence and Attributes of the Deity, Collected from the Appearances of Nature* (1802). In this text, read by the young Waldo Emerson, Paley surveys the intricate harmony and beauty of the design of nature, concluding that only an intelligent creator could fashion such a world: 'Were there no example in the world of contrivance except that of the eye, it would be alone sufficient to support the conclusion which we draw from it, as to the necessity of an intelligent Creator.'[31] Paley's work influenced such grandiose efforts as the *Bridgewater Treatises*, a project commissioned by the Earl of Bridgewater before his death in 1829 that took for its goal to show, with the help of eight distinguished authors, the 'Power, Wisdom, and Goodness of God' in his creation. The most important of these was William Whewell's *Astronomy and General Physics Considered with Reference to Natural Theology.*

Paley and Whewell excited American thinkers, showing them that one could successfully bring Baconian induction to theology, finding 'evidence' for God's grandeur, while avoiding 'metaphysics' or 'hypothesis'. In 1848, Francis Bowen, the famous crusader against transcendentalism, summed up the American appropriation of natural theology in his lecture series 'Applications of Metaphysical and Ethical Science to the Evidences of Religion', in which he confidently told his audience that any study of 'relations of ideas', such as pure reason, is worthless 'metaphysics', while the examination of 'matters of fact', such as the history and divinity of Christ, is true science and theology.[32]

Of course, a major consequence of this emphasis on the physical was the equation of metaphysics – for the Baconians any form of intuition – with infidelity: and this, of course, would cause the famous clash in the late 1830s between the Emerson-led transcendentalists – as eager to explore the invisible landscapes of mind as the visible ones of nature – and the prevailing orthodoxy, of which Bowen was a charter member. Bowen was one of the first orthodox Protestants to find in Emerson's *Nature* exactly what he most condemned – an appeal to intuition as a ground for inquiry. In 1837, he reviewed Emerson's first book in the *Christian Examiner*, clearly drawing battle lines between Unitarian orthodoxy and transcendentalism, between Bacon and Kant, Anglo and German; his account shows exactly why Emerson found the American intellectual landscape of his moment enervated. Bowen oversimplifies transcendentalism, calling it a mere 'revival of the old Platonic school' and thus extremely antithetical to the Baconian method:

> It rejects the aid of observation, and will not trust to experiment. The Baconian mode of discovery is obsolete; induction is a slow and tedious process, and the results are uncertain and imperfect. General truths are not to be obtained without previous examination of particulars, and by the aid of a higher power than the understanding.... Pure intelligence usurps the place of humble research. Hidden meanings, glimpses of spiritual and everlasting truth are found, where former observers sought only for natural facts. The observation of sensible phenomena can lead only to the discovery of insulated, partial, and relative laws; but the consideration of the same phenomena, in a typical point of view, may lead us to infinite and absolute truth, – to a knowledge of the reality of things.

Bowen concludes this attack on intuition by comparing transcendental modes of thought and expression with gambling: their 'indistinct modes of reflection', their 'loose and rambling speculations', their 'mystical forms of expression', their 'utterance of truths that are but half perceived' are grounded on the 'same principle... that influences the gambler, who expects by a number of random casts to obtain at last the desired combination'.[33] It is no wonder, given this strong language, that this controversy between natural theology and transcendentalism would only heat up more in the ensuing years, both sides demonizing the other, whether the issue was miracles, epistemology, or Emerson's volatile 1838 'Divinity School

Address', whether the debaters were Bowen and Emerson or Andrews Norton and George Ripley.

Of course, Bowen, in his fanaticism for the material, oversimplifies Emerson's position. Indeed, Emerson, in his desire to be a naturalist, possessed just as much respect for fact, induction, Bacon, and science as his natural theologian enemies. Yet, he differed from them fundamentally on one issue, of which Bowen is rather hyperbolically aware: for Emerson, the facts of the mind are *equally* as important as those of nature. Emerson, again returning to Coleridge to inspirit him in his materialistic country, was unwilling to reduce Reason to Understanding, cognition to classification, comparison, and arrangement of empirical facts. Likewise, and this is the fact that detractors like Bowen missed, Emerson did not wish to reduce Understanding to Reason either – he wanted both to work in concert, to 'evidence' the intuitions of the Reason with the facts of the Understanding, to prove the insight that matter is the energy of spirit with the scientific facts of Faraday.

Emerson could write in 1830, even before his scientific epiphany in the Jardin, that Bacon 'showed the inanity of science not founded on observation. So he is the Restorer of science' (JMN 3: 216). He went on to praise Bacon in 1835 for the same reasons the natural theologians did: Bacon is an unbiased, honest observer, unwilling to foist unnaturally his favorite views onto facts, wrenching them to fit his preconceptions; on the contrary, '[h]e is content to view them [natural facts] where they lie and for what they are. He does not magnify the facts that make for his view and conceal or neglect all others' (EL 1: 326–7). Emerson welcomes his 'new method', 'namely a slow Induction which should begin by accumulating observations and experiments and should deduce a rule from many observations, that we should like children learn of nature and not dictate to her' (1: 330–1). Bacon's importance is extreme: 'Newton, Davy, and Laplace have put in execution the plan of Bacon. The whole history of Science since the time of Bacon is a commentary and exposition of his views' (1: 333).

BOUNDLESS MIND, DYNAMIC NATURE

However, for all his admiration of Bacon, Emerson found him partial; Bacon used his great imagination, almost as powerful as Shakespeare's, as 'an instrument merely to illustrate and adorn the objects presented under the agency of the Understanding' (EL 1: 321). Bacon's neglect of Reason, of the organizing powers of his mind, leaves his texts lacking in unity: 'All his work lies along the ground, a vast unfinished city. He did not arrange but unceasingly collected facts. His own Intellect often acts little on what he collects' (1: 335). Had he employed his Reason to shape the facts of his Understanding, his legacy might have been that of Shakespeare or Milton, who produced according to the 'higher faculties' and consequently left behind for our inspiration works of 'the mind's own Creation', 'perfect according to certain inward canons which the mind must always acknowledge' (1: 335). The virtues of Bacon and his Scottish and American schools were for Emerson incomplete; as he observes of Stewart, his works are 'all splendour & promise till you enter the gate, then you look before & behind but only cottages and shops' (JMN 3: 198). He went so far as to say of Stewart that he 'has laid down no one valuable principle and established no lasting distinction' (EL 1: 374). Likewise, thinking of Paley's *Natural Theology,* he critically asked '[w]hat matters it to the mind, as far as concerns the evidence how one or another fact looks – what may be the aspect of things toward materialism . . . or any other humbug? Does not every consciousness contain its own evidence?' (JMN 3: 267).

By this time, two magnets had drawn Emerson's mind away from American materialism: the emerging sciences of force, like the above-mentioned astronomy and geology, and Coleridge's meditations on scientific method, his merging of Bacon with Plato. He could not go the way of his American contemporaries, who held open no space for the powers of the mind or the invisible forces of the sublime.

The young Emerson was well aware of the boundless universe being revealed by the sciences mentioned above, especially the astronomy of Herschel and the geology of Hutton. Attending sedulously to these sciences on his return to America, he learned that visible phenomena are condensations of vast system of energy, power, duration. These sciences doubtless fueled his excitement over the related science of electricity as well as prepared him to blend science and the sublime, idealism and empiricism.

His early lectures, delivered between 1833 and the publication of *Nature,* teem with allusions to astronomy and geology. In 1831, he had gathered from reading *Preliminary Discourse on the Study of Natural Philosophy* (1830), by Sir John F. W. Herschel, the famous son of William Herschel, that science leads man to the conception of a Power and Intelligence superior to his own...a Power and Intelligence to which he may well apply the term infinite, since he not only sees no actual limit to the instances in which they are manifested, but finds, on the contrary, that the further he enquires, and the wider his sphere of observation extends, they continually open upon him in increasing abundance.

This superabundant universe opens into 'wonder on wonder, till his [man's] faculties become bewildered in admiration, and his intellect falls back on itself in utter hopelessness of arriving at an end'.[34]

Emerson found the science of astronomy sublime for precisely this reason: it revealed a boundless universe, its vastness and power always beyond anthropocentric conceptions: 'Natural history is elegant, astronomy sublime for this reason – their impersonality' (EL 2: 354). Astronomy demoted man and the earth from the center of the universe to 'diminutive speck[s] utterly invisible from the nearest star' (2: 184). This astronomical decentering is made 'good' by 'the act of Reflection' – Reason is stimulated to earnest vision. The discovery of realms whose 'material grandeur' exhausts 'straining conceptions of possible power, size, and duration' dwarfs and appeases man's petty agitations, forcing him to partake of cosmic magnificence (2: 32).

Emerson groups geology with astronomy as two sciences that 'have been explored with wonderful diligence in our time and have bestowed splendid gifts on men' (EL 2: 32). Geology, like stellar observation, grants man a vision of immense 'multitude and range of spawning life' (2: 33). During 1834, Emerson was keen on geology, reading John Playfair's *Illustrations of the Huttonian Theory of the Earth* (1802) and G.L. Cuvier's *Discourse on the Revolutions of the Surface of the Globe* (1831) (L 1: 404). These two texts would have educated Emerson in the two main and opposing schools of geological thought, uniformitarianism and catastrophism. Hutton and Playfair believed that the causes of the past changes in the earth's surface were uniform with the causes altering earth in the present; Cuvier, on the other hand, attributed changes in the earth's surface to catastrophes (floods and earthquakes) that destroyed living species, which were then replaced by new ones. In their time, Hutton and Playfair bordered on heresy, arguing against creation and for evolution, while Cuvier enjoyed the popularity of orthodoxy, as he supported the idea that God had wiped out the race with a flood only to create it anew.[35]

While Emerson in his early lectures on science in 1833–4 indiscriminately employed the conclusions of both schools to elucidate his ideas, by 1836, after reading Charles Lyell's *Principles of Geology* (1830–3), a book that champions Hutton's views, he moved into the uniformitarian camp.[36] In 1833, he cited the Cuvierean 'conclusion at which general geologists have arrived...that there had been repeated great convulsions of nature previous to the present order of things; that we now stand in the midst of the fourth succession of terrestrial animals...that the present races are not more than five or six thousand years old' (EL 1: 31–2). However, in the same lecture, some nine paragraphs later, Emerson invokes what seems to be Hutton's theory of the formation of coal, which account he likely found in Playfair's *Illustrations*.[37] Coal is a 'vegetable formation, – the relic of forests which existed at unknown antiquity before the era of the creation of mankind – ' that had been buried below the surface of the sea 'at too great a depth to be reached by man'.

By 1836, Emerson clearly endorsed uniformitarianism: 'No leaps, no magic, eternal' account for natural phenomena, calm or convulsive, but 'tranquil procession of old familiar laws'.

> The irresistible destroyers of the old are all the time strong builders of the new – the irresistible destroyers who have rent and shivered the planet being now as near and potent as ever, nay the beautiful companions of man's daily walk, mountains and streams, cloud and frost, sun and moon.

To emphasize this persistence of uniform laws, he summons Hutton: 'In the economy of the world,' said Hutton, 'I can find *no traces of a beginning, no prospect of an end*' (EL 2: 31–2) (italics mine).

Emerson continues in the same lecture to stress the immense durations and spaces introduced by geology: 'In Geology...we have a book of Genesis, wherein we read when and how the worlds were made, and are introduced to periods as portentous as the distances of the sky' (2: 32). Later, in 1844, Emerson celebrates geology in the same mode: geology unveils the 'Efficient Cause, *natura naturans*, the quick cause, before which all forms flee as the driven snow, itself secret, its works driven before it in flocks and multitudes...in indescribable variety' (CW 3: 104). This cause publishes itself in creatures, reaching from particles to spicula, through transformation on transformation to the highest symmetries, arriving at consummate results without a shock or leap. A little heat, that is, a little motion, is all that differences the bald, dazzling white, and deadly cold poles of the earth from the tropical climates. (3: 104)

Force, power, immensity: these were the keynotes of these emerging sciences. The heavens are worlds upon worlds, infinite fires; the bit of coal, a concentration of primeval, vast energies. The science of electricity, as we shall see, subsumed the kinetic concerns of astronomy and geology, making force itself its primary object of serious study. Appropriately, the study of electricity began with the sublime: Benjamin Franklin, avatar of Prometheus, seizing the fires of heaven.[38]

Emerson found in Coleridge (and possibly Wordsworth) a method that could grasp immensity in the minuscule, that could apprehend and articulate these sciences of force, that combined the best of natural theology, its quest for evidence, with the best of speculative thought, its faith in intuition. While the natural theologian trusted in nothing beyond the senses and worked to evidence scripture, the poetic scientist relied primarily on extra-sensual apprehensions of the boundless and worked to evidence intuition; while the speculative thinker trusted only in intuitions, feeling no need to realize them in nature or experimentation, the poetic scientist knew that intuitions were valid only if they could be grounded in things.

Appropriately, in his first effort at thinking with the lights of science, an 1833 lecture entitled 'The Uses of Natural History', delivered a mere month after his return from Europe, Emerson clearly articulates this meeting of Plato and Bacon, propounding the scientific vision that he would eloquently incarnate in *Nature* three years later. After listing the various uses of natural science – 'health; useful knowledge; delight; and the improvement of mind and character' – Emerson announces its most important use: 'to explain man to himself' (EL 1: 23). Emerson is most interested not in relations between scripture and evidence but in connections between mind and nature:

Is there not a secret sympathy which connects man to all the animate and to all the inanimate beings around him? Where is it

these fair creatures . . . find their link, their cement, their keystone,
but in the Mind of Man? It is he who marries the visible to the
Invisible by uniting thought to Animal Organization.   (1: 24)

The laws of mind are incarnated in nature, metaphorized in the
cloud, eagle, and rock: 'the whole of Nature is a metaphor or image
of the human Mind' (1: 24). As chemistry and astronomy, as Davy
and Cuvier and Laplace, have revealed, a more intimate knowledge
of nature yields a deeper knowledge of the mind; indeed, '[n]ature
is a language' that explains to humans the laws of their own mind
(1: 25–6).

Beginning with the lecture in 1833, a prelude to future scientific
inquiry, Emerson made good his vow in Europe, spending the
remainder of his days attempting to marry mind and nature
through the agency of science. He assiduously learned of scientific
discoveries and theories in several fields, acquainting himself, as we
already know, with Goethe's botany, Hutton's geology, Cuvier's
anatomy, Herschel's astronomy, Davy's chemistry, Faraday's physics. He translated this Bacon-inspired scientific education – occurring simultaneously with an intense reading of the hermetic,
neoplatonic masterpieces of Bruno, Boehme, and Cudworth – into
several lectures on mind and nature: 'On the Relation of Man to the
Globe' (1833), 'Water' (1834), 'The Naturalist' (1834), and 'The
Humanity of Science' (1836). In 1836, this concurrent attention to
the avatars of Plato and the men of Bacon resulted in the confluence
of *Nature*. Embodied in this 'little, azure-colored book', as Carlyle
called it (CEC 157), was one of the major (if not *the* major) motifs
of Romanticism on the Continent and in England: the conflation
of intuitive vision and empirical fact. Emerson in *Nature*, dissatisfied with the extreme empiricism of his countrymen, returns
to the synthesizing agenda of the hermeticists, wishing to find
in the turnings of nature a materialization of the meditations of
mind.

EMERSON'S SUBLIME INDUCTION

In about the middle of *Nature*, right after his 'Language' chapter, in
which he claims again that 'nature is a metaphor of the human
mind', and just before his section on idealism, where he claims
that the Reason can see through things to their 'causes and spirits',

Emerson clearly sets forth in the 'Discipline' chapter his version of poetic induction, or Romantic methodology.[39] The chapter is about the disciplining influence of nature on the human as well as about the discipline of inquiry:

> Space, time, society, labor, climate, food, locomotion, animals, the mechanical forces, give us sincerest lessons, day by day, whose meaning is unlimited. They educate both the Understanding and the Reason. Every property of matter is a school for the under-standing, – its solidity or resistance, its inertia, its extension, its figure, its divisibility. The understanding adds, divides, combines, measures, and finds nutriment and room for its activity in this worthy scene. Meantime, Reason transfers all these lessons into its own world of thought, by perceiving the analogy that marries Matter and Mind. (N 46)

While the Reason hypothesizes that '[s]ensible objects conform to the premonitions of Reason and reflect the conscience' (51), the Understanding gathers evidence to test the validity of this intuition. This experiment takes place in *Nature*, in which Emerson begins by deducing a theory and proceeds throughout his text to validate it with induction.

Emerson introduces his essay with a hypothesis; wondering if his present age can behold 'God and nature face to face', he asks 'Why should not we also enjoy an original relation to the universe? Why should not we have a poetry and philosophy of insight and not of tradition, and a religion by revelation to us?' Why should we look to the past for our understanding of nature when we are '[e]mbosomed for a season in nature, whose floods of life stream around and through us, and invite us by the powers they supply, to action proportioned to nature' (N 5)? His intuition is: in our integral relation to nature, we can gain insight into the floods of life animat-ing and connecting mind and matter. His hypothesis, if proven, would involve nothing short of a universal science: 'All science has one aim, namely, to find a theory of nature' (6). In the first chapter, Emerson refines this theory of nature; all natural objects, most obviously the stars, reveal 'the perpetual presence of the sublime' if 'the mind is open to their influence' (10). If the mind is open to the 'flowing in' of nature, to its flux and force, then nature appears as sublime – grand, vast, boundless. Bringing this premonition to studies of nature, one finds proof:

Neither does the wisest man exhort her secret, and lose his curiosity by finding out all her perfection. Nature never became a toy
to a wise spirit. The flowers, animals, the mountains, reflected all
the wisdom of his best hour, as much as they delighted the
simplicity of his childhood.   (10)

Having laid out his theory in the beginning, Emerson proceeds to
structure the remainder of the essay inductively, beginning with
attention to nature on its most material level and, by increasingly
larger generalizations from observed facts, moving toward its spiritual qualities. He starts by considering nature on the level of commodity, studying it as raw material for human use; nature's
economic benefit, he observes, is not a final end, but a prelude to
understanding higher uses. When Emerson begins to see nature not
as an amalgamation of isolated particulars to be appropriated by
humans but as an interaction of parts with each other and with a
larger whole, he begins to appreciate its beauty: 'Nothing is quite
beautiful alone; nothing but is beautiful in the whole' (N 30). Realizing that nature itself is connected by a whole, he proceeds to consider how humans relate to nature: through language. If nature is
metaphor, symbol, text, for the mind, then mind and matter are
inescapably connected, mind dependent on matter for expressing
thought. This insight on the connection between human and
nature leads Emerson to consider how nature disciplines thought
and action; he learns that proper attention to each part of nature
renders an insight into the whole: '[A] leaf, a drop, a crystal, a
moment of time is related to the whole, and partakes of the perfection of the whole' (54). Moving to wider generalizations, Emerson
next attends to idealism, followed by examinations of spirit and
prospects.

In each of these sections, he focuses on connections between the
visible and invisible, matter and spirit, concluding that '[n]ature is
not fixed but fluid. Spirit alters, moulds, makes it. The immobility or
bruteness of nature, is the absence of spirit; to pure spirit, it is fluid,
it is volatile, it is obedient' (93–4). Because nature and human are
transformed, shaped, and constituted by a dynamic spirit, attention
to the visible substantiates the initial hypothesis: each microcosm,
properly seen, is a pattern of a vast, volatile, energetic force. This
initial deduction has been evidenced by reading parts in the light of
the whole: as Emerson observes near the end of the essay, recapitul-
ating his method:

I cannot greatly honor minuteness in details, so long as there is no
hint to explain the relation between things and thoughts; no ray
upon the *metaphysics* of conchology, of botany, of the arts, to show
the relation of the forms of flowers, shells, animals, architecture, to
the mind, and build science upon ideas. (83–4)

Emerson's sense of the whole emerges only through attention to
parts: sublime vision depends on empirical observation.

Emerson clearly expresses this sense of the sublime in *Nature*; after
praising physics for 'degrad[ing]' the material before the 'spiritual'
and the astronomer and the geometer for 'disdain[ing] the results of
observation', he then celebrates the 'sublime' remark of the Swiss
physicist and mathematician Leonhard Euler, which he found in
Coleridge's *Aids to Reflection* (JMN 4: 327, 332): scientific laws 'will be
found contrary to all experience', yet are 'true' (N 69–70). Euler's
remark is sublime because it reverses customary, empirical expecta-
tions, suggesting that not the visible but the invisible is primary. It is
in scientists like Euler and others, notably Faraday, that Emerson
found substantiated the following hermeticist presupposition: spirit
– for Emerson synonymous with life, energy, electricity – is primary,
constituting, generating, shaping, and motivating matter, which is
its pattern, its form. While the discrete entities of matter discerned in
everyday life seem real, substantial, science demonstrates, ironically,
through empirical investigation, that they are manifestations of an
essential underlying power. An insight into this relationship produces the sublime vision.

Emerson opens *Nature* with this crucial idea: 'One might think the
atmosphere was made transparent with this design, to give man, in
the heavenly bodies, the perpetual presence of the sublime' (N 9).
The stars awaken the sublime sentiment because 'they are inaccessible' – invisible, beyond conception; but then, Emerson adds, 'all
natural objects make a kindred impression when the mind is open
to their influence' (10). A few paragraphs later, Emerson offers an
example of the mind opening to the influence – the inflow, the
influx – of natural objects in the 'transparent eye-ball' passage.
Crossing the bare common, attending in empirical fashion to the
snow puddles, the twilight, his own thoughts and feelings, he is
overwhelmed with the contradictory sublime sensations of pleasure
and pain, joy and fear: 'Almost I fear to think how glad I am.'
Simultaneously, he gains insight into the relation between spirit
and matter, becoming a pattern of the 'currents' of the 'Universal

Being', sensing that he and the organs of nature are parts and particles of the circulations of God (12–13). Seeing the stars, the common, all of nature, as visible forms of invisible, inaccessible currents is to sense the sublime, concurrently feeling pleasure over the infinite, pain over limitation.

A third time the word 'sublime' appears in *Nature*, Emerson likewise meditates on the unity pulsing through the many. The activities of the ant, he claims, become sublime when 'a ray of relation is seen to extend from it to man' (N 36). As he learned during his epiphany in the Jardin des Plantes, humankind is related to the universe, including ants, cayman, carp, and eagle, by the 'upheaving principle of life'. When viewed in light of spirit, apprehended by Reason, all particulars, processed by the Understanding, become sublime, related, Emerson writes in his journal, to 'the depth of the Original' (JMN 4: 83). Any phenomenon, from ant to atom to Adam, is, seen with the lights of science, with a mind open to their influence, sublime: 'The sublime enters into every thing even into a baker's score or a school boy's multiplication table, as Light beams into privies & garrets' (JMN 5: 24); each grain of water contains the laws of lightning (W 10: 60); each fact symbolizes 'the Unattainable' (CW 2: 179); '[t]he world globes itself into a drop of dew' (2: 59).

Emerson's desire to find visible patterns for his sublime intuitions of the whole places him well outside of the materialist concerns of his countrymen and in a larger, more ancient tradition of inquiry: hermetic alchemy, a 'science of the soul', in the words of one historian.[40] The hermeticist, prototype, as we shall see, of the Romantic scientist, yearning for the one in the all, was not content to leave his intuitions as castles in the air, but wished, in Thoreauvian fashion, to build foundations under them, in his alembic or furnace conducting experiments – sublimation, distillation – that visibly patterned the workings of spirit. Hermetic alchemist, Romantic scientist, Emerson: all see in their mind the secret of life but know they need diurnal objects to make it live.

THE SECRET MECHANISM OF LIFE AND SENSATION

Emerson, for perhaps no other good reason than historical good luck, began his career as public thinker at about the same time that the intuitions of the Platonist and the facts of the Baconian found themselves more firmly bound together than ever before – when the forces of Kant, the immense spaces and durations of Herschel and Hutton, the sacred unity of the hermeticist were being registered in the laboratories of Davy and Faraday. While Emerson's Romantic forebears, because of the time in which they flourished, had to be content with partial proof and inconclusive evidence for their synthesizing insights, Emerson, fortunately for him, saw his most cherished intuition demonstrated and measured. Goethe, for all his scientific passion, in spite of botanical experiments and anatomical dissections, had to rely primarily on the *Urbilden*, archetypes, he carried in his mind. Coleridge, for all his attention to the science of his day, to the electrochemistry of Davy and the organicism of Steffens, had to resort to brash, *Naturphilosoph* speculation to make his theory of life cohere. Emerson, however, could claim with confidence in 1833, three years after Goethe's death and one before Coleridge's, that Faraday had likely discovered 'the secret mechanism of life & sensation' (JMN 4: 94). In 1831, with his discovery of electromagnetic induction, a discovery to be detailed in ensuing chapters, Faraday found hard, undeniable proof for the sublime conjectures of the poets: he found that the constitution of matter and thus of all other forces is electricity – the ancient mystery of spirit, of the principle of animation, had been solved. His discovery, Sir Karl Popper claims, was more revolutionary than Copernicus's, for it did away forever with the fundamental unit upon which science had always been based: matter. Faraday showed that the world is a vast field of force, matter emerging in condensations of electrical energy.[41]

Between 1832 and 1836, concurrently with his learning about poetic methodology and organicism from Goethe and Coleridge, Emerson was becoming aware of Faraday's work in electromagnetism and Davy's electrochemistry. He found in the British scientists' conclusions an electrified version of Goethe's organicism and a basis for galvanizing Coleridge's poetics of symbol. Drawing on this emerging science, Emerson could transform Goethe's primal leaf into fields of force; he could revise Coleridge's ideal of the poem as plant into an ideal of the poem as a grain of water containing lightning. While the influence of literary organicism on Emerson cannot be discounted, the sciences of electrochemistry and electromagnetism – both of which study the electrical constitution of matter – provided a less idealistic, more empirical way of conceiving of nature as well as rich metaphors for guiding and describing his poetics. Though Emerson could not think outside of the methodologies and presuppositions of Goethe and Coleridge, the facts he brought forth to substantiate his holistic hypothesis were, by virtue of his historical good fortune, *harder* than theirs. While Emerson endorsed and was fascinated by Goethe's and Coleridge's organicism, the central idea of 'Romantic science',[42] he discovered in Faraday's electromagnetics incontrovertible data that made the ideas of Coleridge and Goethe seem more speculative than scientific. His engagement with the work of Davy and Faraday in the 1830s suggested to him that the animating force of nature is electricity, that the organic life celebrated by Goethe and Coleridge is electrical force.

Fittingly, Faraday emerged from the same philosophical traditions and methodologies as Emerson, early choosing science – specifically physics and chemistry – as his *modus operandi* for uncovering the secrets of nature. His scientific quest was likely driven by the same motive that spurred Emerson's interest in science: a thirst to divine the one flowing through the many. Faraday, like Emerson, had been brought up in a devoutly religious household and supplemented his faith with scientific rigor. Faraday grew up worshiping in the Sandemanian Church and never left it. Based on the teachings of the eighteenth-century Scottish dissenter Robert Sandeman, Sandemanians believed, like most dissenting Protestant groups, that the single, devout individual needs only his faith to guide him in sounding the scriptures and the heavens. As Sandeman never tired of pointing out in his writings and sermons, God's existence and presence are evident from the beautifully complex laws of nature – if one looks at nature with a desire to see God, then all doubt will disappear. Certainly, as Faraday's biographer L.P. Williams observes, Faraday's 'deepest intuitions about the physical world sprang from his religious faith in the Divine origin of nature'.[43]

Though Faraday never made his religion at all prominent in his scientific pursuits, it certainly complemented, in its quest for a unifying spirit, the philosophical and scientific traditions out of which he emerged. It is not unfair to say that he is the flower of the seed of Kant's theory of matter, blooming from the stalk of *Naturphilosophie*, Coleridge, and Davy. In 1831, he indeed fulfilled the dreams of poets, philosophers, scientists in discovering electromagnetic induction, demonstrating conclusively that matter is electricity: visible matter is but a pattern of vast, invisible force. The Sphinx of the *hermetica* had been vanquished.

THE INVISIBLE

William Blake memorably announced the relationship between the invisible and the visible, claiming that he could see the entire world in a grain of sand.[44] Emerson was beginning to meditate on this relationship when for the first time in the history of thought the connection between invisible and visible was scientifically shown: the visible is the invisible, nature is force, matter is spirit. Emerson registered this insight just as he was preparing to write his own treatise on matter and spirit.

The science of electricity, like astronomy and geology, convinced Emerson that nature is a presentation of vast, perpetual, infinite forces. With science as his guide, Emerson could see a world in a grain of sand, learning that huge universes of forces animate matter, from the atom to the Andes. He was drawn to scientists, like Faraday, whose explorations divine the 'supernatural force' (EL 1: 80) beneath even the grain of sand, scientists who demonstrate that each organism 'stretch[es] away into that other infinity of minute division which the microscope and laws of polarization and chemistry have been opening to man', who reveal that 'there is as great an interval between a grain of sand and nothing as there is between the visible universe and the space in which it is swallowed as an atom' (EL 1: 78). This insight, indeed the science of electromagnetism as a whole, concretized the insights of hermeticists like Plotinus, who speculated that 'everywhere there is all, and each is all, and infinite glory. Each of them is great: the small is great; the sun there is all the stars; and every star again, is all the stars and sun; each is mirrored in every other.'[45] Likewise, the new science verified the religious visions of Pascal, who, following Augustine, believed that the God-pervaded universe 'is an infinite sphere, the centre of which is everywhere, the circumference nowhere'. Each center, each point from a star in the vast distance to a mite under a microscope, from 'the visible universe' to the 'womb of [an] abridged atom' contains 'an infinity of universes, each of which has its firmament, its planets, its earth.'[46] Pascal's intuition that under the 'smallest point of nature' there is always 'a new abyss' opening is accounted for by fact, rephrased by a more scientific Emerson: '[U]nder every deep a lower deep opens' (CW 2: 179). While we in our century take such scientific information for granted, nineteenth-century thinkers were awed, bewildered, when first looking through a microscope and learning that Plotinus's or Pascal's intuitions were true, or when hearing that Faraday had proved the insights of the Renaissance *magi*.

Obviously, simple empiricism of the American stamp was inadequate for apprehending invisible worlds. Fact was generally reduced by the American Baconians, like Francis Bowen, to visible phenomena, nothing more. Understanding served as the primary cognitive tool in America; Reason was condemned to the realm of soft-headed transcendentalism. Emerson, open to the new currents in European science, knew, however, that the invisible is the true realm of science, that to account for the invisible is to detail the sources, the origins, of the visible fabric of the world. If we, like Bowen, were to indict Emerson for the following 'transcendentalist' statement, he would likely reply, having the new science of force in mind, that he was being *more* scientific than his Baconian peers, that he was detailing, albeit a bit hyperbolically, what happened when Davy and Faraday were in the midst of their discoveries.

> To the senses and unrenewed understanding, belongs a sort of instinctive belief in the absolute existence of nature. In their view, man and nature are indissolubly joined. Things are ultimates, and they never look beyond their sphere. The presence of Reason mars this faith. The first effort of thought tends to relax this despotism of the senses, which binds us to nature as if we were a part of it, and shows us nature aloof, and, as it were, afloat. Until this higher agency intervened, the animal eye sees, with wonderful accuracy, sharp outlines and colored surfaces. When the eye of Reason opens, to outline and surface are at once added, grace and expression. These proceed from imagination and affection, and abate somewhat of the angular distinction of objects. If the Reason be stimulated to more earnest vision, outlines and surfaces become transparent, and are no longer seen; causes and spirits are seen through them. The best moments of life are these delicious awakenings of the higher powers, and the reverential withdrawing of nature before its God. (N 61–2)

To the scientist of forces, this might well be rigorous methodology: studying things so intently that their visible qualities dissolve into the invisible powers constituting them. For Emerson, possibly thinking of Davy and Faraday, scientific attention to the visible culminates in an intuitive vision of the unseen. While Davy and Faraday were meticulous practitioners of induction, generally fearful of theory, they nonetheless dealt in agencies beyond the physical observation and showed that a correct understanding of nature required seeing that visible facts are comprised of vast, unpresentable forces.

Grains of sand, volcanoes, ants, words, a bare common: all are sublime, patterns of boundless force, if seen with the eyes of science. Not religion, not philosophy, not poetry, but science is the lens of the sublime. Suddenly, science had taken over from religion the wonders of the invisible world. Now, the task was, how to manifest the unseen essentials of nature, how to incarnate them. The task required from the scientist beautiful experiments, like Faraday's using copper coils and bits of iron to show how electricity functions; and it required from the poet charged words, like Emerson's tropes and figures, designed to shock and attract readers like the perpetual forces of the universe.

These efforts at incarnating spirit in visible patterns, at designing a scientific Eucharist, revived the projects of the hermetic alchemists, early scientists keen on embodying the flows of spirit in their alembics. Emerson, unable to participate fully in the empirical undertakings of his countrymen, turned to European Romanticism, not to be derivative, but to bring to his own country a bizarre and beautiful blending of the most ancient soundings for spirit and the most recent demonstrations of it, a meshing of Hermes and Faraday, Egypt and the Royal Society. At this strange nexus is where Emerson's sublime science originates.

2
The Hermetic Current

By 1844, fortune's slings and arrows had almost rendered the normally affirmative Emerson a skeptic. The death of his little boy Waldo, killed by scarlet fever, two years earlier had thrown Emerson into dark meditation; he began seriously to doubt those vital truths that had buoyed him through the trials of his youth, ranging from his risky break with the church to his scandalous critiques of orthodoxy. He found himself in the middle of life's way in a dark wood. As he lamented in 'Experience', written at the nadir of this crisis, 'Where do we find ourselves? In a series of which we do not know the extremes, and believe it has none.... Sleep lingers all our lifetime about our eyes, as night hovers all day in the boughs of the fir-tree. All things swim and glitter' (CW 3: 27). He is lost, lethargic, stupefied, bewildered: what on earth, he asks throughout the essay, can redeem man from the despair of the skeptic?

The answer arose from an act of Wordsworthian memory. Emerson returns to his youthful insight to nourish his enervated middle age: though we may not possess perfect bearings, though things flit and fly, though we dream more than we think, all is nonetheless inhabited by a stable, sturdy, permanent power that can, if we open ourselves to it, shock us to wakefulness and energize our wondering: 'Like a bird which alights perpetually from bough to bough, is the Power which abides in no man and in no woman, but for a moment speaks from this one, and for another from that one' (CW 3: 34). 'Life', he remembers, 'is a mixture of power and form' (3: 35). In this insight lies rejuvenation.

Emerson felt this in his blood. He had for years been an adept in power and form, in the boundless energy animating and inhabiting everyday phenomena. He had come to maturity at a time when this ancient hermetic revelation was finding scientific evidence in the laboratories of the scientists. Indeed, all of this young life, a coming of age filled with metaphysical speculation – the Calvinism of his Aunt Mary Moody, William Ellery Channing's poetic Unitarianism, the Swedenborgian orations of Sampson Reed – Emerson had prepared himself to become an adept in the primal mysteries of power and form. It is not difficult to imagine his joy when he found that the secrets he had been contemplating were no longer complete enigmas but emerging facts for which scientists were beginning to account. In the years before he published *Nature*, he was crossbreeding, concocting a hybrid of first philosophers – Plotinus, Bruno, Boehme, Cudworth, Swedenborg, Goethe, Coleridge – and hard scientists – Newton, Davy, Faraday. This mixing would flower into *Nature* and continue to supply vigor, rejuvenating sap, to an aging thinker beset by life's inevitable tragedies.

As early as 1835, in the midst of composing *Nature*, Emerson first proclaimed his life's goal, his quest for the power in form: 'I endeavor to announce the laws of the First Philosophy' (JMN 5: 270). This *prima philosophia* is expounded in his first book, an ambitious quest for the 'sublime idea' suggested by Davy in *Elements of Chemical Philosophy* (1812):

> If that sublime idea of the ancient Philosophers which has been sanctioned by the approbation of Newton, should be true, namely, that there is only one species of matter, the different chemical, as well as mechanical forms of which are owing to the different arrangements of its particles, then a method of analyzing those forms may probably be found in their relations to radiant matter. (CD 4: 164)[1]

This synthesis of science and the sublime, paraphrased and praised by Emerson in an early lecture (EL 2: 29), inspired Coleridge's famous paean to his old friend Davy in 1823, when he hailed him as 'the Father and Founder of philosophic Alchemy, the Man who *born* a Poet first converted Poetry into Science and *realised* what few men possessed Genius enough to *fancy*'.[2] Expounding the philosophic center of this alchemy in 1832, Coleridge reverses the notion that chemistry improves on alchemy: 'alchemy is the theoretic end of chemistry: there must be a common law, upon which all can be each and each can be all' (CC 14: 269). Coleridge here reveals a primary source of Romantic forays into science: the hermetic tradition, or, the ancient science of power and form.

Hermeticism, an eclectic blend of alchemy, Platonism, Gnosticism, and Egyptian theology, is a *science* of mysticism. The hermeticist through his alchemical experiments, like Davy through his scientific ones, labored to *evidence* his intuitions. Like the Romantic scientist of whom he forms an archetype, the hermeticist searched for the 'common law', the 'all in all', by attending not only to his mental travels but also to his laboratory equipment: his alembic, his furnace – he wanted an art for his science. Hermetic alchemy, distinguished from the charlatan alchemy condemned by Ben Jonson, was, like *Naturphilosophie* and the early nineteenth-century electromagnetism that grew out of it, a science devoted to synthesizing oppositions: power and form, matter and spirit, positive and negative, male and female, darkness and light, science and religion. The central concern of hermetic alchemy was to reveal, through experimentation, the spirit coursing through matter, the one animating the many. The hermeticist, like the Romantic scientist, worked toward a grand synthesis, a *Pansophia*, an encompassing wisdom comprised of philosophy, religion, and science.[3] Coleridge is clear about these connections between Hermes and the Romantic scientist; he equates Davy's 'philosophic alchemy' with the hermeticism of Bruno, Boehme, and Swedenborg and with the science of 'modern German *Naturphilosophie*, which deduces all things from light and gravitation, each being bipolar' (CC 14: 269n). As one critic observes, with Coleridge doubtless in mind, ' "Romantic" science is really "hermetist" '.[4]

This is not to say that Romantic science is a *mere* instance of hermeticism; it is to claim that this nineteenth-century form of science cultivated the speculations of the Renaissance hermeticists to a more empirical fruition.[5] The scientific theories of Faraday and Davy indeed do tell us more of Emerson's concerns than hermeticism. However, the proper context for Emerson's sublime science, as well as for the synthesizing projects of Coleridge and Goethe, is hermetic alchemy, science of the spirit. Romantic science, in its desire to marry Plato and Bacon, idea and fact, studio and laboratory, is a new, palpable hermeticism, and Emerson is one of its prime practitioners, repeatedly picturing 'the old Alchemists . . . brooding on the edge of discovery of the Absolute from month to month' (JMN 8: 214).

All is one; the one is a synthesis of opposing forces; the particular is a window to the infinite one; the all is revealed in art, be it alchemy or poetry: these are the ideas flowing from the Renaissance *magi* through the *Naturphilosophen* and electroscientists to Goethe, Coleridge, Emerson. Tracking the hermetic vein running through Coleridge's roster of Bruno, Boehme, Swedenborg, and the *Naturphilosophen* will elucidate the tradition out of which Emerson emerged and which he revised as well as illuminate the fascination Goethe and Coleridge, Emerson's forebears, had with science. More specifically, we shall find in the hermetic philosophy the seeds of Emerson's sublime science, his conflation of nineteenth-century scientific ideas, the sublime, and composition theory. Predicting Emerson's science, the hermeticists held that scientific observation reveals the sublime, the all in each; foreshadowing his art, they believed that the art of sublimation dissolves each into all, exposing the sublime forces generating the universe.

HERMETIC ALCHEMY

In the words of M. A. Atwood, a nineteenth-century hermeticist, 'The Smaragdine Table ... in its few enigmatic but remarkable lines, is said to comprehend the working principle and total subject of the art [of hermetic philosophy and alchemy]'.[6] This table, customarily referred to as the 'Emerald Tablet of Hermes,' is worth quoting in full to introduce hermeticism.

> True, without error, certain and most true; that which is above is as that which is below, and that which is below is as that which is above, for performing the miracles of the One Thing; and as all things were from the one, by the mediation of the one, so all things arose from this one thing by adaptation; the father of it is the Sun, the mother of it is the Moon; the wind carries it in its belly; the nurse thereof is the Earth. This is the father of all perfection, or consummation of the whole world. The power of it is integral, if it be turned into earth. Thou shalt separate the earth from the fire, the subtle from the gross, gently with much sagacity; it ascends from earth to heaven, and again descends to earth: and receives the strength of the superiors and of the inferiors – so thou hast the glory of the whole world; therefore let all obscurity flee before thee. This is the strong fortitude of all fortitudes, overcoming every subtle and penetrating every solid thing. So the world was created. Hence were all wonderful adaptations of which this is the manner. Therefore am I called Thrice Great Hermes, having the Three Parts of the philosophy of the whole world. That which I have written is consummated concerning the operation of the Sun.[7]

This passage, according to Ernest Lee Tuveson, is indeed the 'bible' of the hermetic alchemists, giving 'in summary form the hermetist philosophy of the All and the One'.[8] The 'one' emanates through the cosmos, gathering opposites – 'above' and 'below', 'father' and 'mother', 'Sun' (gold) and 'Moon' (silver) – into concord. It is immanent in matter, the earth, for it 'penetrates every solid thing'; however, its force – its fire, its subtlety – can be separated through the art of alchemy and used to obtain the 'glory of the whole world', the 'Sun', or gold. In the 'Tablet' we find the four persistent ideas of hermeticism: one power emanates through all the cosmos; opposites are brought into concord by the mediation of this force; each microcosm, each form, condenses macrocosmic force; through art, this force can be revealed and channeled. These four ideas contain in nascent form Emerson's theory of the sublime – the all, through proper understanding of nature, is revealed in each – and his sublime practice – the all can be revealed in art. These are the inspirations of his lifelong jubilees on power and form.

The visionary of this hermetic doctrine is the Thrice Great Hermes, Hermes Trismegistus, thought by many to be a pre-Mosaic seer, included by Emerson in a 'band of grandees', a 'high priesthood of pure reason', whose first philosophies make him feel as if he is 'present at the sowing of the seed of the world' (CW 2: 204). In reality, Hermes was an amalgamation of various unknown authors, likely Greek and living in Egypt, flourishing between 100 and 300 AD; these anonymous sages blended Platonism, Gnosticism, ancient Egyptian ritualism, and metallurgical tradition into a wildly eclectic work known as the *Hermetica*.[9] The expansive philosophy aggregated in this text began slowly to take root in Europe in the Middle Ages, primarily by way of Islamic sources, in the form of alchemy.[10] It flowered fully during the Renaissance, when lost ancient texts were rediscovered and translated, and attained its richest bloom in late fifteenth-century Florence, where the neoplatonists Marsilio Ficino and Giovanni Pico della Mirandola, according to one historian of the art, 'adapted ancient hermeticism, prophecy, and natural magic in an intellectual system that would be widely influential throughout Europe for centuries to come'.[11]

The translation of the *Hermetica* by Ficino unleashed a 'new force' on the Western world, for it proposed a cosmos that diverged markedly from traditional Christian views.[12] While Christian doctrine tends toward dualism, a separation between God as maker and the world as made, the hermetic view centers on the more organic apothegm of Hermes that 'the world is a living creature endowed with a body which men can see and a mind which men cannot see'.[13] The philosophy of the *Hermetica* is indeed firmly opposed to dualistic tendencies in Christianity: while the orthodox Christian held that God created matter from nothing, *creatio ex nihilo*, the hermeticist maintained a *creatio ex deo*, from God, believing no opposition to exist between matter and spirit.[14] This anti-dualist current in hermetic thought celebrates the universe as a pattern of God's energy: matter and spirit are continuous, one.[15] The hermeticist intuited what Emerson would most celebrate about Faraday's discovery of electromagnetic induction: matter is energy; polarities are manifestations of the same energy; things, from the largest to the smallest, are patterns of vast systems of force: *Natura naturans* and *natura naturata* are one.

The philosophical side of hermeticism was often inseparable from its practical, alchemical one. Hermeticists practiced alchemy in order to discover and manipulate the spirit pervading matter, the quintessence in essence. The central concern of this alchemy (again, as opposed to the alchemy of charlatans) was the twofold transmutation of metal into gold and the soul into perfection. The hermeticist attempted, through detailed experiments, to separate and recover the spirit animating matter, the golden perfection of the cosmos, and to manipulate it to illuminate his groping soul.[16] The experiments carried out in the alembic or the furnace formed a spiritual discipline: as the alchemist attempted to transform lead, dross, or earth into the purer element of gold, he was also essaying to unleash the spirit inhabiting matter and to convert his soul from impurity to purity. Many alchemists held that matter is comprised of three principles or elements: sulfur, salt, and mercury. These corresponded, respectively, to body, intellect, and spirit; black, white, and red; purgation, illumination, and union. Through a series of dissolutions and solutions prompted by heating, the alchemist would try to 'sublimate' – convert, transmute, purify – sulfur into salt, salt into mercury, and thus attain red, the symbolic color of gold or perfection, the mystic consummation of the marriage of sun and moon, the synthesis of human and divine, the merging of finite and infinite, the perfection of earth and soul.[17]

Indeed, in aiding in the process of transformation of the world into pure gold or spirit, the alchemist participated in God's work. According to Titus Burckhardt, the hermetic philosopher viewed the transmutations he fashioned in his laboratory as miraculous 'leaps' that 'nature by herself can only accomplish in an unforeseeably long time'. While nature may take years to turn lead to gold, the alchemist speeds this process, turning 'chaotic', 'heavy' lead into gold, 'congealed light', an 'earthly sun' – a process that is really the dissolution of matter into spirit as well as inspiration for the soul to merge with God.[18]

Like the scientist, the hermetic alchemist learned his art from close observation of physical process, his motto: 'Follow nature'.[19] Following this imperative, alchemy played a vital role in the growth of science. An attempt to mesh theory and practice, philosophy and craft, the art of alchemy required close observation of natural processes, the base of all experimentation. This science aimed to create in the furnaces of its laboratories the very processes carried out by the God-generated earth, the scientist playing a demiurge. In mimicking the processes of nature, the hermetic alchemist attempted to prove in his alembic his favorite hypothesis: substances are sustained and pervaded by *pneuma*, spirit. Like Bacon, he believed that one had first to obey nature in order to overcome it.[20]

The alchemist, like the scientist of electricity centuries later, discovered two primary principles active in nature, dissolution and coagulation, understanding dissolutions as preparations for new forms. Imitating nature, the alchemist dissolved imperfect coagulations (lead, literally and figuratively) to reduce them to elements and crystallized them into more perfect forms (real and symbolic gold). He often symbolized nature's 'unrollings' and 'rollings', its *solve et coagula*, with a double spiral or with the caduceus, two dragons or serpents winding in contrary directions around a staff or tree.[21] The double spiral of the caduceus is a symbol of the synthesis of opposites, be they solution or dissolution, centrifugal or centripetal force, positive and negative charges. Gathering antinomies, alchemical processes figure not only the electromagnetic universe but also Romantic literary symbols: syntheses of part and whole, multeity and unity, nature and language.

The process of 'sublimation' was key to the *solve et coagula*. The term denotes several processes of conversion.

> [S]ince the fifteenth century, sublimation has had currency in scientific parlance, referring essentially to a complete transformation of matter into purer forms. Thus, in alchemy sublimation described the process of converting matter by fire; in metallurgy it explained the refinement of minerals; in geology it once detailed how matter from the core of the earth dematerialized to move

toward the circumference; and in chemistry it described the direct transformation of matter from a solid to a gas.[22]

These conversions occur when there is a 'leap' over a step in a sequence or when normal cycles of transmutation are accelerated: Ovid's *Metamorphoses* is a treatise on sublimation. The historian of science Eduard Farber observes that the sixth and seventh maxims of 'The Emerald Tablet', already quoted above in a slightly different translation, describe the scientific process of sublimation. 'You will separate the earth from the fire, the subtle from the compact, with great skill. It ascends from Earth to Heaven, then descends again to Earth and receives the force of those above and below'. Farber rightly remarks that this passage conflates the 'physico-chemical process' by which a vapor solidifies into a sublimate without first turning into a liquid as well as the 'original' meaning of the sublime as the lofty. Often confused with distillation, sublimation fascinated alchemists. When they saw vapors in their alembics rise, condense into solids, and then revaporize, they thought they were witnessing the dissolution of matter into a higher resolution of spirit.[23] Sublimation, like distillation, showed the spirit pervading matter, for it transmuted solid matter into a vaporous gas which in turn transformed back into matter. This circular process was often symbolized by the coiled ouroboros, the tail-eating serpent, gathering many into one, yet another potential figure for Romantic ideas of literary symbol.[24]

Sublimation is a vehicle to the sublime: turning matter faster than normal, it reveals the unbounded spirit that immediately dissolves the selfish will of the alchemist, cleansing his doors to perception, readying him for the sublime sensation – fear, fascination, redemption. Appropriately, as we shall see, Emerson uses alchemical language reminiscent of this process to detail the procedure by which the poet tropes the world into word, condensing the boundless significance of the cosmos into the alembic of his essay.

RENAISSANCE HERMETICISM

Emerson's early exposure to hermetic philosophy came from several sources, ancient and modern, ranging from Plotinus, Iamblichus, and Proclus to Bruno, Boehme, and Cudworth to, of course, Swedenborg, Goethe, and Coleridge. To place Romantic science and

Emerson's more empirical sublime science in their proper context, I shall highlight those thinkers who appear on Coleridge's roster of philosophical alchemy. Girodano Bruno, listed early in Coleridge's group, is included by Emerson, who was reading him in the 1830s, in an 1834 list of 'mythological' expounders of 'primal philosophy' comprised of Hermes Trismegistus, Plotinus, and Swedenborg, all of whom are connected with Plato, Bacon, and Coleridge (JMN 4: 354–5). Bruno's hermetic roots have been well demonstrated by the brilliant study of Francis Yates.[25] Here, I shall focus only those Brunian ideas that bridge hermetic thought and Romantic science.

In his dialogue *Concerning the Cause, the Principle, and the One* (1584), Bruno expounds the hermetic philosophy. God is the first cause and principle of the cosmos, emanating through matter in the form of the 'world-soul', the 'innermost, most real, and essential faculty' of the 'universal intellect'. The universal intellect 'fills the whole, illumines the universe, and directs nature in producing her species in the right way'. The *magi*, Bruno remarks, call this principle the sower of seeds, since it 'impregnates matter with all forms'. Bruno himself terms it the 'inner craftsman', and describes its dynamic behavior in language that predicts Coleridge's and Emerson's accounts of organic form:

> it shapes matter and figures it from within, as from within the seed or the root it sends forth and unfolds the trunk, from within the trunk it sends forth branches, from within the branches the formed twigs, and from within the twigs the buds – and within those it shapes, forms, and weaves, as with nerves, leaves, blossoms, and fruits.

This 'intrinsic' power is the same as 'spirit', 'soul', and 'life', all of which are part of the 'one', the life and form of all things. This shaping power, the *natura naturans*, and the matter it shapes, the *natura naturata*, though they may seem to comprise a dualistic universe, are actually reducible to one being and one source. Matter, then, is not to be condemned, but to be considered excellent, for it is part of the one.[26]

The one is infinite. Because the universe is a unity – all parts partake of the whole, the whole participates in the parts – each thing is an infinity. Thus, as Emerson would come to believe, the whole universe, seen properly, is sublime, a window to the infinite. Though the things of the universe are differentiated, each is a pattern of the infinite force pervading the cosmos. To illustrate the relation between the parts and the whole in the infinite cosmos, Bruno resorts to illustrations of time and space. 'Under the comprehension of the infinite, there is no greater part and no lesser part because a greater part does not conform more to the proportion of the infinite than any other smaller part.' For example, in infinite duration, or eternity, 'the hour does not differ from the day, the day from the year, the year from the century, the century from the moment'. Likewise, in infinite expanse, or immensity, 'the foot is not different from the furlong, the furlong from the mile, because the mile does not more conform to the proportion of immensity than does the foot'. While these different units of measurement, like all things, are one with infinity and thus with each other, they retain, as do all things, their individuality in that they differ in their modes of being.[27]

The infinite one gathers opposites into concord; as Emerson would later assert, repeatedly, all is polar. Not only are finite things one with the infinite universe, part with whole, but all opposites are gathered by an underlying unity. 'Heat' and 'cold' are intensities of the same energy; the principle controlling heat is the same as the one governing cold. Transformations, like from heat to cold, are circular, because 'there exists a substratum, a principle, a term, and a continuum and a coincidence of one and the other'. Minimum cold and minimum heat, for example, are one; and at the limit of maximum heat, we understand the 'principle of movement towards the cold'. The same principle generates corruption and generation, destruction and creation, dissolution and solution; love is hate, hate is love.[28]

This *coincidentia oppositorum* is at the heart of the *solve et coagula* of the alchemists. It is to this tradition that Bruno refers when he writes 'he who wishes to know the greatest secrets of nature should regard and contemplate the minimum and maximum of contraries and opposites. It is profound magic to know how to draw out the contrary after having found the point of union'.[29] To study sublimation, the points at which solids transmute to gases, matter to the energy animating it, is to understand that parts are patterns of an infinite whole, to stand awed before the sublime.

Along with attending to Bruno's first philosophy in the years leading up to *Nature*, Emerson was also reading Jacob Boehme's *Aurora* (1612), which prompted him to write in 1835 that 'Jacob Boehme is the best helper to a theory of Isaiah & Jeremiah. You

were sure he was in earnest & could you get into his point of view
the world would be what he describes. He is all imagination' (JMN
5: 75). Boehme, a Prussian shoemaker turned mystic, clearly meant
for his *Aurora* to be the first and last philosophy; its subtitle reads
'The Root or Mother of PHILOSOPHY, ASTROLOGY, and THEO-
LOGY from the True Ground'. This 'pansophic' project is grounded
on an idea, similar to Bruno's, that God is immanent in the cosmos.
Indeed, Boehme pictures God's relation to the world in organic
language reminiscent of Bruno's: 'God the creator rules in everything, just as . . . sap in [an] entire tree'.[30]

Like Bruno, Boehme, in *Aurora*, posits God as the infinite one who
emanates his force through the universe and is thus fully present in
each part: 'For all qualities of nature are one in another as one
quality, in that manner as God is all, and as all things descend and
come forth from him: For God is the heart or fountain of nature,
from him cometh all.' Emanating from God are two qualities, 'a *good*
one and an *evil* one, which are in each other as one thing in this
world, in all powers, in the stars and the elements, as also in all the
creatures'. These qualities, ostensibly two but really one because
they flow from God, are forces that generate 'the mobility, boiling,
springing and driving of a thing'. All things are driven by an interaction of opposite qualities; for example, heat both consumes and
enlightens, destroys and gives life.[31]

A tripartite process, springing from the divine trinity structures
the polarized existence of creatures. God is threefold: He is the
Father, the eternal, changeless source of existence, the ground of
all being, pure potential; He is the Son, who extends from and
reflects the Father as His heart and light, as His 'moving *springing
joy*'; He is the Holy Spirit, which proceeds from the Father and the
Son, causing them to move throughout the cosmos as a 'spring or
fountain of joy'. Because God is all in all, '*All things* in this world are
according to the similitude of this *Ternary*'.[32]

Three qualities animate existence; they are present not only in the
trinity, but, as Ronald Gray explains in detailing Boehme's influence
on Goethe, in the creation of the world, the functioning of matter,
and the spiritual movement of humanity. The first quality of God,
his 'Fatherly' quality, is the abyss. It is the seed of reality, pure,
unformed potential. It tends to contract. In this 'nothing' arises the
desire to be something, an urge to mirror itself. The second quality, a
'Sonly' one, emerges in this filling of nothingness: out of the abyss
arises time, space, extension, opposing contraction. Boehme

believes, as noted above, that these first two qualities eternally conflict with one another; they are like darkness and night, nothing and something, male and female, the wrath of God and the love of God. Indeed, these are the active and passive forces of the universe and humanity, the *solve et coagula* of the alchemists, the opposites of Bruno, the attraction and repulsion of the electromagnetists: interdependent and reconciled by the one. Out of their tension arises the third quality, the motion of the universe, like the 'Holy Spirit' a synthesis of polar movement.[33] This threefold process pervades the inanimate and animate universe, each thing of which is a dynamic tension between contraction – nothingness, the possibility of non-existence, death – and expansion – extension, existence, life. This ternary also encompasses the alchemic salt, mercury, sulfur; body, soul, spirit; purgation, illumination, union; male, female, marriage. From microcosm to macrocosm, the world is a *coincidentia oppositorum*, each element a pattern of the dynamic force of the infinite – each form is a condensation of power.

Because God is all in all, each part of the world corresponds to other parts and to the whole. This idea is expounded fully in his work *The Signature of Things* (1619–20), but also in *Aurora*, where Boehme writes man is a 'similitude' or 'image' of God. It follows that 'The interior or hollowness in the body of man is, and signifieth, the deep between the stars and the earth'; 'The whole body with all its parts signifieth heaven and earth.' The blood signifies water; breath, the air.[34] The physical world is a system of signs, signatures, the decipherment of which leads to an understanding of God. Observation of the physical is requisite for apprehending the spiritual, pulling eyes from heaven to earth, suggesting that each is a *symbol* of the all. This notion not only became the controlling metaphor of Swedenborg's thought; it cleared a path for poets like Goethe, Coleridge, and Emerson to make the step decisive for Romantic poetics: to move symbol from nature to language, where the poet could work his own alchemy to reveal the *solve et coagula*.

ROMANTIC HERMETICISM

Swedenborg's importance in shaping Romantic thought has probably not yet been fully fathomed. This hard scientist turned hermeticist placed infinite power into visible form for such major figures as Blake, Coleridge, and Emerson. In claiming that the invisible can be known only through close observation of the visible, Swedenborg is an important transitional figure, moving hermeticism from speculative philosophy and ecstatic mysticism toward the more palpable organicism of a Goethe or a Schelling, a Coleridge or a Wordsworth. Emerson's preoccupation with Swedenborg has been demonstrated and discussed often.[35] Swedenborg's thought, whether from Swedenborg himself or from his French disciple Guillaume Oegger or his American one Sampson Reed, significantly influenced *Nature*. The scientific rigor Swedenborg brought to hermetic speculation fascinated Emerson, who sensed that Swedenborg was, as Robert D. Richardson, Jr eloquently puts it, 'a sort of eighteenth-century Plato working out his ideas in the Post-Newtonian laboratories of the Enlightenment'. Swedenborg's volumes ranged over mining, smelting, metallurgy, and the animal kingdom as well as anatomy, physiology, and psychology. Richardson observes that 'the overarching principles that unify all of Swedenborg's work are the avowed search for the soul and the idea that everything that exists on the physical plane – our world of space and time – has a counterpart in the immaterial world of mind'.[36] These two principles are markedly hermetic, as is Swedenborg's desire to verify his insights scientifically – in the words of E. A. Hitchcock, author of *Swedenborg: A Hermetic Philosopher*, the Swedish thinker was 'a disciple of Hermes', drawing 'the principles of his spiritual philosophy from the study of Hermetic art'.[37]

In 1832, Emerson read in the *New Jerusalem Magazine*, an American Swedenborgian periodical, that Swedenborg ' "considered the visible world & the relation of its parts as the dial plate of the invisible one" ' (JMN 4: 33). This statement inspired Emerson to attend to Swedenborg the remainder of his days. In *Nature*, he includes Swedenborg in a list of those who have acted on nature with Reason and Understanding, those who are lights in a dark time (N 90). Likewise, in the 'The Divinity School Address' (1838), he distinguishes Swedenborg as the greatest exemplar of the hermetic agenda, finding in the Swedish thinker 'the most imaginative of men, yet writing with the precision of a mathematician.... [H]e saw and showed connections between nature and the affections of the soul. He pierced the emblematic and spiritual character of the visible, audible, tangible world' (CW 1: 68). Emerson most delighted in Swedenborg's inflection of the old hermetic idea that matter is spirit. In his 1850 essay on the mystic, he claims that Swedenborg came to his spiritual truths through observation of nature, not through fancy: 'In the atom of magnetic iron' is 'the quality which would generate the spiral motion of sun and planet' (4: 60).

Though Emerson criticizes Swedenborg's theory of language in the same 1850 essay, Emerson's acceptance of two primary Swedenborgian ideas early in his life amply prepared him to celebrate Faraday's science. One, the visible world is animated and sustained by an influx of spirit. Swedenborg proclaims in *Arcana Coelestia* (1747–58) that all life 'flows solely from the Lord. [He] .... is essential life, and diffuses himself through the universal heaven'. God pulses through the cosmos like the sun, shedding more light on creatures, like humans, high on the chain of being, and less on those lower on the chain. A second, related theory also excited Emerson: the visible, physical world relates to the invisible, spiritual one flowing through it by correspondence. Swedenborg claims, again in *Arcana Coelestia*, that '[n]atural things represent spiritual things ... they correspond .... What is natural cannot possibly come forth except from a cause prior to itself. Its cause is from what is spiritual.... All natural things represent the spiritual things to which they correspond.' For example, Swedenborg observes in *Heaven and Hell* (1758) that 'members, organs, and viscera are used in the Word [the Bible] to denote parallel things; for everything in the Word has meaning according to correspondence'. 'Head' corresponds to wisdom, for instance, and 'chest' to charity.[38]

Though Swedenborg, like Boehme, tends to draw from dualistic, Gnostic currents in the hermetic tradition, he nonetheless stimulated Emerson to conceive of matter as a pattern of spirit and of the relationship between matter and spirit as analogous to that between word and meaning. It is perhaps Swedenborg's theory of language, so firmly in back of Emerson's 'Language' chapter in *Nature*, that prompted Emerson to substitute for literal alchemy a linguistic form of the art – the alembic to the *magus*, so the essay to Emerson.

Swedenborg's scientific hermeticism cleared a path for the powerful syntheses of Goethe and Schelling, the respective seed and flower of German *Naturphilosophie*, or Romantic hermeticism. While Goethe through his botanical, anatomical, and optical studies desired to separate himself from what he thought were the speculative excesses of the overtly hermetic *Naturphilosophen*, his theories of plants and his morphology, expounded most prominently in his *Metamorphosis of Plants* (1790), nonetheless considerably influenced and corresponded to Schelling's thought.[39] Though there are significant differences between the scientific rigor in Goethe and the more speculative efforts of the *Naturphilosoph*, these thinkers undoubtedly share a common hermetic foundation: the young Goethe read deeply in Boehme and practiced alchemy before turning to science, while Schelling drew his *Naturphilosophie* not only from Goethe, but also from Bruno and Boehme.[40] Both thinkers espoused a version of the four primary ideas of hermeticism we have so far been tracking: all is one; the one is infinite; the one brings opposites into concord; the one can be revealed and channeled in art, be it alchemical or linguistic. While it may seem curious that these ideas span thinkers from Bruno to Goethe, Ernest Lee Tuveson observes that '[w]ithout dropping his preconceptions *about* nature, the hermetist could move from the "world-picture" of the Middle Ages and Renaissance to that of the Newtonian ages.' Goethe, Tuveson adds, 'did exactly that; he...became a scientist of the late eighteenth century – all without giving up the very ideas about nature which the alchemists believed in'.[41]

While Goethe may have forsaken the philosopher's stone for the *Urpflanze*, his science retained alchemical motivations, as his study of plants uncovered, he thought, the principle of life, manifesting itself in polarized forces.[42] As Emerson recognized early in his career, Goethe was 'much impressed' with the view that '[t]he whole force of the Creation is concentrated upon every point', that 'agencies of electricity, gravity, light, affinity combine to make every plant what it is' (EL 1: 72). Indeed, Emerson's scientific quest for holistic power may well have begun with Goethe, the exemplar of the poetic scientist. As Emerson made his way through Europe in 1833, one of the few books he carried with him was Goethe's *Italian Journey* (1786–8), the German writer's account of his trek through the Italian landscape in search of the archetypal botanical form.[43] While in Naples, Goethe records that

> [t]he primal plant is going to be the strangest creature in the world, which Nature herself shall envy me. With this model and the key to it, it will be possible to go on forever inventing plants and know that their existence is logical.... [T]hey possess an inner necessity and truth. The same law will be applicable to all living organisms.

Some months later, his quest had ended:

While walking in the Public Gardens of Palermo, it came to me in a flash that in the organ of the plant which we are accustomed to call leaf lies the true Proteus who can hide or reveal himself in all vegetable forms. From the first to the last, the plant is nothing but leaf, which is so inseparable from the future germ that one cannot think of it without the other.

This insight spurs Goethe to wonder if an understanding of how the primal form of the plant, the leaf, unfolds over time might lead to a 'better insight into the fundamental principle of metamorphosis'.[44] After his return to Germany, Goethe systematized his epiphany in *The Metamorphosis of Plants* and *On Morphology* (1817–24), both of which Emerson read soon after his own return from Europe. In these texts, Goethe extended this theory of a primal shaping force to include all life; as Goethe observes in *On Morphology*, organic natures are formed according to an *Urbild*, 'archetype' or 'prototype', an evolving pattern of life springing from an infinite, unknowable source. The botanical *Urbild*, as noted, is the leaf; the anatomical one, Goethe discovered in 1784, the vertebra.[45] These archetypes are not static but dynamic patterns through which organisms unfold over time as energy shapes form, and form, energy – as the whole influences the parts, parts, the whole.

Fittingly, one of Goethe's clearest articulations of the part–whole relationship, the primary element of organicism, comes during an 1817 discussion of Kant's philosophy. Goethe, who admits to admiring Kant's thought, claims that he found Kant's terms 'analytic' and 'synthetic' as well as his ideas on form useful in framing his own concerns. He observes: 'I could not help but notice that nature always follows an analytic course – development out of a living mysterious whole – but then seems to act synthetically in bringing together apparently alien circumstances and joining them into one.' This whole works 'from within', forming the parts like a seed shapes a stalk.[46]

The archetype *becomes*, or, to use Goethe's term, metamorphoses, through an interplay of polar forces. Metamorphosis, the structural force of nature, is a balance of two polar drives – a centrifugal, disruptive drive and a centripetal, formative one. Plants and animals are evolving interactions between the disruptive surge of life and their own form, between centripetal and centrifugal forces. As Goethe intones in *On Morphology*:

The idea of metamorphosis deserves great reverence, but it is also a most dangerous gift from above. It leads to formlessness; it destroys knowledge, dissolves it. It is like the *vis centrifuga*, and would be lost in the infinite if it had no counterweight; here I mean the drive for specific character, the stubborn persistence of things which have finally attained reality. This is a *vis centripeta* which remains basically untouched by any external factor.

The world is a tense and creative interaction of opposites; each organism is a *coincidentia oppositorum*, emerging 'out of a living, mysterious whole' that synthesizes 'apparently alien circumstances' into 'one'.[47] For example, plants are generated by the polarized interplay between a vertical and spiral principle: the vertical principle is the durable, stable, centripetal principle that maintains form; the spiral principle is the developmental, nourishing, centrifugal principle entwining itself around the vertical principle, pushing toward excess. These two opposing forces, however, fuse into form: 'Neither of these two systems can be considered as working alone; they are always and forever together. In complete balance they produce the most perfect development of vegetation'.[48] In the short note 'Polarity', published posthumously, Goethe lists several examples of the polar principles – such as subject and object, light and dark, spirit and matter, ideal and real, systole and diastole – claiming, in language that predicts Schelling and Hegel, that antitheses of opposites intensify toward higher syntheses as nature evolves, metamorphoses.[49]

Following Swedenborg, Goethe extends this model of Romantic, organic hermeticism to art, asserting that the 'inner life of art and nature' 'work from within'.[50] Goethe's own definition of symbol draws on this organicism: he emphasizes the part-whole relationship of the literary symbol, which places the 'general in the particular', the particular representing the 'more general not as a dream or shadow, but as a living momentary revelation of the Inscrutable'.[51] The symbol, like the organism, is an assimilation of polarities, general and particular, part and whole. His *Faust* draws its exuberance from plants, from organisms. Goethe, like Emerson, replaces the alembic with words to mimic and reveal the processes of nature in tropes and figures. Goethe's literary symbols, like the alembics of the alchemists, reveal the power coursing through form.

Goethe's organicizing of the hermetic tenets supplied rich soil for Schelling to cultivate his own natural hermeticism. While Goethe may have scorned their excesses, the *Naturphilosophen* thinking in his wake, Schelling foremost among them, borrowed from him just as he took from Boehme. Endeavoring to ground hermetic thought in the physical world, Schelling, influenced by Bruno to the extent that he entitled a book in his honor (*Bruno: or On the Natural and Divine Principle of Things* (1802)), wanted, like Goethe and Swedenborg before him, to *evidence* hermetic thought. Emerson's 1835 *precis* of Schelling's thought, in which he is quite aware of its hermetic, Boehmean background, introduces the basic form of the German's *Naturphilosophie.*

> The Germans believe in the necessary Trinity of God, – the Infinite; the finite; & the passage from Inf. into Fin.; or, the Creation. It is typified in the act of thinking. Whilst we contemplate we are infinite; the thought we express is partial & finite; the expression is the third part & is equivalent to the act of Creation. Unity says [Boehmean] Schelling is barren. Duality is necessary to the existence of the World. Shall I say then that the galvanic action of metals foreshows from afar the God head, the zinc the metal & the acid; or the marriage of plants the pollen the ovary, & the junction? (JMN 5: 30)

Emerson here focuses on the Boehmean tendency in Schelling, his attention to the three-step dance perpetually synthesizing thesis and antithesis. In 1797, Schelling in his *Ideas for a Philosophy of Nature* indeed meditated on the dynamic relationship between the subjective, infinite pole and the objective, finite one, emphasizing the natural (objective) pole. Subject and object are diverse forms of the absolute: when the absolute (God) is pure thought, invisible, formless, it is subjective; when it decides to embody its thought, to give thought a visible form, it is objective; this move from subjective to objective pole produces a synthesis of the two, the world as we know it, a blending of ideal and real, infinite and finite. Schelling likens this passage of infinite into finite to thinking, in which boundless conceptions gain more definite forms, synthesizing into ideas. The cosmos itself is an idea of the absolute, each element, from the minute to the magnificent, simultaneously a finite embodying the infinite and an infinite embodied by the finite. As Emerson notes in the journal entry, *pure* unity, as opposed to *dynamic* unity, is barren because there is no movement into an opposite.[52]

The absolute, then, moves in the same polar rhythm as Bruno's one, as Boehme's God, as Goethe's organisms. This process

structures micro- and macrocosm, constituting the primary principle of physics and metaphysics alike:

> in virtue of the eternal law whereby absoluteness becomes subject
> and object, the universe, not only as a whole, but also in detail (in
> Nature, for example, and again even in individual spheres within
> Nature), divides into two unities, of which we have designated
> one as real, the other as ideal. The *in-itself* [the thing, nature,
> Kant's *Ding an sich*] is always the third unity in which the other
> two are equated.

For example, just as the universe is the expression (synthesis) of
infinite and finite, matter is a gathering of the forces of attraction
and repulsion, and forces themselves, such as light, gravity, magnetism, electricity, are mergings of opposing tendencies.[53] Artistic forms
embody the same structure: as Schelling declares in his essay *On the
Relation of Plastic Arts to Nature* (1807), just as the absolute combines
infinite and finite into nature, the artist does the same in his composition of the art product.[54] It is this idea that Emerson cites in the
journal entry: perhaps drawing from Schelling's *System of Transcendental Idealism* (1800), a work emphasizing the self over nature,
Emerson observes that humans participate in the thinking of the
absolute in their own reflections, expressing subjective, infinite
thought in language, an objective, finite form, merging polarities
in linguistic symbols. The artist, a demiurge, an alchemist, creates
worlds in his words.[55]

The latter notion of course is a primary Romantic idea, one
repeatedly summoned by Coleridge. Coleridge, notorious for his
'plagiarisms' of Schelling, was fascinated by the 'dynamic' philosophy theorized by Schelling's *Naturphilosophie*. He attempted to combine the philosopher's ideas with, as one historian of science put it,
'a detailed knowledge of the natural sciences, especially the non-
mathematical ones'.[56] Schelling is not only firmly behind the philosophical passages of the *Biographia Literaria* (1817), which Coleridge
likened to the *System of Transcendental Idealism* in calling it a 'sketch
of the *subjective* Pole of the Dynamic Philosophy;[57] he is also at the
back of Coleridge's *Theory of Life* (written 1816–17, published 1848),
what could be called a sketch of the *objective* pole, in which he
explores the force generating nature: 'the principle of individuation,
or the power which unites a given all into a whole that is presupposed by all its parts' (CC 11: 510–11).

Like Schelling, Coleridge (Emerson's most immediate hermetic father) was deeply read in the canon of 'Philosophic Alchemy', wishing to find embodied in nature the intuitions of a Bruno.[58] In the *Biographia*, Coleridge maintains that nature and mind are 'different degrees or modes' of a 'common substratum' (CC 7.1: 129–30), which is comprised of two contrary yet interacting forces, 'one of which tends to expand infinitely, while the other strives to apprehend or find itself in this infinity' (7.1: 130). Likewise, in *Aids to Reflection* (a book, remember, Emerson admired immensely), Coleridge, as usual attacking Newtonian mechanism, observes that organisms differ from machines because the organ is 'evolved from the central invisible power', generated by an 'unseen agency', an 'invisible energy' that 'weaves its magic eddies', forming leaves, blood, bones (9: 398). For Coleridge, as for Goethe, organs are assimilations of wholes – archetypes, invisible powers – by parts, sites of polar intensity. The philosopher's task is first to use 'discursive reason', the Understanding, to understand how these forces function, and then to 'contemplate intuitively', with the Reason, the 'one power' out of which polarity arises and which unifies nature and mind (7.1: 295). This knowledge is a marriage, as is all of nature, between subject and object, *natura naturans* and *natura naturata* (7.1: 254–94).

Both nature and mind are eddies of an immanent living principle, dynamic patterns of polarity. Just as the plant and animal are spirals turning the whole into their parts, so the imagination organizes 'the flux of the senses by the permanent and self-circling energies of the reason'. Out of this churning emerges a system of symbols, 'harmonious in themselves and consubstantial with the truths of which they are the conductors' (CC 6: 29). The symbols produced by the imagination are alembics, *loci* where the forces of nature are revealed. Like a living organism, in which the visible part is merged with the invisible whole that shapes it from within, a symbol 'always partakes of the reality which it renders intelligible: while it annunciates the whole, it abides itself as a living part' (6: 30). In merging part and whole, a symbol is a 'multeity in unity', figured, aptly, by 'the polished golden wheel of the chariot of the sun' (11.1: 372). In the symbols of Shakespeare, as we already know, we find 'nature idealized into poetry' – as natural objects substantiate the ideas of the Bard – while in the symbols of chemists like Humphry Davy, we discover 'poetry, as it were, substantiated and realized in nature' – as the ideas of the scientists course through the universe (4.1: 471).

EMERSON'S HERMETICISM

The young Emerson reveled in the bright solutions of hermeticism, both Renaissance and Romantic, enriching his forays into science with the philosophical alchemists. Of course, he was not the first American to dabble in the esoteric art. The Thrice Great Hermes, always lauded in Europe, also found ample disciples in America. In the seventeenth century, George Starkey and John Winthrop, Jr, son of the famous first Governor of the Massachusetts Bay Colony, practiced the sacred art; the poets Anne Bradstreet and Edward Taylor and the divine Cotton Mather employed alchemical imagery in their writings. During the latter half of the eighteenth century, the influence of Swedenborg, already hermeticizing England, grew steadily in New England, flowering in the transcendentalist movement in the nineteenth century, making, in the words of Tuveson, '[a] kind of hermeticism... an important part of the idealistic ferment we know as New England transcendentalism'.[59]

Emerson, the spring of this American transcendentalism, early embraced hermeticism, primarily that of Swedenborg, Goethe, and Coleridge, but not neglecting Bruno, Boehme, Plotinian and Cambridge neoplatonists. He studied these thinkers for the same reason he grasped science at about the same time: to embody his intuitions in the practice of his art, to substantiate Reason in the facts of the Understanding, to clothe thought in symbol. Emerson was not content to let the invisible remain unseen but would have it made manifest in the alembic of his essays. In his very first published paragraph, the famous opening of *Nature*, Emerson demands a hermetic blending of theory and practice, calling for a 'philosophy of insight' into nature's 'floods of life' as well as for dynamic, fluid forms, to render these currents visible.

One of Emerson's earliest meditations on science takes as its focus a line from Goethe's hermetic organicism. In *On Morphology*, Goethe had exclaimed 'Nature has no system; she has – she is – life and development from an unknown center to an unknowable periphery'.[60] In 'The Humanity of Science', an 1836 lecture, Emerson closely rephrases this passage. Observing that recent scientific discoveries point to a synthesizing force, he writes, 'all these [scientific ideas] whether they are premature generalizations or not, indicate a central unity, the common law that pervades nature from the deep centre to an unknown circumference' (EL 2: 29). Goethe's language and name show up often in Emerson's early writings, helping him to formulate his own hermetic organicism in the form of the four interrelated ideas described above: form is power; the world is polar; parts are patterns of infinite, holistic power; symbols reveal the infinite. These ideas consistently stimulated Emerson, preparing him for his initiation into electromagnetic rites. As Robert D. Richardson, Jr observes, Emerson's reading of Goethe's *Metamorphosis* inspired him to lament 'We have no theory of animated nature. When we have it, it will be itself the true Classification' (JMN 4: 288–9). This passage divulges Emerson's desire 'to understand not only matter but the directing and organizing of matter'.[61]

Emerson's search for a holistic power coursing through the parts, for a 'central unity' pervading nature from the 'deep center to the unknown circumference', was greatly aided by the organic hermeticism of Goethe and Coleridge. In one of his earliest lectures after returning from Europe, Emerson cites a view, quoted earlier, that 'much impressed Goethe': 'The whole force of the Creation is concentrated upon every point... [A]gencies of electricity, gravity, light, affinity combine to make every plant what it is' (EL 1: 72). Emerson learned from Goethe that this part/whole relationship unfolds in plants in the metamorphosis of the leaf:

[I]s not every part of a plant a transformed leaf? a petal is a leaf, a fruit is a leaf, a seed is a leaf, metamorphosed, and slow-paced experiment has made good this prophetic vision, that is, it may be demonstrated that a flower is analogous in its structure to a branch covered with leaves, – is a branch of metamorphosed leaves. (2: 24)

Emerson also celebrates this idea in a human context: just as 'the eye of a leaf' is the unit of botany that is converted into multitudinous forms of leaves, so the 'one vertebra of the spine' is the unit of the skeleton, the head being 'only the uppermost vertebrae transformed' (CW 4: 158).

With Goethe's scientific notions likely in his mind, Emerson reveled in detailing how the whole is immanent in parts, opening his career in 1836 as a published writer by exclaiming that nature's 'floods of life stream around and through us' (N 5). A few years later, in the 'Method of Nature', he sounds a similar note: 'In all animal and vegetable forms, the physiologist concedes that no chemistry, no mechanics, can account for the facts, but a mysterious principle of life must be assumed, which not only inhabits the organ, but makes the organ' (CW 1: 125). Just as 'agencies of electricity, gravity, light, affinity, combine to make every plant what it is' (EL 1: 72), so '[s]pirit alters, moulds, [and] makes' nature (N 93).

This relationship between holistic principle and individual parts translates for Emerson, as it did for Goethe and Coleridge, into polarity: there is a great principle of 'Undulation in nature', 'known under the name of polarity' 'that shows itself in the inspiring and expiring of breath; in desire and satiety; in the ebb and flow of the sea . . . and as yet more deeply ingrained in every atom and every fluid' (CW 1: 61). All of *Nature* explores this doctrine, attempting to show the reciprocity between not only whole and part, or energy and form, but also between subject and object (the 'ME' and the 'NOT ME'); spirit and matter ('the currents of Universal Being' and the 'transparent eye-ball'); and, of course, nature and language ('nature is a symbol of spirit'). Emerson found polarity helpful in resolving not only epistemological and ontological questions, but also in accounting for artistic genius, observing in an early lecture that great works must possess two poles: the particular genius of the poet and the needs of the times, the energy of the Reason and the restraint of the Common Sense, or Understanding (EL 2: 62).

Like the hermeticists Goethe and Coleridge, Emerson invoked the symbol to account for strong writing, believing that art, literary or otherwise, should bear the organic qualities of nature. As he observed in his first lecture after Europe, and as he was fond of pointing out throughout his career, language arose from nature because 'the whole of Nature is a metaphor or image of the human Mind' (EL 1: 24), a material manifestation of invisible thoughts. Nature as symbol is the model for language as symbol. Emerson cites Coleridge's 'The Destiny of Nations: a Vision' to verify this idea: ' "For all that meets the bodily sense I deem/Symbolical, one mighty alphabet/For infant minds" ' (1: 25). Later, in 1850, in his final assessment of Goethe in *Representative Men*, he still emphasizes the symbolic quality of nature: 'Nature will be reported. All things are engaged in writing their history . . . The air is full of sounds; the sky, of tokens; the ground is all memoranda and signatures; and every object covered over with hints, which speak the intelligent' (CW 4: 261). Nature's writing inspires man, who is 'born to write', to record nature in a 'new and finer form of the original'. This record will be 'alive, as that [nature] which is recorded is alive' (4: 261). A few years earlier, he had given his definitive account of natural language in 'The Poet': the symbolic language of poetry is 'alive' 'like the spirit of a plant or an animal'. It has 'an architecture of its own, and adorn[s] nature with a new thing' (3: 6).

Aptly, the only times Emerson uses alchemical imagery in substantial detail is to describe his composing process, the practice by which he symbolizes his thoughts. In *Nature*, for instance, he considers the process by which the writer converts the energy of nature and thought into language: 'The beauty of nature reforms itself in the mind, and not for barren contemplation, but for new creation' (N 29). Put another way, '[a]rt ... [is] a nature passed through the alembic of man' (30). This process, Emerson explains in 'Divinity School Address,' involves sublimating 'life ... through the fire of thought' (CW 1: 86). Stanley Cavell has shown the importance of this alchemical 'conversion' in Emerson's thought, observing that it is the process by which he transmutes his intuitions into tuitions, detailed also in 'The American Scholar': 'A strange process, ... this by which experience is converted into thought, as a mulberry leaf is converted into satin' (CW 1: 59). This alchemical conversion is, according to Cavell, 'to be taken as a rhetorical operation, Emerson's figure for a figure of speech ... the conversion of words'.[62] Just as an alembic transmutes liquids into purer forms, so the creative mind metamorphoses the raw materials of experiences into golden words.

Emerson's reading in hermeticism in the 1830s no doubt fostered this sense that the production of language is alchemical, a version of sublimation. The hermetic alchemist mimics nature in his alembic, trying to mirror its conversionary processes; however, he speeds these processes, agitating them with the flame, attempting to do in minutes what nature does in centuries – turn lead to gold, matter apocalyptically into spirit. He makes nature work faster than usual, altering (turning, troping) its visible rhythms to reveal the invisible music to which it dances. This alchemical sublimation corresponds to Emerson's troping, detailed fully in later chapters. Emerson, like the alchemist, chose to model his art on nature, essaying to make his words function like things; he also, though, like his hermetic sources, had to minimize and quicken nature, condensing it into an essay, turning it more quickly with his dynamic tropes. He agitates the material of his words into sites of intensity, of spirit. His turnings (spiraling snakes, circling serpents) resemble literary symbols, confluences of polar energies. The sublime requires sublimation, the invisible the visible, seeing saying.

Fittingly, just as Emerson came to embrace electromagnetism at the same time he became a hermetic adept, so he began to equate strong writing with electricity at about the same time that he started to account for composition alchemically. For Emerson the eclectic, thirsty for synthesis, there would be little difference in kind between the alchemist demonstrating that matter is spirit in his alembic and Faraday showing the same relationship with the copper coils he wound around an iron ring to illustrate electromagnetic induction; or the steel filings he employed to show that electromagnetism occurs in lines of force; or the beakers he filled with solutions to be decomposed with Voltaic electricity. When the alchemist or the scientist reveals the forces generating nature, he becomes a poet, his experiments his tropes. Just as Davy and Faraday through electrolysis shock matter to uncover its essentials, so the alchemist in the alembic heats matter to reveal spirit, so the poet tropes words into patterns of energy. Alchemist, scientist, poet: all three turn materials – be they metal, water, or language – from their ordinary courses in order to find the sublime forces immanent in them. These turnings are intense alterations of the ordinary, like a whirlwind or a storm. They inspire moments of heightened awareness: once one sees a tornado, vast pattern of limitless energy, he never quite sees nature the same way again. After Faraday's discovery of electromagnetic induction, one could never see the world in the same way again; from then on, it is a field of force, its things condensations of vast systems of force, its very water drops, sublime. So with Emerson's language, which works to shock readers into an awareness that even the most ostensibly static elements are really sites on infinite force. This is the key to the hermetic art of Emerson's sublime science; it will unlock, as we proceed, his theory of the sublime as his practice of sublimation, his poetics and rhetoric.

Having filled out Coleridge's roster of hermeticism from Renaissance neoplatonism to Romantic organicism, we are now ready to test his bold claim that Davy, a hard scientist, is the father of philosophic alchemy. We shall find that hermeticism remains vital, albeit in a disguised form, in Davy's electrochemistry and Faraday's electromagnetism. And it is this hermetic vein in the science of electricity, this search for the one, that converts Emerson from a pure organicist to an electromagnetic poet, that stimulates him to revise the organicism of Coleridge and Goethe in light of electricity. This highly ambitious and interdisciplinary effort is the core of Emerson's sublime science.

Emerson's gathering of alchemy and chemistry, religion and science, nature and art, rendered him, depending on one's view, either wildly eclectic or grandly synthetic. As the next chapter shows, Emerson truly did want to inaugurate a Renaissance in America, a rebirth of ancient spiritual impulses in the new forms of modern sciences. While we may scoff at these highly interdisciplinary efforts in our more specialized climes of thought, we might do well to recall the cosmologists of this century, including not only Einstein and Heisenberg, but also James Joyce and Wallace Stevens. If we may look askance at the prospect of a poem containing everything, we always stand in awe when everything becomes a poem.

3
Electric Cosmos

With increasing age, Emerson would struggle more and more with limitation, necessity, fate. As a man of 33, he could energetically conclude *Nature* with the golden possibility that we could '[b]uild... [our] own world' (N 94). By 1860, however, in writing 'Fate' a 57-year-old Emerson realized that though we may build it, the materials are limited, the tools scarce: 'Once we thought, positive power was all. Now we learn, that negative power, or circumstance, is half.' We go always in danger of losing positive power, of falling helpless victim to circumstance, the laws of nature that allow scant possibilities for creativity. Nature itself seems but an iron hoop, an insoluble boundary dictating our narrow field of action: 'The book of Nature is the book of Fate.' With what force, Emerson asks, can we resist these 'torrents of tendency?' (W 6: 15).

He would again return to the sublime science for his answer, his solace. He would remember his forays into electricity, his electromagnetic hermeticism. The cosmos, he recalled, is animated by polarized power: if Fate is strong, so is its opposite, power. Positive balances negative: 'Thus we trace Fate, in matter, mind, and morals, – in race, in retardation of strata, and in thought and character as well. It is everywhere bound or limitation. But Fate has its lord, limitation its limits' (W 6: 21). This limitation is power: 'For though Fate is immense, so is power, which is the other fact of the dual world, immense. If Fate follows and limits power, power attends and antagonizes Fate.' This polarity is our redemption, saving us from utter biological determinism: 'Man is not order of nature, sack and sack, belly and members, link in a chain, nor any ignominious baggage, but a stupendous antagonism, a dragging together of the poles of the Universe' (6: 22). Polarity and power are not mere speculation, but, as Emerson learned some twenty years earlier, scientific fact: our resilience to strict necessity is part of our 'chemistry': '[W]hen a strong will appears, it usually results from a certain unity of organization, as if the whole energy of body and mind flowed in one direction. All great force is real and elemental.... Where power is shown in will, it must rest on universal force.' Sympathy with this universal physics brings 'infinite force' (6: 28).

The young Emerson likely had no idea that his excursions into the hermetic mysteries of electricity would train him so thoroughly in the arts of redemption. Yet, perhaps he was fully aware, even at this early moment of his career, of the philosophical power granted by the emerging science of electricity. As Coleridge suggested, Davy, father of philosophic alchemy, had begun to bring the speculations of neoplatonic and organicist organicism to empirical fruition. It remained for Davy's brilliant disciple Faraday to bring the hermetic tradition to an apocalyptic end. Bruno, Swedenborg, were right, and Faraday proved it: matter is electrical energy; electricity is polar; each atom condenses the energy of the solar system; alembic and symbol are to be replaced by the electric trope. Such a sublime science could not fail but to nourish Emerson a lifetime. With the advent of Faraday, matter gave way to force. The world would never be the same. For Emerson, dark matter had been dissolved into luminous possibility.

ELECTROMAGNETIC HERMETICISM

While he was becoming acquainted with Renaissance and Romantic hermeticism, Emerson was also entering into the mysteries of electricity, finding in the work of Davy and Faraday a basis for improving Goethe's and Coleridge's organicist conjectures with hard scientific data. The science of electricity pulled the sublime from the realm of philosophical and aesthetic theory to fact. In what we might call 'electromagnetic hermeticism', Emerson found revealed for the first time the secret of life – the one had been uncovered and measured.

The nineteenth-century science of electricity was the finest flower of the hermetic tradition. Indeed, as Tuveson observes, 'survival of hermetism in the eighteenth century... coincided with the beginning of the study of electrical phenomena. (Indeed, one suspects that there may have been a cause-effect relationship.)'[1] He refers assuredly to the experiments of scientists like Davy, Oersted, and, of course, Faraday. Davy is paramount not only for his influence on the famous discoveries of his prize student, Faraday, but also for his presence in the thought of the young Emerson, who had a passion for Davy's 'sublime conjecture' that there is 'but one matter in

different states of electricity', a 'central unity' (EL 2: 29). This supposition of Davy, articulated in *Elements of Chemical Philosophy*,
gained impetus from the scientist's friendship with Coleridge at
the turn of the century, when he learned from the poet, freshly
returned from Germany, the 'dynamic philosophy' of Kant, who
in *Metaphysical Foundation of Natural Science*, remember, theorized
that matter is comprised only of forces. This idea, of course, became
momentous for *Naturphilosoph* and scientist alike, stimulating in
Davy, by way of the hermeticist Coleridge, a desire to uncover the
prima philosophia.

Emerson himself perhaps learned of connections between chemistry and alchemy in reading Davy's *Elements of Chemical Philosophy*
during the 1830s. This book contained a brief history of chemistry,
tracing the science from its roots in alchemy and alembics to Davy's
own discoveries of chemical affinity with the technique of electrolysis. While Davy repeatedly condemns alchemy as a pseudo-
science, he does credit it with offering the first excursions into
experimentation. He finds most of the European alchemy to be
'fabulous'; yet, certain noble figures occasionally emerge as bright
lights from its overall obscurity, like Roger Bacon of the thirteenth
century, whose alchemical project remained strictly philosophical,
and Paracelsus, the alchemist who became the first public lecturer of
chemistry in Europe (CD 4: 7–14). Davy, summing his view of the
ancient art, seconds Francis Bacon's, who 'described the Alchemists
as similar to those husbandmen who in searching for a treasure
supposed to be hidden in their land by turning up and pulverizing
the soil, rendered it fertile; in seeking for brilliant possibilities they
sometimes discovered useful realities; ... he [Bacon] says a new philosophy has arisen from the furnaces' (4: 15).

The furnaces, the alembics, of the hermetic alchemists served for
them as the voltaic piles and beakers did for scientists of electricity,
who found brilliant possibilities in the reality of the spark. At the
end of his history, Davy sketches recent work in chemical decomposition made possible in 1800 by Alessandro Volta's primitive battery, called a pile, comprised, literally, of a pile of unlike metals, like
zinc and silver, alternatively stacked one on the other. The pile
produced an electric current capable of decomposing compound
bodies into their elements as it separated positively charged elements from negatively charged ones. By running a current from a
voltaic pile into solutions and decomposing them, chemists in
the early part of the nineteenth century were able to explain the

composition of matter in terms of electrical affinities, to discover new elements (as Davy did in 1807, finding potassium and sodium), and to find out which elements are positive and which negative (CD 4: 38–9; 117).

Chemical decomposition, later called electrolysis by Faraday, was the chemist's version of alchemical process. Like sublimation or distillation, the alchemical processes meant to burn compounds down into primal elements in order to uncover the relationship between solid and gas (matter and spirit), electrolysis was a means of shocking compounds into their electrically charged essentials, a mode of revealing the nature of matter. As F. Sherwood Taylor observes in his history of alchemy, the one common factor in alchemy and chemistry is their technique: both work to separate and combine the constituents of bodies.[2] Davy's own definition of chemistry extends this link; for him, the chemist's task is to 'ascertain the causes of all phenomena of this kind [of the chemical kind] and to discover the laws by which they are governed' (4: 1). Davy and Paracelsus, sweating in different laboratories hundreds of years apart, nonetheless strained their eyes for the same causes: the laws of the one.

Davy not only helped bring hermeticism to fruition, but he also worked to complete Kant's speculations on forces. Indeed, the young Davy was reading Kant just about the time he first met Coleridge. Fresh from a reading tour of Locke, Berkeley, Reid, and, according to his brother, 'Kant and the Transcendentalists', Davy was one of the first to welcome Coleridge home from his pilgrimage to Germany. Davy and Coleridge met in the fall of 1799 at the Pneumatic Institution near Bristol, where Davy was working on the chemistry of air with Thomas Beddoes. The two men immediately became enamored of one another, passionately talking, walking, and working together, the scientist learning philosophy from poet, the poet garnering chemistry from the scientist. Coleridge could not have come to the young Davy at a more propitious time.

Just months before Coleridge's arrival, Davy had written optimistically about an active force coursing through all matter:

The supposition of active powers common to all matter from the different modifications of which all the phenomena of its change result, appear to me more reasonable than the assumption of certain imaginary fluids alone endowed with active powers, and bearing the same relation to common matter, as the vulgar philosophy supposes spirit to bear to matter.[3]

This vulgar philosophy was of course Newtonian mechanism, which supposed matter to be passive, moved by external spirit; many Newton-influenced chemists of Davy's time presupposed that electricity, magnetism, heat, and light were imponderable fluids, comprised of atomic corpuscles, behaving according to Newtonian mechanics.

Coleridge's own rendering of Kant no doubt gave Davy more fuel for this hypothesis, perhaps inspiring him to spend the rest of his career attempting to show that forces were unified and non-material. By 1807, after many experiments that involved decomposing substances into elements with an electric current, Davy felt sure that chemical reactions are electrical ones and that the constitution of elements is electrical (CD 4: 39–40). In his *Elements of Chemical Philosophy*, he wondered if the Newtonian view of matter, matter consisting of 'invisible corpuscles', was obsolete and if matter instead could be 'physical points endowed with attraction and repulsion', their powers 'capable of being measured by their electrical relations' (4: 39).

By 1812, Davy was ready to make other bold suggestions in his *Elements*, positing, for example, that the alchemist's dream of the one may find its waking truth in chemistry: 'Matter may ultimately be found to be the same in essence, differing only in arrangements of its particles, or two or three *simple* substances may produce all the varieties of compounds' (CD 4: 132). Later in the book, as we have already seen, he restated this conjecture more grandly: 'If that sublime idea of the ancient Philosophers which has been sanctioned by the approbation of Newton, should be true, namely, that there is only one species of matter, the different chemical, as well as mechanical forms of which are owing to the different arrangements of its particles, then a method of analysing those forms may probably be found in their relations to radiant matter' (CD 4: 164).

Davy of course had reason to offer these optimistic visions. In 1807, he had discovered that the forces controlling chemical affinity between elements are electrical and that elements themselves possess an electrical charge. By chemical decomposition with voltaic electricity Davy isolated the elements sodium and potassium, showing along the way that 'chemical qualities are shewn to depend upon the electrical powers' (CD 5: 137). This hint led him to hypothesize elsewhere that electrical affinity – attraction and repulsion – is 'the power by which different species of matter tend to unite in one compound' (CD 7: 202) and to ask rhetorically '[i]s not

what has been called chemical affinity merely the union or coales-
cence of particles in naturally opposite states? And are not chemical
attractions of particles and electrical attractions of masses owing to
one property governed by one simple law?'[4]

In suggesting that the building blocks of matter are electrical,
Davy not only extended the hermetic tradition as well as the great
work of Lavoisier in elemental chemistry, but he also revised the
atomic theories of his countryman John Dalton. In *A New System of
Chemical Philosophy* (1808), Dalton had questioned the corpuscular
theory of atoms held by Newton. Though Dalton, like Newton,
proposed that atoms were indivisible and indestructible, he
diverged from his scientific forebear in hypothesizing not that
atoms are made of one homogeneous material, but that there are
as many different kinds of atoms as there are elements. Also, in
ascribing to atoms relative weights he found a way, for the first
time, of accounting numerically for the qualities of atoms. As the
historian of chemistry William H. Brock observes, he thus 'married
the theory of atoms with tangible reality'.[5] Through his experiments
in electrical decomposition, Davy was able to suggest that Dalton's
atoms are electrical phenomena, wondering whether atoms are
corpuscular or 'physical points endowed with attraction and repulsion' (CD 4: 39). Conjectures like these provided a foundation on
which Faraday could build in proving that atoms are in fact electrical
points. As Oliver Sacks points out, Davy's work was central in
permitting scientists to trope the word 'energy' away from its customary meaning of 'intellectual and moral vigor' to its modern,
scientific connotation.[6]

While Coleridge would waver in his celebration of Davy as the
father of hermetic alchemy in 1812, condemning him as a Newtonian atomist (CC 12.1: 572), for most of his life he remained
enthusiastic about the electrochemist. In 1825, two years after he
had dubbed Davy the father of hermetic thought, he praised him in
Aids to Reflection, observing that Davy, along with H. C. Oersted, a
Danish scientist, had revealed 'the dynamic spirit of the physical
sciences' by showing that the matter we perceive is 'the translucence
of invisible Energy' (CC 9: 398). Coleridge is correct to mention
Oersted with Davy. In Oersted we find a trained scientist steeped
in German thought, the man who took the first step in conclusively
electrifying hermeticism. In revealing that electrical and magnetic
forces are different manifestations of the same force, Oersted
brought Davy's conjecture of the electrical nature of matter one

step closer to fact. Oersted, as Emerson was aware, opened 'wonders' with his discovery of electromagnetism (EL 2: 38). Indeed, his experiments in the physics of electricity impacted the young Faraday as strongly as did Davy's electrochemistry.

In 1799, the same year Davy became aware of Kant, Oersted, a student in natural science raised, he said of himself, on the 'charm of chemistry', completed his doctoral thesis at the University of Copenhagen on Kant's *Metaphysical Foundations of Natural Science*. Soon after receiving his degree, he went on a *Wanderjahr* round Europe, briefly coming under the tutelage of the German Romantic physicist Johann Wilhelm Ritter, whose experiments in galvanism and belief in the connection between electricity and magnetism highly impressed the young Kantian. He likewise attended lectures by Fichte and read, not uncritically, Schelling, Fichte's disciple. On his return to Denmark, he made the guiding principle of his fledgling researches the search for the unity and polarity in nature.[7] Significantly, he placed himself in the class of natural philosophers who 'are guided by a sense of unity throughout nature'. These philosophers always observe phenomena with an eye to 'the harmony of the whole', believing that 'all phenomena are produced by the same power', one that, as Oersted wrote in 1806, 'appears in different form, as, for example, Light, Heat, Electricity, Magnetism, etc'. By 1813, Oersted was trying to account for this notion scientifically, hypothesizing that this power is polar, manifesting itself in bodies in opposing forces: 'Each of these forces has an expansive and repulsive action in the volume which it dominates; but each attracts [the other] and produces a contraction when it acts on the other. When these forces act most freely, they produce electrical phenomena'.[8] Attending further to electricity, he found that electrical currents attract their opposites and repel currents of the same kind.

Finally, in the winter of 1819–20, he discovered the principle underlying the magnetic behavior of electricity. In an article for *The Edinburgh Encyclopaedia* (1830), Oersted, writing of himself in the third person, recalled his thoughts just before he discovered electromagnetism:

[H]e proved that not only chemical affinities, but also heat and light are produced by the same two powers, which probably might be only two different forms of one primordial power. He stated also, that the magnetical effects were produced by the same powers.... His researches upon this subject were still fruitless, until the year 1820.

In April of that year, during an evening lecture, he accidentally put a wire containing an electric current parallel to a magnetic needle and noticed that the needle was deflected. After repeating the experiment several times, he finally concluded that magnetism and electricity are related. They behave in the same manner – just as two magnets set side by side deflect each other, so do two galvanized wires – and are possibly manifestations of the same underlying force, as are, perhaps, heat and light.[9]

He had proved that electricity and magnetism are manifestations of the same force. As L. P. Williams describes the effect of this discovery: 'The faith of those who believed in the essential unity of all natural forces had been justified'.[10] Yet, in spite of his groundbreaking discovery and provocative theories, Oersted still presupposed, in a Newtonian manner, that electricity was comprised of particles of matter that conflicted with one another in space.[11] While he had pushed hermeticism closer to fruition, he still bogged force in Newtonian materiality, as did his immediate follower, André-Marie Ampère.

About a week after Oersted's discovery, the French scientist Ampère revealed the relationship between positive and negative forces by demonstrating that two parallel, electrified wires attract each other if the currents run in the same direction, and repel each other if the currents travel in opposite paths. On the basis of this experiment, he established the electrodynamic law that forces of attraction and repulsion between galvanized conductors are directly proportional to the currents in the conductors. He believed that magnetism and electricity behave in the same way because magnetism is electricity: 'a magnet is only a collection of electric currents', he wrote in his account of his discovery, and positive and negative electric currents are different fluids running in opposite directions. Though Ampère extended and modified Oersted's discovery, he still maintained that electricity is propagated by a fluid. Like Oersted, he grounded electricity in Newtonian matter.[12]

The stage was now set for Faraday to take matter out of force, to prove that matter is a field of force, a pattern of boundless energy. Like a hermetic alchemist, he would use his art to reveal the life of things. His pile, wire, compass, and beaker: these became modern alchemical apparati, meant, like the alembic, to disclose the all; the all in each; the coincidence of opposites. Faraday's new magic culminated hermeticism. In 1831, he unconsciously proved its most powerful practitioner when he discovered, with a pile and coiled wires (a new alchemical ourobouros, caduceus, Romantic symbol: harvests of opposites), electromagnetic induction, the key to the revelation of the 'secret mechanism of life & sensation'.

FARADAY'S ELECTROMAGNETIC INDUCTION

Faraday not only brought hermeticist speculation to fact; he also completed Kant's work on forces. Coming to maturity under Davy's guidance, Faraday would have learned of Kant, *Naturphilosophie*, and Coleridge through the philosophical meditations of his master, coming no doubt to understand the importance of Kant's powerful critique of Newton's theory of matter. The first time the 21-year-old Faraday heard Davy lecture, in 1812 at the Royal Institution, the older scientist indeed suggested that all matter is electrical. Fervently taking notes, Faraday heard Davy proclaim the following:

> In solids the matter exerts its attractive powers and remains fixed. In fluids there is an equilibrium between attractive and repulsive powers. In Gasses the repulsive power preponderates over the Attractive but is not sufficiently strong to overcome the specific nature of the body and in Radient matter the repulsion is free and unconfined and projects the body in right lines.[13]

Physical states of matter, Davy here proposes, are merely functions of the powers of attraction and repulsion. Fascinated by this possibility, Faraday attended the other three lectures Davy delivered that year; in his enthusiasm for science in general and Davy in particular, he meticulously copied down notes for each of his hero's four lectures. In late December of the same year, he applied to Davy for a position in science, sending along the bound notes. Luckily for Faraday, Davy's present assistant had recently been discharged for brawling, so Davy took him on. Thus began perhaps the most fruitful union in the history of science.[14]

Within eight years, Faraday, through diligent work and brilliant experimentation, equaled his master in scientific fame and was fully aware of the importance of Oersted's and Ampère's work in 1820. News of Oersted's discovery and Ampère's modification did not reach him quickly, however; he learned of it as late as October, some six months after the fact. On the first day of October, 1820, Davy hastened into the laboratory of the Royal Institution to tell his brilliant protégé the news. The two men immediately began to repeat Oersted's experiments; both were eager to interpret the results that seemed to confound both Oersted and Ampère. The excitement aroused by this new science of electromagnetism in England prompted a friend of Faraday's, one R. Phillips, to request that the young natural philosopher write a history of this new branch of science for the *Annals of Philosophy*.

This undertaking proved monumental. It first of all allowed Faraday to see clearly weaknesses in the idea, propounded by both Oersted and Ampère, that electrical and magnetic currents are material, a liquid of some sort. For Faraday, the conception of currents as liquids in conflict was both cumbersome and unsubstantiated. In the midst of drafting his history, Faraday was briefly sidetracked by a curious discovery that made him once and for all reject the notion that currents are liquids flowing in rectilinear paths. He found that a galvanized wire would rotate around a magnetic needle, and that, in turn, a magnetic needle would circle around the wire. He concluded that these forces are not simply liquid flows pushing and pulling against one another, but rotary powers, positive poles circling one way, negative ones the other. Not only had Faraday converted electricity into work, contriving the first electric motor, but he had also broken new ground for thinking about electromagnetic currents as non-material forces, forces that perhaps exist separately from matter. This was his first scientific achievement of international importance. He had discovered electromagnetic rotation.[15]

After his great success of 1821, Faraday devoted himself to concerns largely unrelated to electromagnetism, returning to consider it again in 1831, the *annus mirabilis* during which he discovered electromagnetic induction. This revelation proved conclusively against the notion of a material electric current; instead, it depended on 'seeing the forces between currents in terms of the magnetic *field* produced by the currents in the intervening medium' (italics mine).[16] Based on his experiment, in which he showed that changing the current in one conducting wire can change the current in a neighboring wire, Faraday proposed that electrical energy is a field of force independent of matter and that matter itself is essentially an electric medium. In August of 1831, he wound copper wire around one side of an iron ring (side A) and wound another copper wire around the other side (side B). Between each of the coils was the bare iron ring. The wire coiled around side B was attached to a galvanometer. Faraday found that when he charged the wire on side A, a current could be detected in the wire on side B. He concluded that a 'wave of electricity' traveled through the iron ring and charged the wire on side B (ER 27).[17]

Faraday labored over the next few years to understand his great experiment. He initially thought he could attribute induction to the 'electro-tonic' state of the wires wrapped around the ring: 'The electrical condition of matter has not hitherto been recognized, but it probably exerts a very important influence in many if not most of the phenomena produced by currents of electricity.... I have... ventured to designate it as the *electro-tonic* state' (ER 60). This hypothesis still attached electricity to matter, but importantly kept the current from Ampère's fluidity. He quickly abandoned, however, this theory, as he conducted further experiments in induction throughout 1831–2. After finding that neighboring conductors separated only by space and not by material mediums, like iron, induced electromagnetic currents in one another, he reached the striking conclusion that 'a *singular independence* of the magnetism and the bar in which it resides is rendered evident' (220). In realizing that electromagnetic lines of force are independent of matter, he came to introduce a new concept: electromagnetic currents occur in fields of force that extend progressively through space. When a charged wire induces a current in a distant one

the magnetic curves themselves must be considered as moving... across the wire under induction, from the moment at which they begin to be developed until the magnetic force of the current is at its utmost; expanding as it were from the wire outwards, and consequently being in the same relation to the fixed wire under induction as if it had moved in the opposite direction across them, or toward the wire carrying the current. (238)

This finding allowed Faraday to do away with the 'electro-tonic' state once and for all: space itself is a plenum of force.[18]

This discovery of induction and its corollaries in the early 1830s led Faraday to ponder, for the next thirty years, two problems: how electric and magnetic forces are transmitted through space and how these forces are related to matter. Through a series of further experiments throughout the early 1830s, he eventually concluded by 1833 that magnetic and electric energy are lines of force that cut through the ether that fills all space – a theory that decisively called into question the Newtonian, mechanical worldview of atoms in a void and forces acting at a distance and evidenced, as one historian of science observes, 'notions of the electromagnetic field as a nonmaterial, continuous plenum and material atoms as discrete products of the plenum'.[19] Faraday articulated this iconoclastic vision in 1844 in 'Speculation touching electric conduction and the nature of matter':

> The view now stated of the constitution of matter would seem to involve necessarily the conclusion that matter fills all space, or, at least, all space to which gravitation extends (including the sun and its system); for gravitation is a property of matter dependent on a certain force, and it is this force which constitutes matter. In that view matter is not merely mutually penetrable, but each atom extends, so to say, throughout the whole of the solar system, yet always retaining its own centre of force.[20]

This vision, fully implied as early as 1831, proves the sublimity of the universe. Each atom of matter is a point of force, retaining its own 'centre of force' yet extending throughout 'the whole of the solar system'. Each microcosm literally contains the vastness of the cosmos. Matter is energy. Faraday had evidenced the first two components of Goethe's and Coleridge's organicism and provided a model for revising the third: he proved that each part is connected by force to the vastness of the whole and that this whole manifests itself in polarized energies. Likewise, in illustrating that matter is a pattern of electricity, he provided a model for electrified writing, symbol galvanized.

EMERSON'S STATES OF ELECTRICITY

While attending to the sublime speculations of organicism, Emerson learned of the sublime proofs of electromagnetism. Significantly, his first mention of the science of electricity in public, in the 1836 lecture 'The Humanity of Science', delivered only three months after the publication of *Nature*, not only shows a keen awareness of recent discoveries in electricity but literally revises with electricity Goethe's statement in *On Morphology*, quoted earlier, that life progresses 'from an unknown center to an unknowable periphery'. The following passage combines several recent scientific discoveries and ideas to form a grand scheme of unity.

> The phenomena of sound and of light were observed to be strikingly similar. Both observed the same law of reflection, of radiation, of interference and harmony....
>
> It is then observed that the same laws might be translated into laws of Heat; that all the principle phenomena of heat might be illustrated by a comparison with those of sound. The analogy is followed out, and Light, Heat, Sound, and the Waves of fluids are found to have the same laws of reflection, and are explained as undulations of an elastic medium.
>
> This analogy is followed by others of deeper origin. Light and Heat are analogous in their law to Electricity and Magnetism. Magnetism and Electricity are shown to be identical, – the spark has been drawn from the magnet and polarity communicated to the needle by electricity. Then Davy thought that the primary cause of electrical effects and of chemical effects is one and the same, – the one acting on masses, the other on particles. The phenomena of crystallization resemble electric laws. The famous experiment of Chladni demonstrates a relation between harmonic sounds and proportioned forms. Finally the sublime conjecture sanctioned by the minds of Newton, Hooke, Boscovich, and now of Davy, that the forms of natural bodies depend upon different arrangements of the same particles of matter; that possibly the world shall be found to be composed of oxygen and hydrogen; and that even these two elements are but one matter in different states of electricity; – all these, whether they are premature generalizations or not, indicate the central unity, the common law that pervades nature from the deep centre to the unknown circumference.   (EL 2: 29)

This remarkable passage is dense with recent science and must be unpacked slowly. Let us begin by considering the last statement, important for its almost word-for-word paraphrase of Davy's own language and for its revision of Goethe with the science of electricity. Perhaps because of the favorable mention of Davy in Coleridge, Emerson came to read the British scientist early in his career, even before going off on his *Wanderjahr* in 1832. As early as 1828, he perused Davy's *Elements of Chemical Philosophy* and continued his study of his science throughout the early 1830s, reading *Elements of Agricultural Chemistry* in 1832. By 1833, he was praising Davy for revealing nature's deepest laws, approaching the 'elemental law, the *causa causans*, the supernatural force' (EL 1: 80). In the above passage, he practically plagiarizes the following passage from *Elements of Chemical Philosophy*:

> That the forms of natural bodies may depend upon different arrangements of the same particles of matter has been a favourite hypothesis advanced in the earliest era of physical research, and often supported by the reasonings of the ablest philosophers. This sublime chemical speculation sanctioned by the authority of Hooke, Newton, and Boscovich must not be confounded with the ideas advanced by the alchemists concerning the convertibility of elements into each other.   (CD 4: 364)

This passage no doubt drew Emerson because of its unifying hypothesis and because each scientist in the roster hypothesized a theory of the essentials of matter: Thomas Hooke, a contemporary of Newton, proposed a kinetic theory of matter, maintaining that constantly vibrating invisible particles constitute matter; Newton conjectured that gravity was the unifying force of all matter; Boscovich, closer to Emerson's time and an important influence on Faraday, was the first to suggest, in 1763, that atoms were not solids, but points of force.[21] Including Davy in this stellar company, Emerson shows a clear understanding of the British scientist's work in chemical affinity. In *Elements of Chemical Philosophy*, Davy details his most important discoveries and conclusions to date, emphasizing the electrical nature of chemical affinity, reporting on his decompositions of substances into their elements with electrolysis. In wondering if the world may be 'found to be composed of oxygen and hydrogen' and if 'even these two elements are but one matter in different states of electricity', Emerson goes to the heart of Davy's genius, garnering the same ideas from him that Faraday did. The common law of nature, coursing from the 'deep centre to the unknown circumference' is to be revealed not by Goethe's organicist speculations but by the science of electricity.

Emerson likely drew his remarks on analogies among heat, light, sound, waves, crystallization, electricity, and magnetism from John Herschel's *Preliminary Discourse on the Study of Natural Philosophy* (1831), which he read as early as 1831 and valued highly, comparing it favorably to *Paradise Lost* (S 4: 157). This book is an exciting and lucid introduction to the most recent scientific discoveries, detailing, among other things, the breakthroughs of Davy, Oersted, and Ampère. In it, Emerson learned much of the information he packs into his passage. He found out that the propagation of sound and light are analogous, both moving through space like undulatory waves. In this section, he read of Ernest F. F. Chladni, the German physicist who made the motions of sound waves visible by 'strewing sand over the surfaces of bodies in a state of sonorous vibration, and marking the figures it assumes'. Later in the book, Emerson discovered that light and heat correspond in their motion and behavior, suggesting to him, as his passage shows, that heat is analogous not only to light but to sound and waves as well.[22]

In a most important section of *Preliminary Discourse*, the one entitled 'Magnetism and Electricity', Emerson would have been struck by Herschel's account of almost universal correspondences among electricity, magnetism, light, heat, and crystallization – correspondences that suggested a unifying force. Herschel writes with great excitement of the recent discovery of the blending of the sciences of electricity and magnetism: 'All the phenomena of magnetic polarity, attraction, and repulsion, have at length been resolved into one general fact, that two currents of electricity, moving in the same direction repel each other, and in contrary directions attract each other.' Writing only about a year before Faraday's great discovery of induction, Herschel claims that the 'communication of magnetism in its induced state, alone remains unaccounted for', though Ampère may be on the verge of explaining it. Nonetheless, great breakthroughs have been made: not only has Davy shown that chemical affinity is electrical affinity, but Oersted, in disclosing the 'wonderful phenomena of electro-magnetism', teaches us to rely 'on those general analogies and parallels between great branches of science by which one strongly reminds us of another, though no direct connection appear'. Other such analogies have been disclosed in researches into electricity and magnetism: heat, light, magnetism, and electricity combine in lightning; the heat of friction and electricity correspond; crystallized minerals gain electricity by being heated and consequently become magnetic.[23]

While Herschel, solely because of the time he wrote, did not mention Faraday, he did, along with Davy, help to prepare Emerson to apprehend the full import of Faraday's revelations. Herschel limned a world coursing with corresponding polarized flows. If light and heat and sound are manifestations of the same holistic, underlying structure and force, then the entire world is sublime: a pattern, part, and particle of the polarized circulations of the Universal Being.

While Herschel did not describe electromagnetic induction and remained content to call, with Ampère, electricity an imponderable liquid, he nonetheless kept Emerson up to date on the emerging sciences of electricity. Sometime between his reading of Herschel back in 1831 and the 1836 lecture in which he drew from Herschel's book, Emerson had become aware of Faraday's great discovery. He mentions Faraday for the first time in public in that very lecture, praising 'the wonders opened by Faraday, Ampère, Oersted in Magnetism and Electricity; a finger-pointing at laws and powers of unrivaled simplicity and extent' (EL 2: 38). Three years earlier, in 1833, he disclosed his full understanding of Faraday's importance, quietly recording in his journal the wonderful import of Faraday's Copernican disclosure. The speculations of the philosophers may have been verified, at long last, he wrote, by the 'great long expected discovery of the identity of electricity & magnetism lately completed by Dr. Faraday obtaining the spark from the magnet & opening almost a ... door to the secret mechanism of life & sensation in the relation of the pile of Volta to the electrical fish' (JMN 4: 94). Emerson's source for this information is unclear, as the lists of his reading compiled by Kenneth Walter Cameron and Walter Harding contain no mentions of texts related to Faraday before 1833; possible sources, however, are many for '[n]ews of the discovery [of electromagnetic induction] caused a tremendous reaction around the world'.[24]

Emerson clearly understands Faraday to have revealed the elusive principle of life, the unifying force. He must have been aware of, through whatever source, two of Faraday's papers that would eventually appear in volume one of *Experimental Researches in Electricity*. The reference to a 'spark' may allude to the famous November 1831 paper reporting on the discovery of electromagnetic induction, in which Faraday explains his inaugural induction experiment with coils wrapped around the iron ring. By rubbing one of the coils with charcoal, he obtained a spark when a current ran through the wire (ER 32). After describing his induction experiments, Faraday suggests that all matter probably has an electrical condition, the 'electro-tonic' state mentioned earlier: since the wire used as a conductor both carries and produces a current, it seems likely that all matter is capable of conducting and generating a charge (60).

Indeed, in the second paper to which Emerson likely refers, first read 10 January 1833, Faraday relates the electricity from Alessandro Volta's pile, the precursor of the battery, to the electricity located in animals like the Torpedo fish; he then goes on to correlate all forms of electricity (265). He also refers to a spark several times in this paper in describing the effects of various sorts of electricity, ranging from voltaic to animal. In considering each form of electricity, he registers its tension of positive and negative forces, motion, magnetism, chemical decomposition, physiological effects, and spark. This paper is nothing less than an introduction to the science of electricity, from which Emerson could have learned about electromagnetism, electrical decomposition, the correspondence between heat and electricity, and the identity of different forms of electricity. Faraday's rather hermetic finding here must have struck Emerson: 'The *general conclusion* which must...be drawn from this collection of facts is that *electricity, whatever may be its source, is identical in its nature*' (360).

Whether Emerson was familiar with only the second paper or both, it is clear that he knew of Faraday's groundbreaking discovery and intuited its implications well before Faraday announced his mature field theory in 1844. Remarkably, he anticipated the determination that matter is continuous energy while scientists were in the process of establishing this fact.[25] With this new scientific information in his head, Emerson began to rethink the virtues of organicism in the years leading up to *Nature*. In 1835, two years after his recording of Faraday's revelation, he suggests that Goethe's formulation of the principle of life is no longer an adequate description of the forces of nature. He compares the '[t]rifles' of wishing to know 'why the star form is so oft repeated in botany' or 'why the number five is such a favorite with nature' to the 'laws' opened by the 'two wonders of electromagnetism & of the polarisation of light' (JMN 5: 42). This passage comes close to an outright critique of Goethe's archetypal morphology, his belief in a primal botanical form. Emerson calls the search for such a form a 'trifle' and compares it to Sir Thomas Browne's overt geometrical Platonizing in *The Garden of Cyrus*. (Like Plato, who in the *Timaeus* attempts to locate a geometrical figure in each of the four elements, Browne looks for an archetypal geometrical form pervading nature.) Indeed, the recent historian of biology Ernst Mayr agrees with Emerson, asserting that Goethe's archetypes are imbued with Platonic idealism. Goethe did perform dissections, but, as Mayr notes, his efforts were not so much real science as a search for an underlying Platonic form.[26]

For Emerson, organicism, at least in Goethe's version, is not free of Platonism, a philosophical paradigm he wished to avoid. He wanted scientific laws.

Emerson here contrasts the scientific 'laws' of electromagnetism and the polarization of light to these Platonist conjectures. The principles of the polarization of light, developed most notably by Augustin Fresnel and Sir David Brewster (about whom Emerson learned in Herschel's *Preliminary Discourse*) in the early nineteenth century, were based on the theory that light waves move forward in transverse vibrations, whether vertical or horizontal, perpendicular to the direction of irradiation.[27] In other words, light waves move in several directions at the same time, forward as well as up and down or side to side. In this way, as noted earlier, they resemble electromagnetic waves. Faraday himself drew upon the theory of polarization of light in 1834 to illustrate the structure of polar tensions in electrolytic conductors (ER 951), and he proposed in 1838 that electromagnetic waves, like light waves, proceed transversely and are polarized into currents of attraction and repulsion (1653–65). These findings prompted him to hypothesize that '*All polar forces* act in the same general matter' (1665). Some years later, in the middle of the nineteenth century, James Clerk Maxwell proved Faraday correct, substantiating the connection of electromagnetism and light by mathematically identifying optic and electromagnetic vibrations.[28]

Remarkably, in 1833, some months after recording Faraday's discovery, Emerson intuited this hypothesis of Faraday and subsequent proof of Maxwell when he noted in his journal, 'Elementary forms of bodies revealed by polarization of light', and listed 'Polarity of matter. light. electricity. galvanism. magnetism' (JMN 4: 416). For Emerson, electromagnetism and polarization of light provided hard scientific proof for organic form. From 1833 through the writing of *Nature* in 1836 until near the end of his life, he found in these branches of the science of electricity that the force of life is palpable, electric, verifiable. The work of Faraday pulled organicist speculations about the nature of matter from the realm of imagination to the environment of fact. Though Goethe and Coleridge were right in conjecturing that parts contain the whole, that the unifying force is polar, they remained too much in the mind and not enough in matter.

Throughout his career, Emerson continued to 'galvanize' organicism. Already in 1834, he could invoke the sciences of force to explain polarity: '[W]e seem to be approaching the elemental secrets of nature in finding the principle of Polarity in all the laws of matter, in light, heat, magnetism, and electricity' (EL 1: 48). Also in 1834, Emerson would cite a Goethean view that he would later reconceive with the help of electromagnetics: an idea that 'much impressed Goethe' is that '[t]he whole force of Creation is concentrated upon every point', that 'agencies of electricity, gravity, light, affinity combine to make every plant what it is' (EL 1: 72). Emerson revises this in the 1854 lecture 'Poetry and English Literature', which would develop to become a substantial part of the 1876 essay 'Poetry and Imagination':

> Nature is...on wheels, in transit, always passing into something else, streaming into something higher;...matter is not what it appears;.... chemistry can blow it all into gas. Faraday, the most exact of natural philosophers, taught that when we should arrive at the monads, or primordial elements...we should not find cubes or prisms, or atoms, but spherules of force.   (W 8: 4)

Likewise, Goethe's 'point' upon which the 'force of Creation [is] concentrated' would become in 1877, in a lecture printed as 'Perpetual Forces', Faraday's electrified grain of water:

> What agencies of electricity, gravity, light, affinity combine to make every plant what it is, and in a manner so quiet that the presence of these tremendous powers is not ordinarily suspected. Faraday said, 'A grain of water is known to have electrical relations equivalent to a very powerful flash of lightning'. The ripe fruit is dropped without violence, but the lightning fell and the storm raged, and strata were deposited and uptorn and bent back, and Chaos moved from beneath, to create and flavor the fruit on your table today.   (10: 60)

Emerson had earlier learned of this 'grain of water' from a newspaper report describing a Faraday lecture of 1857 on the conservation of force (JMN 14: 158). In this lecture, Faraday stated an insight he had expressed as early as 1834: 'What an enormous quantity of electricity...is required for the decomposition of a single grain of water' (ER 861) – a quantity 'equal to a very powerful flash of lightning' (853). These revisions show in large relief the reassessments Emerson was beginning to make just before crafting *Nature*, showing that for him the sublime was increasingly conceived as the lightning crackling through the fields of the world.

Emerson's interest in Faraday did not wane, as shown by his attending a lecture by the British scientist on his second trip to Europe in 1848, as well as by the references in journal entries, lectures, and essays of the late 1850s and 1870s. After hearing Faraday lecture in London in April of 1848, four years after the scientist had proposed his field theory, Emerson wrote in his journal that Faraday had discovered a nature comprised not of 'ultimate atoms' but of 'forces' (JMN 10: 225). Emerson would write years later in the 1876 essay 'Greatness' that Faraday had asserted that 'every chemical substance would be found to have its own, and a different, polarity'.[29] This Emerson translated to mean that each mind too had its own attraction, its own genius – an idea whose forceful impact extended to his views on the power of individual expression. Indeed, in an 1871 journal entry, Emerson includes Faraday in a list of poets in science, those whose expression is as powerful as their insights (16: 250).

Electromagnetism provided Emerson with a sublime model of matter that he would imitate in his written forms – a model of matter that resembles those of twentieth-century science more than those of the nineteenth. The idea that matter is comprised of spherules of force prefigures the subatomic universe of quantum physics, in which the world is comprised of bundles of dynamic, unpredictable, volatile energy. Indeed, Albert Einstein and Werner Heisenberg, despite their differences, credited Faraday with having provided a new picture of reality that led, respectively, to relativity and quantum theory.[30] Gay Wilson Allen succinctly sums up this link among Faraday, Emerson, and twentieth-century physics when he writes that Emerson's and Faraday's 'spherules of force' correspond to the atom uncovered by physicists of our century, which is 'not something stable and solid but [a bundle] of energy' that exists 'in fields of energy'.[31]

Apprehending the electrical undercurrent in Emerson's thought, we now suspect that when he praises 'energy', 'life', 'force', 'attraction', 'spirit', he may well have specific scientific information in mind. Electromagnetism is certainly always in the background not only of his passages on polarity, noted above, but also of his celebrations of the energy of nature and of his assertions that things are not stationary, solid, but 'emanations'. In *Nature*, the 'floods of life stream[ing] around and through us', the 'currents of the Universal

Being', the 'causes and spirits' underlying and constituting the 'outlines and surfaces of things', the 'spirit' 'alter[ing], mould[ing],
mak[ing] matter' – all of these may well be figurative registers of
literal electromagnetic fact.

By 1841, in two pieces especially, the lecture 'The Method of
Nature' and the essay 'Circles', Emerson is more overt in his praises
of nature's 'perpetual forces', turning the gists of 1836 into full-
voiced paeans. In 'The Method of Nature', Emerson claims that for
the scientist, 'a mysterious principle of life must be assumed, which
not only inhabits the organ, but makes the organ' (CW 1: 125). This
principle could well recall Goethe's concept of life, but Emerson's
characterization of it suggests fields of force. In nature, generated by
this principle, 'smoothness is the smoothness of the pitch of the
cataract. Its permanence is perpetual inchoation. Every natural fact
is an emanation, and that from which it emanates is an emanation
also, and from every emanation is a new emanation. If anything
could stand still, it would be crushed and dissipated by the torrent it
resisted...' (1: 124). In nature, one finds no distinction between
matter and energy. Things in nature are not discrete entities, but
related to all other things, patterns inhabited by the same energy:
'This refers to that, and that to the next, and the next to the third,
and everything refers' (1: 125). In 'Circles' nature is not permanent
and stable, but a field of continuous force: 'There are no fixtures in
nature. The universe is fluid and volatile' (2: 179); '[n]othing is
secure but life, transition, the energizing spirit' (2: 189).

Moreover, in 'Spiritual Laws', also published in 1841, Emerson
specifically locates this unifying force in the human sphere, attribut-
ing the potency of great leaders to their electricity. Figures like
Caesar and Napoleon open themselves to the currents of force
running through nature. 'Their success lay in their parallelism to
the course of thought, which found in them an unobstructed channel; and the wonders of which they were the visible conductors,
seemed to the eye their deed. Did the wire generate the galvanism?'
(2: 79). These men are conductors to galvanized charges; in other
words, they are synchronized with nature. Later in the same essay,
Emerson likens the power of nature, its spiritual laws, to 'divine
circuits', conductors of electricity. He continues in this electromagnetic mode in the 1844 'Nature', observing that '[w]ithout electricity
the air would rot' (3: 107). And earlier in that work, he indirectly
alludes to Faraday's 'grain of water': 'The whirling bubble of the
brooks, admits us to the secret of the mechanics of the sky' (3: 105).

Emerson in the same year compares universal truths to magnetism: 'The magnetism which arranges tribes and races in one polarity, is alone to be respected; the men are steel-filings...Let us go for universals; for the magnetism, not for the needles' (3: 135). If the earth is a great electromagnet, then men who wish for power, rhetorical or otherwise, must open themselves to the sublime currents.

Emerson, a tireless *rhetor* in quest of verbal power, could not think of an electromagnetic cosmology without simultaneously conceiving of an electromagnetic composition. If, as Coleridge and Goethe urged, good writing approaches the qualities of nature, then writing in a universe of perpetual force should be charged, electric. It should attract readers only to shock them into a recognition of spirit. A sublime cosmos required a sublime style. To articulate his sublime poetics and rhetoric, Emerson again had to look away from his countrymen, who wished words to point to a meaning like a static sign, and toward the continent, where poets and scientists showed that words could be lightning.

4
Electric Words

In 1832, Emerson began using the heading 'Theoptics' to index certain journal entries. The term, Emerson's own (JMN 3: 263n), marks a moment in which one sees God's spirit coursing through matter. In one such entry, he laments his inability to experience the 'divine principle that lurks within', 'of which life has afforded only glimpses enough to assure me of its being'. One glimpses this principle in observing nature, conversing, or reading, suddenly feeling the shock of the sublime sensation.

> We know little of its laws...but we have observed that a north wind clear cold with its scattered fleet of drifting clouds braced the body & seemed to reflect a similar abyss of spiritual heaven between clouds in our minds; or a brisk conversation moved this mighty deep or a word in a book was made an omen of by the mind and surcharged with meaning or an oration or a southwind or a college or a cloud lonely walk – 'striking the electric chain, wherewith we are darkly bound'.
> (4: 28)

Lord Byron in *Childe Harold's Pilgrimage* refers to the body as an 'electric chain' during a description of how abruptly and unexpectedly we are reminded of past griefs, which like lightning renew the shock of pain.[1] Emerson appropriates Byron's image to detail a more exhilarating experience of speaking with the divine 'out of the clouds and darkness'. After we are jolted by this insight into the divine principle for which we and all else are 'vehicles', we are transformed: we feel wretched in our inability to sustain the vision, yet we yearn always for another initiation into the sublime.

In another entry labeled 'theoptics', Emerson again details the sublime moment, this time emphasizing more intensely how language may prompt it. Like 'A prophet waiting for the Lord in vain', Emerson feels exiled from the 'immense powers' that are his heritage. These powers are 'mysterious', 'painful' laws that strike us 'suddenly, in any place; in the street, the chamber, will heaven open & the region of boundless knowledge be revealed...The hours of true thought in a lifetime how few!' (JMN 4: 274). This knowledge is proclaimed by William Shakespeare, John Milton, Thomas Carlyle, who '[call] us up into the high region, [where] we feel & say "this is my region, they only show me my own property – I am in my element, I thank them for it".' Writers like these craft the 'words in a book' 'surcharged' with meaning. They are versions of the 'poets of science' Goethe and Faraday who likewise inspire the sublime sensation.

These passages on theoptics illustrate not only the nature of the sublime moment but also the ability of language to engender it by surcharging the mind with significance. Emerson wishes to be to his readers as Shakespeare, Milton, and Carlyle were to him. He essays to stun them into a recognition of their place in and as the currents of spirit – after which, they will live differently, become more attentive, more open. Robert D. Richardson, Jr correctly observes that Emerson's choice of the term 'theoptics' was likely motivated by his reading in natural history. As Emerson turned 'slowly but inexorably from theology to science', he needed a term like 'theoptics' to replace 'pantheism'. Scientific attention, not passive reception, taught him how to see the mechanics of lightning in a grain of water. Science instructed Emerson, Richardson remarks, to see with Walt Whitman that 'A mouse is miracle enough to stagger sextillions of infidels'.[2] Emerson's visionary moment in the Jardin des Plantes taught him to see differently, to understand the most ordinary as a window to the extraordinary. *Nature* surcharges readers with 'sextillions' of significances, teaching them the miracle of the mouse, the cosmos in the ant.

Once Emerson realized that matter is energy, that the mouse and the ant contain the vast forces pulsing through the universe, he not only never saw nature the same way again. He never wrote the same way again either. To be an adequate writer, he thought, his words would have to be as electric as nature. His agitated style, his linguistic vigor derive from his inflection of the turbulent universe of Faraday. Soon after learning of Faraday's model of matter, he began to equate strong writing with electricity, wishing his words to imitate the scientist's grain of water by containing the charges of lightning. The result of this electromagnetic poetics is *Nature*, whose tropes are conductors of electricity acting upon one another as if they are electric charges of force, not units of a linear argument. *Nature*'s electric tropes work to shock readers into theoptic moments. They suggest in their extreme linguistic multivalence a boundless, and hence God-like, semantic richness. The *logos* becomes electric.

LOCKE'S SIGNS

However, Emerson again had to renounce the theories of his fellow Americans to find his own creative force. Just as he had to reject the scientific methodology of his fellow Americans, he also had to throw off their notions of words. Bacon's reign extended not only over science but also language. Inflected through Locke and Stewart, Bacon's dreams of a transparent language stripped of figure had firm control over language theory in Emerson's America. In his search for a poetics and rhetoric of the sublime, of electricity, he would again have to turn to Europe.

In his infamous review of Emerson's *Nature*, Francis Bowen not only attacks the young transcendentalist's rejection of observation; he also assaults his ambiguous style: 'though [w]e find beautiful writing and sound philosophy in this little book', 'the effect is injured by occasional vagueness of expression, and by a vein of mysticism, that pervades the writer's whole course of thought'; while it is a 'suggestive book', the reader nonetheless finds that his 'effort of perusal is often painful, the thoughts excited are frequently bewildering, and the results to which they lead us, uncertain and obscure'.[3] Bowen attributes this linguistic obscurity to the same source to which he attaches Emerson's blurry thought: the rejection of Bacon.

For Bacon, stripping the mind of speculation was one with divesting language from figure. He urged his empiricist disciples to 'set everything forth, as far as may be, plainly and perspicuously (for nakedness of mind is still, as nakedness of the body once was, the companion of innocence and simplicity)'. Bacon's call for clear, precise language to express equally lucid, empirically-based thoughts inspired the Royal Society, an offspring of Bacon's new science and the arbiter of scientific study in England, to make official rules for controlling prose in the second half of the seventeenth century. The Society wished to reduce written expression to 'mathematicall plainness'. Rebelling against figurative language and the potential ambiguity it caused, seventeenth-century Baconians endeavored to reduce language to a system of transparent signs, each with a significance as plain as a mathematical mark. Indeed, John Wilkins, in an extreme case of longing for precision, yearned in his *Essay towards a Real Character and Philosophical Language* (1668), a treatise sponsored by the Royal Society, for a universal language. He believed that the primary evil to induction, rationality, and truth was 'the ambiguity of words by reason of Metaphor and Phraseology.'[4] He craved, along with his fellow Society members, all Baconians, a perfectly univocal language, a mode of expression, as one historian of prose put it, 'devoid of literary qualities all together, including aphorisms, antithesis, paradoxes, neologisms, and metaphors'.[5]

Locke's theory of language in his *Essay Concerning Human Understanding* (1690) participates vigorously in this worship of denotation, construing, like the Society member, words as no more than mere tools, useful when they cleanly denote a crystalline meaning, useless when they do not. For Locke, 'The use of words is to be sensible marks of ideas; and the ideas they stand for are their proper and immediate significations.' In Locke's philosophy, ideas are representations of sensible objects, things, in the mind; these ideas remain private until we attach a linguistic sign to them and make them public by speaking or writing them. Words, Locke adds, are made the signs of ideas 'but by a voluntary imposition, whereby such a word is made arbitrarily the mark of such an idea'. The meanings of words come not from God or nature but from the '[l]ong and familiar' use of a sign in connection with an idea.

When men abuse these meanings, breaking the linguistic conventions of their culture, they are likewise abusing thought: if language is a tool for making ideas public, then the tool must be efficient not only for efficacious communication, but, indeed, for successful philosophy. Locke repeatedly claims that philosophical disputes arise when words are not clearly attached to ideas; if they are not univocal and do not 'excite in the hearer exactly the same idea they stand for in the mind of the speaker', then they are disservicable, indeed, harmful, potentially inciting confusion and disagreement. Consequently, Locke takes great pains to warn against the misuse of words, devoting an entire chapter to numerous abuses of them. One involves 'taking [words] for Things'. Locke, a nominalist, maintaining that words are arbitrary signs for things, would never believe that words correspond to reality in any way. Further, firmly taking the Baconian stance, he asserts that another of the abuses is figurative language specifically, eloquence generally. While he feels strained in indicting felicitous phrasing, which 'like the fair sex, has too prevailing beauties in it to suffer itself ever to be spoken against', he nonetheless declares that it and its twin rhetoric are used not to enlighten the understanding but to inspire passion and to muddy judgment.[6]

Dugald Stewart, the philosopher of moment in the Common Sense schools of early nineteenth-century Princeton, Harvard, and Yale, took the mantle from Locke, by way of Reid, not only for his epistemology but also for his related theory of language. In his *Elements of the Philosophy of the Human Mind* (1792–1827), he boils down Locke's philosophy of language into a brief chapter whose title reveals its Lockean origins: 'Inferences with respect to the Use of Language as an Instrument of Thought, and the Errors in Reasoning to which it occasionally gives rise.' Grounding his remarks in George Campbell's *Philosophy of Rhetoric* (1776), yet another effort in the Common Sense school that found a home in American college curricula, Stewart, a nominalist like Locke, explains language as the vehicle of the reasoning process, words as signs of ideas. To insure the clarity of thought, he warns against the three most pernicious linguistic abuses: 'exuberance of metaphor'; the attempt to 'denote things which are of a complicated nature, and to which the mind is not sufficiently familiarized'; and the employment of terms which are 'very abstract, and consequently of a very extensive signification'.[7]

For prudent Unitarians like Bowen and Andrews Norton, the linguistic school of Bacon, Locke, and Scottish Common Sense was, like its inductive course, a precise weapon against sundry forms of infidelity, ranging from Calvinist trinitarianism to Concord transcendentalism. This weapon was most often wielded on the battleground of scriptural hermeneutics. If one were to find evidence for one's dogma, one had to find it in the Bible. Though the Bible is a highly figurative, polysemantic text, hopelessly resistant to univocal interpretations, Norton persistently attempted to reduce the scriptural 'voice of many waters' to one meaning. In response to his orthodox opponents at the trinitarian Andover Theological Seminary, who held that God's grandeur could only be approximated by the figurative language of the Bible, Norton brought out his Locke-inspired *Statement of Reasons for Not Believing the Doctrines of Trinitarians* (1819), in which he endeavored to show that one can find exact meaning in the Bible, Unitarian of course, if one only employs the proper methods. This method involved inflecting Lockean language theory through the recently emerging German-born hermeneutics of Johann G. Herder and J. G. Eichhorn. Herder and Eichhorn interpreted the Bible not so much as scripture as a sublime literary work, a myth or poem, to be read with the techniques of literary criticism, primarily philology and historical contextualization. Norton is quick to point out that these German methods potentially question the 'authority and value' of Scripture, disclosing as they do poetic connotations that could upset dogma. However, if handled cautiously, these hermeneutical strategies can shed 'much light upon the history, language, and contents' of the Bible. Using Locke's theories to brake those of Herder and Eichhorn, Norton urges that one can ascertain an accurate, univocal meaning of the Bible if one can reveal the historical and philological contexts surrounding it. Figurative and symbolic discourse, he believed, could easily be reduced to one meaning: '[W]hen the words which compose a sentence may be used to express more than one meaning, its meaning is to be determined SOLELY by a reference to EXTRINSIC CONSIDERATIONS'. For example, for Norton, the cornerstone of trinitarianism 'I and my Father are one' is merely a figure of speech that clearly means, after careful study of Biblical idiom through attention to the proper contexts, 'I am fully empowered to act as His representative.'[8]

The American brand of Baconian induction is here at work. Just as the Baconian scientist or theologian reduces nature only to what was most obviously before his eyes, so the Baconian hermeneuticist flattens the poetry of the Bible to mathematical precision. In both cases, the Understanding is used at the expense of the Reason. Intuition, the invisible, the sublime are anathema. Bowen so roundly abused Emerson's *Nature*, Norton so fervently attacked the 'Divinity School Address', because both texts bear traits of the most vatic, oracular Biblical scripture without being authorized by the sound institutions of God and godly men. To be sure, by the mid-1830s, Emerson, burning to behold the sublime, had already moved far from the reductive induction and interpretation he had undergone at Harvard, having turned to Europe for his poetics just as he did for his science.

SWEDENBORG'S SYMBOLS

In August of 1821, an 18-year-old Waldo Emerson, just a few days before he was to graduate from Harvard, heard an MA candidate named Sampson Reed deliver an 'Oration on Genius'. In this cryptic yet electric speech, which Emerson would copy and 'keep as

a treasure' (JMN 16: 184), Reed condensed Swedenborg's theory of
language into charged patterns that would stimulate Emerson's
thoughts on language for the rest of his days. Having spent his
college years arduously reading the Swedish mystic's visions of
invisible worlds, Reed found the unfailing devotion to the visible
in his Unitarian professors not only inadequate to account for religious experience, but likely blasphemous. In his 'Oration', a speech
bound to disqualify him for the Unitarian ministry, Reed bluntly
claims that we gain knowledge not from empiricism but from intuition, the 'innate strength of the human intellect': 'The mind of the
infant contains within itself the first rudiments of all that will be
hereafter, and needs nothing but expansion; as the leaves and
branches and fruit of a tree are said to exist in the seed from
which it springs.' One need not use Locke to apprehend that nature
is in unison with spirit; one need only employ the innate genius
of one's mind. To the pure of heart, the insight 'nature is full of
God', grows naturally in the mind, like a spreading tree. Induction
is unnecessary; insight is all. The mind 'returned to its God' understands that '[t]he arts have been taken from nature by human
invention'. They are not 'arbitrary,' but grow from nature, and,
like nature, are 'in their origin...divine'. Indeed, the arts, like
nature, are forms for spirit – for God and the mind's intuitions
of God.[9]

In 1826, Reed expanded these ideas, focusing specifically on relationships among nature, language, and spirit in his pamphlet *Observations on the Growth on the Mind*, lauded by Emerson as 'the best
thing since Plato of Plato's kind, for novelty & wealth of truth' (L 1:
176). In this similarly oracular work, Reed counters Locke with
beautiful concision: 'There is a language, not of words, but of
things.' Everything, he explains, 'is, whether animal or vegetable,...full of expression'. The world is a vast poem: '[T]he visible
creation then, can not, must not...be anything but the exterior
circumference of the invisible and metaphysical world.' The poet,
if he wishes to attain beauty, must understand the meanings of
nature's words, seeing them as symbols of the divine, and deploy
them in his own works:

> The true poetic spirit, so far from misleading any, is the strongest
> bulwark against deception. It is the soul of science. Without it, the
> latter is cheerless, heartless study, distrusting even the presence
> and power of whom to which it owes its existence. Of all poetry

which exists, that only possesses the seal of immortality, which presents the image of God which is stamped on nature.[10]

In Reed, Emerson found Swedenborg's provocative blending of epistemology and poetics. If one gains proper insight, through intuition, into the invisible spirit generating visible nature, then one simultaneously gleans two further insights: that nature is an expression or language of the divine and that the poetry that draws its figures and tropes from this nature partakes of and expresses the divine. Happy to detect in this impressive proposition an alternative to the aridity of the American Lockeans, Emerson became attracted to Swedenborg in the early 1830s, drawn by Reed's magnetic orations as well as by the voice of New England Swedenborgism, *The New Jerusalem*, and by the *The True Messiah* (1829), a seminal transcendentalist treatise by Guillaume Oegger. From these sources, Emerson garnered the Swedenborgian idea that endlessly fascinated him: correspondence. '[T]he visible world', he quotes in an early lecture, 'and the relation of its parts is the dial plate of the invisible one' (EL 1: 25). Language is not arbitrary, not merely a collection of univocal signs for empirical ideas: it is, like nature, a symbol of spirit, a metaphor for the intuitions of Reason.

Concurrently with his nascent courtship with Swedenborg, Emerson found this blending of Reason and language theory in another hermeticist, Coleridge. James Marsh's 1829 edition of Coleridge's *Aids to Reflection* was partly an orthodox response to Unitarians like Norton; Marsh, like his fellow trinitarians in Andover, would have found it blasphemous to reduce God's word to the Understanding. Marsh's 'Preliminary Essay' repeatedly invokes Reason to show that mere empiricism, simple Understanding, cannot account for spiritual ideas, the invisible world. While the Understanding, representing things, may be signed in univocal marks, the Reason, approximating the sublime, requires flexible, polyvocal symbols to gesture towards, without exhausting, its grandeur. Coleridge's conviction that words should be elevated into things and 'living Things, too' in order to symbolize intuitions of spirit inspired Emerson to reflect on a sublime language. Emerson wanted his language to be as sublime as nature, as the mind. He wished for readers to say of his prose what Horace Bushnell claimed of the polyphony of the Bible: 'the second, third, the thirteenth sense of [its] words – all but the physical first sense – belong to the empyrean, and are given, as we see in the prophets, to be inspired by'.[11]

The Bible, nature, the mind: these cannot be represented by signs but must be approximated by symbols. Significantly, Emerson's first mention of Coleridge in public directly follows his citation of Swedenborg's theory of correspondence – the visible is a dial for the invisible. To demonstrate further that nature is a metaphor for the human mind, he quotes Coleridge's 'Destiny of Nations: A Vision': 'For all that meets the bodily sense I deem/Symbolical, one mighty alphabet/For infant minds.' Coleridge's theory of symbol fed the burgeoning Swedenborgianism of the young Emerson. Coleridge, like Swedenborg, looked to the woods and saw words. In contrast to mechanical form, a rigid structure imposed on passive materials from without, organic form shapes from within, merging energy and form, generated by '[n]ature, the prime genial artist, inexhaustible in diverse powers...equally inexhaustible in forms' (CC 5: 495). For Coleridge, the symbol arises when the artist mimics the prime demiurge, nature, finding a fluid form to pattern his dynamic thoughts. Symbol and nature are visible parts in communion with the invisible whole that shapes them from within; symbol, as we already know, 'always partakes of the reality which it renders intelligible: while it annunciates the whole, it abides itself as a living part' (CC 6: 30). Coleridge here corresponds to Goethe, for whom a symbol is a particular thing or event that represents a more general thing or event 'as a living momentary revelation of the Inscrutable.'[12]

Emerson, again returning to European Romantic fecundity to counter American dearth, harvesting from Swedenborg and Coleridge, realized as early as 1831 that '[i]n good writing, words become one with things' (JMN 3: 271). However, he was to concretize this equation in his own writing only after he learned from nineteenth-century scientists how the 'things' of nature function. Through his reading in Davy and Faraday, he came to understand 'things' not as static entities but as evolving patterns of electric force. His words would belong to and mimic this reality. Like his vision of nature, Emerson's theory of language is a dynamic synthesis of organicism and electromagnetism, Coleridge and Faraday. Emerson merges Coleridge's symbol with Faraday's grain of water containing lightning. For Emerson, the symbol is to be electric.

This confluence of hermeticism, Romanticism, and science is amply illustrated, again, by Emerson's first lecture after returning from Europe, 'The Uses of Natural History'. Two paragraphs after conflating Swedenborg – the visible is a dial to the invisible – and

Coleridge – nature is 'symbolical, one mighty alphabet' – Emerson
hails the language of science, recalling no doubt his epiphany in the
Jardin: 'I look to the progress of Natural Science as to that which is
to develop new and great lessons of which good men shall understand the moral. Nature is a language and every new fact we learn is
a new word; but it is not a language taken to pieces and dead in the
dictionary, but language put together into a most significant and
universal sense' (EL 1: 26). Predicting this idea earlier in the essay, he
overtly recalls his vision in Paris: 'Moving along these pleasant
walks [in the Jardin], you come to the botanical cabinet, an inclosed
garden plot, where grows a grammar of botany – where the plants
rise, each in its class, its order, the genus ... arranged by the hand of
Jussieu himself' (1: 8). Plants pattern invisible natural laws just as
words manifest their meanings. Moving from flora to fauna in the
Jardin, Emerson boldly asserts that natural organs manifest the
source of all natural law: 'The universe is a more amazing puzzle
than ever, as you look along this bewildering series of animated
forms, the hazy butterflies, the carved shells, the birds, beasts,
insects, snakes, fish, and the upheaving principle of life every
where incipient, in the very rock aping organized form' (1: 10).

Science is the key to hermeticism and organicism: the 'things' of
nature, in giving form to the currents of universal Being, constitute a
bewildering, cryptic text – a *Corpus Hermeticum*, a Bible – to be
deciphered by the scientist. The words of this text are not signs,
marks standing for univocal meaning; they are not even symbols,
parts standing for the whole; they are spherules of force, condensing, containing, and manifesting the currents that make and sustain
them.

ELECTRIC CIRCUITS

Right around 1836, Emerson began equating good writing with
electricity, literally electrifying Coleridge's theory of symbol to fashion an electromagnetic poetics. While Emerson's poetic *theory* came
primarily from Coleridge, his *practice* issued from the science of
electricity.

Emerson could agree with Coleridge's Romantic revolt against the
Locke-inspired literary theory of the eighteenth century, which was
primarily concerned with how the Understanding and its sense
perceptions imitate the physical world and how words in turn

copy sense impressions.[13] Turn-of-the-century poets like Coleridge and later Emerson found eighteenth-century literary theory unjust to the Reason-driven power of the imagination; Coleridge and Emerson, having digested Kant, believed that nature does not shape a passive mind, but adheres to the *a priori* structures of an active one. For Coleridge and Emerson, to borrow the phrases of M. H. Abrams, the artist's mind, imbued with the shaping power of Reason, is not a mirror reflecting reality, but a lamp illuminating new creations.[14] The Romantic poet is not an imitator, but a demiurge, reshaping nature in his mind, creating a new organism.[15] As Emerson observes in his first book, art is nature transformed through the creative imagination: the *'creation* of beauty is Art' (N 29; italics mine). The poet *'forges* the subtile and delicate air into wise and melodious words, and gives them wings as angels of persuasion and command' (51; italics mine). The imagination, 'the use which the Reason makes of the material world', is constructive, as it conforms not 'thoughts to things', but 'things to thought'. The sensual man, who uses only the fancy, 'esteems nature rooted and fast'; the poet, using imagination, sees nature as 'fluid, and impresses his being thereon. To him, the refractory world is ductile and flexible' (65). He 'delights us by animating nature like a creator' (68).

Later, in 'Intellect', Emerson designates this creative power the 'intellect constructive': it is 'the generation of the mind, the marriage of thought with nature', the producer of 'thoughts, sentences, poems, plans' (CW 2: 198). This intellectual faculty is a version of the Reason, for it is the genius that receives a revelation of nature and publishes it in words. The product of this process, Emerson observes in 'The Poet', 'adorns nature with a new thing' because the poet's words are deeds, 'modes of divine energy', 'actions' (3: 6); his 'expression is organic', the form things themselves take – a sonnet should be a sea-shell or a group of flowers, the ode a tempest (3: 15).

While Emerson concurs with Coleridge on poetic process, he wants for his product more electricity than his Romantic forebear. Significantly, Emerson, aroused for galvanism, asserts in 'The Poet' that the poet can create only by becoming 'the conductor of a whole river of electricity' (CW 3: 23). Similarly, he avows in a late lecture that man's vocation is to translate nature's immense currents into his own creative power:

> His whole frame is responsive to the world, part for part, every sense, every pore to a new element.... No force is but his force.

He does not possess them, he is a pipe through which their currents flow. If a straw be held still in the direction of the ocean current, the sea will pour through it as through Gibraltar.

(W 10: 60)

The poet and the book of nature speak by means of a unifying force, manifesting their meanings in electricity:

There is one animal, one planet, one matter, and one force. The laws of light and of heat translate into each other; – so do the laws of sound and color; and so galvanism, electricity, and magnetism are varied forms of the selfsame energy. While the student ponders this immense unity, he observes that all things in Nature, the animals, the mountain, the river, the seasons, wood, iron, stone, vapor, have a mysterious relation to his thoughts and his life; their growths, decays, quality and use so curiously resemble himself, in parts and wholes, that he is compelled to speak by means of them.

(8: 8–9)

Emerson translates the sublime grain into sublime words.[16] In the 1844 'Nature', likely with Faraday in mind, Emerson contends that each element of nature is a version of the water grain, inhabited by the sublime: 'The whirling bubble on the surface of a brook, admits us to the secret of the mechanics of lightning.... [S]tar, sand, water, tree, man, it is still one stuff, and betray the same properties' (CW 3: 105). Believing that in good writing, words become things, patterns of electrical energy, Emerson could claim in 1838 that good oration is like magnetism, electricity (JMN 5: 449). At about the same time he began to associate powerful spoken words with electricity, a connection he would consistently make (W 8: 115; JMN 7: 224–5), he also started to claim electric status for writing: the written text should 'become a new & permanent substance added to the world', arranged and charged like matter by 'chemical affinity' (JMN 5: 92) – which, as Emerson knew from Davy and Faraday, is electrical affinity. Writing that does not cohere is akin, he wrote to Carlyle in 1838, to an array of 'infinitely repellent particles' (CEC 185). The power of good poetry, and by extension all good writing, resides in 'the magnetic tenaciousness of [the] image', affecting readers like an 'explosive force' (W 8: 27, 64). Eloquence, written or spoken, vitalizes its audience with electricity: it 'thrills and agitate[s] mankind' (8: 70, 73). Emerson wanted words that were charged with the creative, electric forces of nature, 'initiative, spermatic, prophe-sying, man-making words' (JMN 8: 148; W 8: 294). The controlling idea of his composition was that particular words or characters, like things, are impotent without electric charge: '[T]he needles are nothing, the magnetism all' (JMN 9: 229).

Electric writing is sublime, a condensation of vast systems of signification, its words 'spherules of force' containing worlds. Wishing his words to be charged like Faraday's grain of water, Emerson believed that the 'virtue of rhetoric is compression' (W 12: 290). The writer should compose 'dense', 'contracted' sentences resembling the human face, 'where in a square space of a few inches is found room for every possible variety of expression' (12: 348). Every word in a perfect sentence should be packed, dense – like the words of Thomas Carlyle, whom Emerson praised for 'crowd[ing] meaning into all the nooks and crannies of his sentences' (JMN 5: 291). Each word in such a sentence is stressed, italicized: 'In good prose, every word should be underlined' (3: 271). Powerful thinkers should 'write that which cannot be omitted; every sentence a cube, standing on its bottom like a die, essential and immortal' (15: 259).

Like sublime scenes in nature – the tornado, the whirlpool – electric writing is a vector of immense force, not an aggregate of words but a dynamic deed. The speech of the great orator, Emerson wrote later in life, 'is not to be distinguished from action. It is the electricity of action. It is action, as the general's word or command, or chart of battle, is action' (W 8: 115). Powerful language

> is an organ of sublime power, a panharmonicum for a variety of note. But only then is the orator successful when he is himself agitated & is as much a hearer as any of the assembly. In that office you may & shall (please God!) . . . let the electricity to part from the cloud & shine from one part of heaven to the other.
>
> (JMN 7: 224–5)

These late, summary statements found form much earlier in Emerson's career; in 1844, he sounded his rallying cry: '[w]ords are also actions and actions are a kind of words' (CW 3: 6). While he remained drawn to Swedenborg, Emerson would criticize him in *Representative Men* (1850) for believing symbols to be univocal, for neglecting to endorse the fact that words, be they natural or human, are 'waves' that cannot be 'chained' by 'hard pedantry' (4: 68).

Powerful writing should be a kinetic field of polar force, like nature, *'one thing and the other thing,* in the same moment', not to be 'orbed' in a single thought (3: 139).

The primary vectors of Emerson's sublime style are his tropes: 'The value of a trope is that the hearer is one; and indeed Nature itself is a vast trope, and all particular natures are tropes. As the bird alights on the bough, – then plunges into the air again, so the thoughts of God pause but for a moment in any form' (W 8: 15). Emerson here equates troping with the 'incessant metamorphosis' of nature, specifically drawing on the word's etymology of 'turning'. Tropes 'turn' univocal words into multivalent vectors. Nature is constantly troping as it proceeds in 'rapid metamorphosis' (CW 1: 124), converting 'every sensuous fact' into a 'double', 'quadruple', 'centuple', or 'much more manifold meaning' (3: 3–4). So Emerson's tropes, aspiring to be one with things, to 'flow with the flowing' of nature, are 'fluxional', 'vehicular and transitive', expressing 'manifold' meanings (3: 20).

Not only do tropes convey the flowing of nature; they also conduct the shock of its electrical force. In 'The Poet', he declares that 'An imaginative book renders us more service at first, by stimulating us through its tropes' (3: 18–19). 'Nothing', he notices, 'so works on the human mind ... as a trope':

> Condense some daily experience into a glowing symbol, and an audience is electrified .... Put the argument into a concrete shape, into an image, – some hard phrase, sound and solid as a ball, which they can see and handle and carry home with them, – and the course is half won. (W 7: 90)[17]

As we shall see in ensuing sections, Emerson's tropes are the conductors of his electromagnetic style. Like electric circuits, they gather and channel the electricity, the semantic richness, of the cosmos; they bear polar meanings, positive and negative poles; and they influence other circuits, other tropes, attracting some, repulsing others. Condensing several traditional tropes, like metaphor, metonymy, synecdoche, into the same sentence, sometimes the same word, Emerson expresses a linguistic vigor akin to an electrical storm, a sublime scene. Like Faraday's electrical 'spherules' of force, his tropes constantly turn words from one meaning to another, keeping his essay active, oscillating between poles. To prepare for the following sections devoted to Emerson's poetics and rhetoric, I would suggest that Emerson's tropes perform three inter-related activities, each of which bears an electromagnetic resonance: they *turn* words in innovative ways, keeping them polar, oscillatory; they *condense* multiple strands of meaning into a concentrated passage, mimicking in semantic richness the vast forces of nature; and they *act* on one another reciprocally, attracting some nearby tropes, repulsing others, holding the language in constant vibration.

Ultimately, Emerson wanted the tropes in his prose to approach the condition of poetry – any composition, in whatever form, is poetry if it is electric: '[A] poem...shall thrill the world by the mere juxtaposition & inter-action of lines & sentences that singly would have been of little worth and short date. Rightly is this art called composition & composition as manifold the effect of its component parts' (JMN 5: 39). Like Wordsworth, who affirmed that there is no 'essential difference between the language of prose and metrical composition', and like Shelley, for whom 'the distinction between poets and prose writers is a vulgar error', Emerson made no critical distinction between poetry and prose, claiming that 'it is not metres, but metre-making argument that makes a poem' (CW 3: 6) and that '[t]here are also prose poets' (W 8: 50).[18]

CHEMICAL DECOMPOSITION

Emerson's *Nature*, the visible dial of his newly discovered invisible world of perpetual forces, is an electric prose poem, a vector of immense polarized force. In it, Emerson translates the vast forces of nature into the formal elements of his composition. He practices an electromagnetic poetics, resulting in a galvanizing rhetoric. A poetics always implies a rhetoric, an investigation of the relationship between the poetic product and the audience, of the effects of the essay.

Stanley Cavell provides the key to Emerson's rhetoric. He claims that Emerson's language provokes readers into thinking by 'averting' them away from 'conformity' while simultaneously 'converting' them to attend the complexities of every word. When Emerson's language engenders these two effects, it provokes readers to become self-reliant thinkers, to convert his words into vehicles for their own thoughts. The controlling maxim of Emerson's rhetoric appears in the 'Divinity School Address': 'Truly speaking, its is not instruction, but provocation that I receive from a great soul' (CW

1: 80). Emerson's own conversions, his turnings of words, stimulate readers to redeem words, to convert them not into safe, univocal signs, but into sites of intellectual agitation. While Emerson, according to Cavell, appears to be playing 'fast and loose with something like contradiction in his writing', his contradictions can be seen as 'the countering of diction', the 'genesis of his writing of philosophy'. The contradictions in Emerson's style oppose 'dictation', 'avert[ing]' readers from conforming to the linguistic meanings handed down from philosophical, religious, cultural traditions while 'converting' them to attend to each word closely in order to redeem it from the past and make it live in the present. Each word, Emerson implies, must be converted, transfigured, reattached to the world; must be led home, 'as from exile', to the living speech of fresh ideas.[19]

In the lecture 'Art and Criticism', Emerson registers the qualities of a strong rhetoric, emphasizing how words stimulate thought. First, the *rhetor* should use living words – the vernacular, idioms, slang, 'convey[ing] his meaning in terms as short and strong as the smith and the drover use to convey theirs' (W 12: 285). Using the *lingua franca*, the orator, like a magnet, attracts his audience, speaking in the vivid words by which they describe their world; like a voltaic battery, he charges them with voltage, manipulating the mother-tongue into vigorous figures. The second 'virtue of rhetoric is compression' (12: 290). As mentioned above, for language to be powerful, it must be dense, crammed with significance – writing is 'the science of omitting' (12: 290). Using the vernacular, the *rhetor* opens a familiar world to his auditors, establishing comfort and trust. Yet, suddenly, he shocks them into thought with his dense sequences designed to defamiliarize and overwhelm. The primary vehicle of this sublime overload is the third 'principal power of rhetoric': troping, called here metonymy, 'using one word or image for another' (12: 299–300). The trope is inherently surcharged with meaning, bearing at least three significations – that of the vehicle, the tenor, and their relationship.[20] When several tropes gather around one idea, like bits of steel around a magnet, then multitudinous meanings arise, overcoming auditors and readers with semantic force, requiring them to counter by calling their own minds to action.

This rhetorical eloquence, fittingly, is magnetic: it is 'attractive', requiring a rare 'coincidence of powers, intellect, will, sympathy, organs, and, overall, good fortune in the cause' (W 7: 76). The pole of the orator attracts the pole of the audience; they merge in a meeting of personal powers: eloquence occurs 'wherever the polarities meet'

(7: 95). However, this attraction is not free of tension. Indeed, once the orator has drawn the audience to his words, he shocks them: the eloquent man 'is...no beautiful speaker, but...is inwardly drunk with belief. It agitates and tears him, and perhaps also bereaves him of articulation. Then it rushes from him in short, abrupt screams, in torrents of meaning' (7: 92). These two qualities, magnetism and electricity, make eloquence 'the order of nature itself, and so the order of greatest force, and inimitable by any art' (7: 93).

Emerson wished his lectures and essays to be voltaic piles, batteries sending electrical currents to decompose his audience's habits of thought, in turn forcing them to recompose new, more attentive ways of thinking and interpreting – to be creative. Emerson knew well that 'decomposition is recomposition', signaling 'new creation' (CW 4: 46), hoping his words would 'smite' and 'arouse' his readers with 'shrill terms', breaking their 'whole chain of habits', urging them to 'open' their eyes 'on [their] own possibilities' (2: 185).

The voltaic qualities of this rhetoric make it sublime, a part containing a whole of vast force, capable of overwhelming attentive readers with signification while stimulating their minds with a sense of the infinite. As we shall see, *Nature*, the first pure product of Emerson's electromagnetic poetics, is indeed a site of the sublime, inducing currents in active readers like Faraday's copper coils induced them in surrounding conductors during his famous 1831 experiment. The turnings of the scientist's coils, so the turnings of Emerson's tropes. Faraday needed the coils to shock the world into an awareness that matter is energy: he altered matter, bending (troping) normally straight wire, in order to demonstrate the nature of all matter, to jolt us out of our habitual way of seeing nature. 'Common sense' tells us that Newton's worldview is correct, that things are discrete and acted on by external force from a distance. However, we are occasionally jostled from this habitual view when patterns become agitated, when the immense forces underlying matter are revealed in lightning, whirlwinds, tornadoes. Like these events, Faraday's copper wires show that even the most static seeming-stuff is charged. Likewise, the spiralings of the proleptic electromagnetist, the hermetic alchemist, alter normal processes of matter in order to disclose its true nature. In his alembic, he intensely agitates matter, dissolving it into the vast spirit generating it. His dissolutions are aptly pictured by the spiraling caduceus, the coiling ouroboros. God's whirlwinds, Faraday's coils, the alchemist's sublimations: all are turnings that reveal the boundless, that break down matter to unveil its underlying energy. These decompositions inspire a similar breakdown in the mind of the beholder, forcing him to recompose new conceptions of the cosmos. So Emerson's electric tropes, turning language quickly, dissolving words into patterns of energy, overloading readers with boundless signification to teach them that the fabric of the universe is sublime.[21]

METALEPSIS

Before moving to an example from *Nature* to illustrate Emerson's sublime troping, we must face our own linguistic problem. The theory of language I am locating in Emerson seems resilient to traditional classifications: its collocation of electromagnetics, the sublime, and sublimation render it a bizarre concoction. It merges Romantic symbol and something like modernist vorticism, a religious quest for spirit and a scientific one for fact, not to mention words and things. What to call his style?

We might readily term his style 'metaleptic'. Metalepsis, or 'transumption' (the Latin form), describes language in which one trope or figure is added to another 'with extreme compression', usually in 'rhetorical situations of maximum drama and interest'.[22] The use of this trope has been dismissed, most notably by Quintilian, because it resembles catachresis, which is a confusing, mixed metaphor, and *abusio*, or an unnatural wrenching of the meanings of words.[23] John Hollander, however, has recently shown that metalepsis is useful in formally describing rhetorically charged passages, like Milton's similes, that, as Samuel Johnson put it, '"crowd the imagination"'.[24] Indeed, Angus Fletcher claims that a metaleptic style is a sublime one, for it overtaxes the faculties like the infinity of the cosmos.[25]

I would submit that metalepsis is the key to Emerson's verbal labyrinths. The trope formally describes Emerson's most sublime passages, where he fuses several figures, tropes, and allusions. Indeed, in his discussion of the trope, Hollander pauses to consider Emerson's remark in 'The Poet', that 'We are far from having exhausted the significance of the few symbols we use. We can come to use them yet with a terrible simplicity' (CW 3: 11). Hollander notes that 'The beautiful complexity figured in this last phrase is that of revisionary, interpretive transumption'.[26]

For Hollander, metalepsis refers primarily to 'diachronic, allusive figures'. He takes a cue from Fletcher's claim that Milton has a 'transumptive style' because he saw nature, as Dr Johnson wrote, 'through the spectacles of books'. Hollander, in turn, revives metalepsis to designate tropes that echo past literary texts. The word derives from *metalambano*, which covers a wide range of meanings: 'to partake in, succeed to, exchange, take in a new way, take in another sense [of words], and even to explain or understand...'. Taken together, these semantic dimensions suggest, Hollander notes, both meanings of the modern 'to take after', to mimic and to come after in time. In Patristic Greek, the word primarily meant 'to interpret' in the sense of translating or transferring from a literal to a spiritual level. Quintilian translated the word to the Latin *transumptio*, 'to adopt' or 'to assume'. This term became the basis for the English 'transumption', which has meant, since the fifteenth century a 'copy or quotation'; 'transfer or translation'; 'transmutation or conversion'.[27]

These meanings underline a diachronic relationship between an earlier and a later text. But the relationship, Hollander observes, is not one of overt literary allusion; the metaleptic relationship is elliptical, covertly echoing the past. It is 'elusive and allusive' at once. Moreover, the metaleptic echoing is interpretive. The later text always revises the earlier one. For example, Milton's famous trope of the 'blind mouths' in *Lycidas* alludes to and revises Sophocles's trope of 'blind feet' in *Oedipus at Colonus*. On a more complex transumptive level, Satan's spear in *Paradise Lost* (1.292–6) – 'to equal which the tallest Pine/Hewn on Norwegian hills, to be the Mast/Of some great Ammiral, were but a wand' – echoes the club of Homer's Polyphemous (as rendered by Chapman), 'being an Olive tree...so vast/That we resembl'd it to some fit Mast/To serve a ship'; the club of Goliath; the one of the Polyphemous of *The Aeneid*, who holds a 'lopped pine'; the pine tree described in the Golden Age of Ovid's *Metamorphoses*, in which pine trees still rooted in the earth, unlike Satan's uprooted tree, symbolize unspoiled innocence. This wide and complex range of covert, yet 'charged' allusion packs maximum meaning. Milton's Satan is not only Goliath, but a rebellious giant who is blind (Virgil's Polyphemous is 'a horrid monster, shapeless, huge, bereft of light') and who spoils what is natural (the echo of Ovid suggests that Satan's spear 'reeks of implicit technology'). In echoing these past texts, Milton transcends them by making his tree bigger and richer. Satan's tree makes that of Polyphemous seem like a mere wand.[28]

Metalepsis in its 'broadest sense' is 'the process of taking hold of something poetically in order to revise it upward... cancelling and transforming' it.[29] Indeed, Harold Bloom uses metalepsis for his ultimate trope of revision, and applies it to Emerson's relationship to his poetic predecessors. For Bloom, transumption is 'a total, final act of taking up a poetic stance in relation to anteriority of poetic language, which means primarily the loved-and-feared poems of the precursors. Properly accomplished, this stance figuratively produces the illusion of having fathered one's own fathers'.[30] Transumption is the most powerful revisionary trope because it not only allows the poet to hide his influences but to cancel them as well. It resists the anxiety of influence.

Certainly Satan's spear is, as Hollander notes, 'imaginatively crowded' because of its dense pattern of diachronic, historical allusion. Yet we find that metalepsis features a related synchronic, ahistorical modality as well. Quintilian writes:

> It is the nature of metalepsis to form a kind of intermediate step between the term transferred and the thing to which it is transferred, having no meaning in itself, but merely providing a transition. It is a trope with which to claim acquaintance, rather than one which we are ever likely to require use. The commonest example is the following: *cano* ['sing' Homerically] is a synonym for *canto* ['recite', 'declaim', 'repeat'] and *canto* for *dico* ['to write'], therefore *cano* is a synonym for *dico*, the intermediate step being provided by *canto*.[31]

Explaining this definition, Hollander observes that metalepsis can be a 'trope of a trope', a synchronic 'combination of figures', that often leads to a catachretic, or thoroughly mixed, metaphor. In other words, the metaleptic trope can often allude intertextually as well as historically. Milton's celebrated catachresis, 'blind mouths', a historical transumption of Sophocles, is also dense intertextually. While Sophocles's 'blind feet' is simply a synecdoche for a blind man, in 'blind mouths' Milton's metaphoric 'blind' describes the synecdoche 'mouths', with a metalepsis occurring in the unstated middle term of 'preachers'. 'Blind' is synonymous with 'preachers'; 'preachers', with the 'mouths' they use to preach. Within the text, the metaleptic trope opens a circuit of hidden associations, its two tropes – metaphor and synecdoche – reciprocally acting on one another to produce additional meanings. The classic example of synchronic, or intertextual, metalepsis is Virgil's *Aeneid* 1: 60. It occurs in several medieval and Renaissance rhetorics, namely Susenbrotus's sixteenth-century *Epitome tropam et schematum*. Drawing from Virgil's line 'the father omnipotent hid them in gloomy caverns', Susenbrotus writes that transumption occurs in 'gloomy', because 'gloomy means black; black, shadowy; and shadowy, deep'.[32] While this example is a bit confusing because 'gloomy' isn't really a trope but a literal adjective, still we can understand the basic component of intertextual metalepsis: an interaction of tropes that produces several simultaneous meanings.

Both historical and intertextual metalepsis function in the same way, and are, as we see with Milton's 'blind mouths', often simultaneous. Just as synchronic metalepsis operates on elided middle terms, so does diachronic. Just as one must move from 'gloomy' to 'deep' by way of the elided middle terms of 'black' and 'shadowy', so one proceeds from Satan's spear to Polyphemous's club by means of the elided allusion to Homer's *Odyssey*. Fletcher's description of metalepsis suggests this correspondence between synchronic and diachronic metalepsis; transumption, he theorizes, is a device 'in which commonly the poet goes from one word to another that sounds like it, to yet another, thus developing a chain of auditory associations getting the poem from one image to another more remote image'.[33] If we expand the definition to include semantic as well as auditory associations, we realize that metalepsis constructs a chain, with hidden links, by which a poet, and the reader, get from one image, be it synchronic or diachronic, to another 'more remote image'.

Emerson in his most charged, sublime passages employs both modes of metalepsis, synchronic and diachronic. Intertextually, he packs trope on trope, figure on figure, to conduct the electric forces of nature into his words. Historically, he alludes to the Bible to revise its revelations in light of science. Issuing from a Romantic tradition that endeavored to revise Judeo-Christian religion with secular concepts,[34] Emerson in *Nature* transumes scriptural passages, revising them with scientific ideas. He suggests that the Bible is unable to account for nature's perpetual forces, which he endeavors to reveal in the fecundity of his own words.

Metalepsis aptly figures the three primary activities of Emerson's electromagnetic tropes: it details their turnings, the endless oscillations of meanings; their condensations of multiple significances; and their actions on one another. It is the copper coil patterning Emerson's linguistic vigor.

LINGUISTIC SUBLIME

Emerson's metaleptic sites are sublime. They are theoptic moments in which words reveal the world, parts the whole, the grain of water lightning. The oscillating force of his metaleptic tropes, acting on both Biblical scripture and on other passages in Emerson's text, reveal a boundless, Godlike, semantic expanse. Before moving to consider one of these sublime sites, we must pause a bit longer to articulate more clearly the relationship between metalepsis and the sublime. We can schematize the relationship between these two terms in Emerson by drawing on Thomas Weiskel's study of the Romantic sublime and language. Weiskel theorizes that the sublime occurs in the mind of the poet in three phases, in the course of which his linear, comprehensible reading patterns are suddenly disrupted by the sublime – be it in the form of disruptive language or nature – which forces him to create his own tropes. These phases can take place not only in the poet but also in the ordinary inter-preter of language or nature. In the first phase, the mind is in a harmonious relationship to the object it attends, in a state of 'normal perception or comprehension, the syntagmatic linearity of reading or talking a walk or remembering or whatnot'. This 'habitual rela-tion of mind and object' suddenly is disconnected in the second phase, when '[e]ither mind or object is suddenly in excess' and the relationship between mind and object, word and meaning, becomes indeterminate. This rupture occurs, for example, when 'a text... ex-ceeds comprehension,...seems to contain a residue of signifier which finds no signified in our minds' – or, using our terminology, when the reader confronts metalepsis. In the third and final phase, the mind recovers a balance between itself and the world or the text, by realizing that the indeterminacy that erupted in phase two sym-bolized 'the mind's relation to a transcendent order'. In this phase, we realize that our inability to present or to image the world in phase two was an intuition of a beyond, a 'meta' world, the unat-tainable.[35]

Weiskel details the transition from phase two to phase three as a process of troping. Faced with the indeterminacy, the poet or reader can recover a sense of balance with the world or text either meta-phorically or metonymically. The metaphorical sublime 'resolves the breakdown of discourse by substitution.' By substituting the 'trans-cendent', 'the spiritual', the 'daemonic', etc., for the indeterminacy, one is able to identify with it, restore some sort of relation to it. The metaphorical sublime occurs when one is overwhelmed with an overabundance of meaning in trying to grasp a religious mystery, unbounded nature, or a difficult text, and then makes this over-taxing profusion significant by substituting 'God' or the 'absolute' for it. Weiskel notes that the metaphorical is generally the reader's sublime because it is the mechanism by which one reads obscure texts and enigmatic nature.[36]

The metonymical sublime works by displacing 'its excess of signified into a dimension of continuity which may be spatial or temporal'. The metonymical is typically the poet's sublime, the process by which he diffuses the energy of the sublime disruption into language to distribute its force into his text. When Words-worth's mind is 'overwhelmed by meaning', he not only meta-phorically substitutes for the disruption but also displaces the excess meaning, by way of metonymy, throughout nature. In 'Tin-tern Abbey', Wordsworth is overcome by disruption, which he immediately metaphorizes into a 'presence' that 'disturbs' him, an 'elevated thought', a 'sense sublime/Of something far more deeply interfused'. Simultaneously, he spreads this presence by metonymy, diffusing it to 'the light of setting suns', 'the round ocean and the living air', 'the blue sky', the 'mind of man', indeed, to '[a]ll thinking things', 'all objects of all thought', and 'all things'. According to Weiskel, the most powerful, original poets follow Wordsworth here, occupying both positions – reader and poet – at once. They simultaneously substitute their 'genius' for the disruptive power and express it by distributing it in their words.[37]

Metalepsis instances this tripartite framework. It transports read-ers from phase one to two, disrupting typical reading habits with its semantic fecundity. Bewildering readers in such fashion, the metaleptic sequence inspires troping. Alert readers will substitute for their overtaxed state an interpretive metaphor and then spread the excess of signification metonymically in the lines of their explication.[38]

GOOD WRITING AND BRILLIANT DISCOURSE

Now we can turn to a metaleptic passage in *Nature*. The sequence, in the 'Language' section, functions on two levels. First, it exhibits a speaker undergoing the tripartite process of the sublime moment.

Overwhelmed by sublime energy, he employs tropes to restore calm. Second, the stylistic density of the passage works to inspire a sublime moment in readers, urging them to perform interpretive activities like those of the speaker. In other words, Emerson depicts a speaker initially in a habitual, ordinary relation to his environment; suddenly, he is overwhelmed by the sublime; after, by making his own tropes, he fashions a new way of relating to his environment. The same threefold process is likely to take place in readers attending actively to Emerson's own language.

After lamenting the recent decay of language into meaningless abstraction, Emerson asserts that wise men can again fasten words to visible things, so that 'picturesque language' shows that one is 'in alliance with truth and God'. He continues, detailing the process by which good writing and brilliant discourse are made.

> The moment our discourse rises above the ground line of familiar facts, and is inflamed with passion or exalted by thought, it clothes itself in images. A man conversing in earnest, if he watch his intellectual processes, will find that always a material image, more or less luminous, arises in his mind, cotemporaneous with every thought, which furnishes the vestment of the thought. Hence, good writing and brilliant discourse are perpetual allegories. This imagery is spontaneous. It is the blending of experience with the present action of the mind. It is proper creation. It is the working of the Original Cause through the instruments he has already made. (N 39)

The passage features a speaker experiencing a sublime moment. His habitual relation to the world is disrupted. He is elevated above the ground line, overtaxed by thought and emotion. Immediately, he 'clothes his thought in images', or transmutes the indeterminate energy of his mind and heart into images, or tropes.

These lines work to stimulate similar activities in readers. Through intertextual metalepsis, tropes acting on tropes, Emerson's language is agitated, imitating the fiery passion and expanding thought of the discourser. Emerson tries to cast readers as good writers and brilliant discoursers. His language, like that of this poet, swells with excitement, rises above the ground line of familiar facts. 'Ground' is a pun, signifying the earth, a foundation, and a zero charge of electricity. When language rises above the ground, it is charged, electrified, becoming both volatile, 'enflamed', and increased in power and size, 'exalted'. It is sublime, above the ground, lofty, extraordinary, not 'grounded' in the habitual.

This energy arising from the ground must be 'clothed' in images. The 'clothing' is a catachretic metaphor, as the idea of fire being clothed strains logic. Expanding fire and electricity will be 'clothed' only momentarily by images, for the cloth will be consumed or ripped by the flames. The energy of the discourse, then, will and will not be clothed; words will and will not express. This strained metaphor is a paradox. It taxes logic.

This Emersonian vector stimulates readers with auditory effects as well. Emerson uses subtle repetitions of sounds to reinforce his more overt message, wishing to get 'under the skin' of readers, to pierce their unconscious.[39] 'The moment our discourse rises above the ground line of familiar facts, and is inflamed with passion or exalted by thought, it clothes itself in images.' The key word in the passages is 'rises', for it details the direction of inflamed passion, exalted thought, and brilliant language. The word itself seems to rise, as its long 'i' sound rhymes with 'high'. Several 'i' sounds throughout the passage, primarily short ones, sustain this echoing. Each of these 'i' words is key in the semantics of the sentence. The 'line' is the monotony of habit that the sublime 'rises' above. 'Inflamed', connected to rising discourse by 'is', figures the energy of the sublime. '[I]t' and 'itself' refer to 'rising' discourse that is clothed in 'images' by one experiencing the sublime.

'S' sounds, prominent in 'rises', likewise pervade the passage. These sounds cause the passage to hiss with the smoke of the flames as the inflamed 'i's' rise. Also, just as 'i' rhymes with 'high', 's' rhymes with *esse*, Latin for 'to be'. For Emerson, 'to be' truly is 'to rise', to feel the upwelling of sublime energy. Likewise, 'to be' is to 'essay', to write, to clothe fiery thought in images. Taking a cue from Emerson's claim that he would 'essay to be', Joel Porte has shown that Emerson in his essays 'dares, endeavors, tries, attempts...to create himself'.[40] Indeed, throughout the passage we hear a faint rhythm of *I-esse*, a nexus expressing the heart of the passage and Emerson's overall project: the *I is* by *ess*aying the sublime.

The next sentence in the passage proceeds to describe this complex process by which one experiences the sublime: 'A man conversing in earnest, if he watch his intellectual processes, will find that a material image, more or less luminous, arises in his mind, cotemporaneous with every thought, which furnishes the vestment of that thought'. A man 'conversing' finds that a 'material' image – a visible furnishing, a massy vestment – rises in his mind along with thought – invisible and weightless – to provide the clothing of that thought. Another paradoxical, catachretic metaphor appears: a *material* image is made to rise as if it were invisible and weightless like thought. This material image 'furnishes' the vestment for thought. 'To furnish' is a catachretic metaphor as well; it means to provide, but also to furnish, to place furniture in a house. Does the material image then provide a perfectly fitting garment for thought or does it clutter the mind with unnecessary furniture? Other questions riddle us: why is the image more or less luminous? Is it more or less consumed by the flames of fiery thought?

In calling the material image that arises with thought 'luminous', Emerson practices diachronic metalepsis. He elliptically alludes to the Bible. The brilliant discourser is in a position similar to God in the first chapter of *John*, where God's creative Word is made flesh. God's *logos*, his Son, is his Word clothed in material: 'In the beginning was the Word, and the Word was with God, and the Word was God'. In him 'was life; and the life was the *light* of men' (1: 1–4; italics mine). Like God's *logos*, the words of this speaker clothe the invisible and are luminous. However, unlike the *logos*, which fully embodies and represents God on earth, the words of the brilliant discourser do not fully incarnate and depict their meaning. Indeed, their meaning consumes and destroys them, burning them with fiery passion, ripping them with expanding thought. Ironically, the words are 'vestments', robes worn by priests in celebrating the Eucharist, a festival that commemorates the relationship between *logos* and God, a communion of symbol and meaning. But the discourser's 'vestments' do not symbolize union between word and meaning, visible and invisible. The discourser's words are really *anti*-vestments. They suggest a problematic *logos*. Emerson has revised the *logos* in light of his idea of the scientific sublime. The book of nature is not comprised of univocal signs but by electrical forces.

This process of clothing thought is spontaneous, as fiery and exalted discourse 'clothes itself'. However, Emerson seems to contradict this statement in claiming that if a man '*watch* his intellectual process' (italics mine), he will find that the image rises with the thought. The process is paradoxical, both spontaneous and conscious.

At this point, the language has become indeterminate, bewildering. It seems as if Emerson senses this indeterminacy in his own language, for the remainder of the passage is comprised of simple sentences meant to clarify the baffling process of turning fiery thought into words. He calls this complex process an act of 'conversing'. He then follows 'conversing' with a series of seven metonymic displacements that associate 'conversing' with 'good writing', 'brilliant discourse', 'perpetual allegory', 'spontaneous imagery', 'blending of experience with present action of the mind', 'proper creation', 'working of the Original Cause'.

The seven metonymies restore a balance between dissolution and solution, centrifugal and centripetal, *solve et coagula*. Emerson has moved from the indeterminacy of his own language by troping: he has substituted the metaphor of 'conversing' for the process of sublime composition and displaced his surplus of meaning with a litany of metonymies. The metonymies literally 'slow down' the quick turnings of the agitated site, as each of the seven sentences is monotonously patterned with 'subject–copula–complement' structures. This syntactic parallelism itself is slowed down by the anaphora of the last three sentences, each of which begins with 'It is...', further reinforcing the return to stasis. Emerson like an alchemist has turned down the flame under the alembic of his essay, settling the fluid after the vigorous sublimations of language.

Attentive readers would be in the same position as the brilliant discourser and Emerson. They would be overwhelmed by linguistic force. Emerson has compressed several tropes and figures into this brief passage, essaying to affect readers on semantic, syntactic, and auditory levels, his sentences constituting a voltaic pile or an alembic. In embodying sublimation, his tropes have worked to sublimate – to dissolve and diffuse – the habits of readers. He would urge his readers to refigure fresh hermeneutic practices, to create new tropes by which to pattern his style.[41]

READER'S MUSE

Emerson's *Nature*, aspiring to pattern the sublime forces of nature, is a hermeneutic invitation. His tropes emancipate the understanding from the tyranny of one meaning for one word. They work against lethargy, habit, stagnation. They stimulate self-reliance. Under each word and thing is a million worlds. Emerson's trope or symbol

> has a certain power of emancipation and exhilaration on all men. We seem to be touched by a wand, which makes us dance and run

about happily, like children. We are like persons who come out of a cave or cellar into the open air. This is the effect on us of tropes, fables, oracles, and all poetic forms. Poets are thus the liberating gods. Men have really got a new sense, and found within their world another world or nest of worlds; for the metamorphosis once seen, we divine that it does not stop.   (CW 3: 17)

This theory of language produces what B. L. Packer has called Emerson's 'deep' style, 'one that challenges the reader to intellectual activity'. As Packer notes, an early reader of Emerson, W. C. Brownell, correctly observed that interpreting an Emerson essay 'requires virtues much more strenuous than passive receptivity' because '[e]verything means something additional. To take it in you must go beyond it. The very appreciation of an essay automatically constructs a web of thought in the weaving of which the reader shares.' Packer emphasizes that this appreciation requires great energy; for inactive readers, Emerson's sentences 'lie upon the page like steel filings when no magnet is present', while active readers are rewarded with a 'certain electric tingle'.[42] Alan Hodder agrees with Packer in claiming that Emerson deliberately frustrates 'a habitually discursive reading'. His sentences were 'not composed to yield up meaning passively, for the meaning is wound tightly in each sentence structure'. In order to make sense of *Nature,* Hodder continues, we 'need to adjust our normal reading habits'. Instead of searching for discursive continuity, readers must meditate on individual sentences, 'small models that contain the wholes', and forge the links, the transitions, between them. *Nature* is replete with what Wolfgang Iser calls 'gaps', locations of indeterminacy that engage readers to communicate with a text, to participate in the construction of its meaning. The more gaps, the more readers are engaged. There is not a more gap-ridden text, as Hodder claims, than *Nature.*[43]

Emerson's *Nature,* becoming itself a reader's muse, engenders creative interpretation. In it, Emerson 'muses' readers, inspires them away from slavish, paraphrased interpretations and toward creative ones. Opposed to the 'silkworm' who creatively tropes, who turns mulberry leaf into satin, the uncreative reader is the 'bookworm'. He is the 'meek young m[a]n' who believes it is his 'duty to accept the views' of those he reads. He values books 'as such; not as related to nature and the human constitution, but as making a sort of Third Estate with the world and the soul'. He restores readings, emendates, is a bibliomaniac (CW 1: 56).

The bookworm does not read that he may write, but that he may memorize.

Creative readers, conversely, treat texts not as signs but as provocations to thinking. As Emerson claims in 'The American Scholar':

> One must be an inventor to read well...There is...creative reading as well as creative writing. When the mind is braced by labor and invention, the page of whatever book we read becomes luminous with manifold allusion. Every sentence is doubly significant, and the sense of our author is as broad as this world.
>
> (1: 58)

Creative readers discover the text to be highly figurative, dense with manifold allusion, luminous with energy. They are no longer inhabited by thought, but 'Man Thinking'. This insight into the relationship between word and meaning should inspire new creation, as books 'are for nothing but to inspire' (1: 56). Readers should not read simply to learn facts but to create. Proper interpretation should be as creative as the text being interpreted: 'Every scripture is to be interpreted by the same spirit which gave it forth' (N 44).

Emerson's rhetorical effects do not merely, as Kenneth Burke argues, carry readers across the bridge from the natural to the supernatural,[44] but work to convert them into trope-makers. Several readers have turned writers after engaging Emerson's prose. Moncure Conway's account of reading Emerson sounds like a conversion narrative. After lamenting over his lack of prospects, the young Conway gives into depression by going alone into the woods.

> Utterly miserable, self-accused amid sorrowful faces, with no outlook but to be the fettered master of slaves, I was then wont to shun the world, with a gun for apology, and pass the hours in this retreat. So came I on a day, and reclined on the grass, reading a magazine casually brought...Nature had no meaning, life no promise and no aim. Listlessly turning the printed pages, one sentence caught my eye and held it; one sentence quoted from Emerson, which changed my world and me.
>
> A sentence only! I do not repeat it: it might not bear to others what it bore to me: its searching subtle revelation defies any analysis I can make of its words. All I knew is that it was the touch of flame I needed. That day my gun was laid aside to be resumed no more.

While Conway feels the flames of Emerson's words in his conversion, John Albee undergoes agitation and satiation. He recalls that upon picking up *Representative Men* in a book store:

> I read a few pages, becoming more and more agitated, until I could read no more. It was if I had looked in a mirror for the first time. I turned around, fearful lest someone had observed what had happened to me; for a complete revelation was opened in those few pages, and I was no longer the same being who entered the shop. These were words for which I had been hungering and waiting.[45]

John Jay Chapman described his experience of reading Emerson even more concretely: 'His words...sparkle in the mind, or you may carry them off in your pocket. They get driven into your mind like nails, and on them catch and hang your own experiences, till what was once his thought has become your character.'[46]

Each of these readers responded to Emerson's prose by writing his own. Indeed, it is fascinating to note how many writers, like Whitman, were simmering until Emerson's words brought them to a boil. This list would include not only Thoreau, Whitman, Dickinson, the three writers mentioned above but also William James, John Dewey, and Wallace Stevens. Attentive readers of Emerson, like these writers, open themselves the the tingle of the prose. Doing so, in the oven of their own imaginations, they sublime sensations into tropes of gold.

5

The Electric Field of *Nature*

Though Emerson broke from the Unitarian Church in 1832, casting off his ministerial office in favor of the poet's vocation, he continued to preach, the lyceum his pulpit, the essay his sermon. In substantiating religious intuitions with scientific facts, Emerson, suckled on the scripture, tutored by his intensely devout Aunt Mary, never thought to reject Christianity but to revise it, to improve upon it. This he did by redeploying in scientific contexts the religious ideas, patterns, structures he most valued: God's animating breath became the scientific principle of life; prophecy, apprehension and expression of natural law; the grandeur of scripture, the sublime. Again, Emerson was about synthesizing, blending, in hermetic fashion, a religious sensibility with scientific rigor. He wished to bring the minister's speculations to fruition in the laboratory.

In reviving Christian concerns within secular contexts, Emerson once again participates in one of the primary traditions of European Romanticism: natural supernaturalism, a coinage from Carlyle, described memorably by M. H. Abrams. Emerson, like his European forebears, never trades religion for science but instead 'reformulates' 'traditional concepts, schemes, and values which had been based on the relation of the Creator to his creature and creation' within the frameworks of science.[1] Emerson, casting himself as a sort of American Wordsworth, fashions himself in his essays as a prophet, not simply of scripture or merely of nature, but of a new revelation – the poetry of scripture realized in nature, nature's exuberant truths embodied in agitated words.

Emerson, remember, came to his study of natural philosophy steeped in scripture; indeed, the majority of his hypotheses concerning nature were shaped by his religion. Alan Hodder correctly observes that 'Emerson hardly learned anything from the Book of Nature that he had not already learned from the Book of Revelation'.[2] While the epiphany in the Jardin des Plantes inspired Emerson to redistribute emphasis from the book of scripture to the book of nature, he essentially discovered the same insights in each. In *Nature*, his youthful spiritual preoccupations still hanging on him like the remnants of a dream, Emerson often looks at nature and sees scripture: 'All things are moral; and in their boundless changes have an unceasing reference to spiritual nature' – especially natural processes: '[F]rom the sponge up to Hercules, shall hint or thunder the laws of right and wrong, and echo the Ten Commandments.... Nature [is] ever the ally of Religion; [she] lends all her pomp and riches to the religious sentiment' (N 51–2). We find statements of this kind sprinkled throughout his first book: 'Every natural process is a version of a moral sentence'; a farm is a 'mute gospel', with its 'chaff and wheat, weeds and plants, blight, rain, insects, sun' (53). As Emerson never tired of saying, the 'axioms of physics translate the laws of ethics' (41).

Emerson the hermeticist blurs the office of prophet and scientist: with his faith-driven deductions and empirically minded inductions, he searches for God in nature through both devotion *and* reason. He takes for his models naturalist prophets and religious scientists. The prophets he most respected – 'David, Isaiah, Jesus' – drew 'deeply from [nature]' (N 52) in proclaiming their teachings. Likewise, the scientists he most admired – 'the heroes of science' Kepler, Galileo, Newton, Linnaeus, Davy, Cuvier, Humboldt – 'are persons who added to their accuracy of study a sympathy with men, a strong common sense; and an earnest nature susceptible of religion' (EL 2: 37). These men creatively combined rigor and vision, fulfilling Emerson's requirement: the 'rapt saint' is the 'only logician' (CW 1: 122). These men were what Emerson strove to be: ideal teachers who showed that 'the Ought, that Duty, is one thing with Science, with Beauty, and with Joy' (1: 93). According to Emerson, Jesus himself could not be this teacher because he had 'no love of natural science' (JMN 5: 71–2). The 'prophetic vision', he believed, could be made good only by 'slowpaced experiment' (5: 220). For Emerson, 'religion by revelation to us' is a vision not of Jesus, but of the causes of nature that 'stream around and through us' (N 5).

Nature remains Emerson's first and most powerful vehicle for these syntheses, not only in content but also in form, aspiring to be a hermetic revelation: 'an instantaneous and radical alteration of sight' in which 'man's imaginative vision, suddenly liberated, penetrates to the inner forms, both of man and his world, which had been there all the time, beneath the veil'.[3] For Emerson, this apocalypse occurs with 'more earnest vision' through the surfaces of things, rendering them 'transparent' to their 'causes and spirits' (N 62). The religious model, of course, for Emerson's synthetic apocalypse is

John's Revelation, in which the prophet sees 'a new heaven and a new earth' (Rev. 21: 1). Indeed, readers as far back as Carlyle have read Emerson's 'little, azure-colored book' as a version of Revelation, both in theme and structure.[4] Not only are both thoroughly visionary; each is crafted in vatic, highly figurative language, dense in literary allusion. Both are indeed metaleptic, John revising past prophecies in wildly figurative poetry, Emerson refiguring scripture itself, including John's book, with similar linguistic vigor.[5] Both are not only about revelation in content but *are* revelation in form: while John writes the book of God in heaven, Emerson translates nature's dynamic text. What Austin Farrar says of Revelation pertains to *Nature*; both boast 'an astonishing multiplicity of reference ... [and endeavour] to be that of which [they] speak, and imitate reality by multiplicity of [their] significance'. John and Emerson both know that 'exact prose abstracts from reality, symbol presents it. And for that very reason, symbols have some of the many-sidedness of wild nature'.[6]

Emerson is clear about his desire to write a bible of his own, a hermetic text condensing God and nature: 'We too must write Bibles, to unite again the heavens and the earthly world' (CW 4: 166). More specifically, he calls for a new Revelation: One should make one's own Bible, by 'hearkening to all those sentences which ... thrill ... like the sound of a trumpet' (JMN 5: 476) – the angel-blown trumpets in Revelation that signal the apocalypse. Since the revelatory sentences of the Bible are not sufficiently powerful for his age, Emerson must create his own:

> The Hebrew and Greek Scriptures contain immortal sentences, that have been the bread of life to millions. But they have no epical integrity; are fragmentary; are not shown in their order of the intellect. I look for the new Teacher that shall follow so far those shining laws that he shall see them come full circle; shall see their rounding complete grace.   (CW 1: 92–3)

Emerson himself will be this new teacher. His sentences will reveal the shining laws that generate the universe. Drawn from the 'book of Nature', containing the 'Natural history of the woods', they will join 'astronomy, botany, physiology, meteorology, picturesque, & poetry together' (JMN 5: 25).

Emerson coalesces scientist and saint throughout *Nature*, but especially in three visionary passages. Out of each, Emerson emerges as new prophet of science, revising scripture through historical metalepsis, inscribing nature's forces through intertextual metalepsis. He overwhelms readers with sublime disruption, urging them to fashion creative hermeneutic practices. Each of these visionary passages comprises a unit of what might be called an electromagnetic revelation. Each vibrates with semantic complexity, dissolving into intense forcefields of signification.

BUILDING

The opening paragraph of *Nature* is electric, seemingly boundless in meaning, polarized. Within eleven tightly wound sentences are numerous tropes and other rhetorical devices, no less than five echoes of the Bible, and statements about Emerson's relationship to nature and his poetics.

> Our age is retrospective. It builds the sepulchres of the fathers. It writes biographies, histories, and criticism. The foregoing generations beheld God and nature face to face; we, through their eyes. Why should not we also enjoy an original relation to the universe? Why should not we have a poetry and philosophy of insight and not of tradition, and a religion by revelation to us, and not the history of theirs? Embosomed for a season in nature, whose floods of life stream around and through us, and invite us by the powers they supply, to action proportioned to nature, why should we grope among the dry bones of the past, or put the living generation into the masquerade out of its faded wardrobe? The sun shines to-day also. There is more wool and flax in the fields. There are new lands, new men, new thoughts. Let us demand our own works and laws and worship. (N 5–6)

The passage is foremost about building, by extension writing;[7] as Emerson once wrote in his journal, rhetoric is the 'Building of Discourse', a 'temple, soaring in due gradation, turret over tower to heaven, cheerful with thorough lights, majestic with strength desired of all eyes' (JMN 5: 409). Elsewhere, he equates composition with 'a foundation of a new superstructure' (5: 198), and calls the 'maker of a sentence ... [one who] launches out into the infinite & builds a road in Chaos and Old Night' (4: 363). Indeed, Emerson ends *Nature* by requiring his readers to 'Build ... [their] own world'

just as nature builds its own, by altering, molding, and making
(N 93–4). In this passage, Emerson teaches readers how properly
to trope: not by constructing stark terms that house the dead, but by
fashioning fluid words that fit the electric fields of nature.

Emerson's 'retrospective age' looks backward to the past, and in
doing so, builds certain kinds of texts. Activating the trope of prosopopoeia, Emerson personifies his age into a builder: 'It builds the
sepulchres of the fathers.' This personification acts on the synecdoche of 'sepulchres of the fathers', which stands for all celebrations
of the dead, the past. Indeed, as Joel Porte has shown, '[s]epulchres'
recall those built by the spiritually dead enemies of Jesus, for these
structures echo and revise Luke 11: 46–8, in which Jesus chastises
the Pharisees: 'Woe unto you! for ye build the sepulchres of the
prophets, and your fathers killed them. Truly ye bear witness that
ye allow the deeds of your fathers: for they indeed killed them, ye
build their sepulchres.'[8] While Porte draws attention to Emerson's
indirect echoing of Jesus in this passage, he does not consider the
idea of building; Emerson not only fashions himself as a new Jesus
in attacking his age for killing revelation, but he also links certain
forms of building with blindness and death. The next sentence
details the sepulchres of Emerson's age, the ones that bring spiritual
death, loss of vision, to his own times; they are 'biographies,
histories, and criticism'. This third sentence is a metaphor for the
second; writing is analogous to building; certain kinds of writing, to
sepulchres.

In these first three sentences, Emerson has drawn contrasts. Writing that celebrates or commemorates the past is blind to revelation
and associated with static structures that house the dead. By impli-
cation, writing that celebrates the present and its prospects will
be visionary, dynamic, alive, electric. The linguistic vigor we have
so far seen in these sentences is itself an example of this revelatory
writing. The sentences, far from static, urge activity in readers, bring
them to life.

The next sentence elaborates these contrasts, as Emerson opposes
immediately 'beholding' God and nature face to face to viewing
God and nature mediately through the eyes of the fathers: 'The
foregoing generations beheld God face to face; we, through their
eyes.' 'Behold' is a pun; it not only means 'to look upon', but also
etymologically suggests 'to hold, have, occupy, possess, guard or
preserve', as well as 'to belong', or 'to signify'. To behold something
is not only to see it, but to participate in it actively and palpably and

to represent it, synesthetically combining the faculties of sight and touch. This sentence is also packed with diachronic meaning, echoing, as Porte shows, I Corinthians 13: 'When I was a child, I spake as a child, I understood as a child, I thought as a child: but when I became a man, I put away childish things. For now we see through a glass, darkly: but then, face to face'. Porte is correct to suggest that this echoing predicts one of the primary themes of the 'Divinity School Address'. Subverting the traditional Christian idea that full apprehension of the divinity will come only at the end of time, in that address and in *Nature* Emerson claims that one can have a vision of God in the present.[9] Yet Porte here again does not focus on the idea of building; a dark glass is a constructed form – like a sepulchre, history, biography, and criticism – that hinders direct revelation. Avoiding this, Emerson as a seer and builder must construct texts that reveal the forces of nature, their workings and significance. His *Nature*, far from darkening spirit, will be a conduit through which it flows.

This echoing of Corinthians sets up another contrast; vision, life, and dynamism are associated with the child, with youth, while blindness, death, and stasis are related to the father, to age. As Emerson will claim later in *Nature*, 'In the woods...a man casts off his years...and...is always a child. In the woods, is perpetual youth' (N 12) – 'Infancy is the perpetual Messiah' (88). The adept, the one prepared for a vision of nature, is as an infant, without words, yet prepared, like Peter at the Pentecost, for the language of God. The infant, ears free of the heavy words of the past, is a portal for the muse. As in the parable of Nietzsche's Zarathustra, the infant is not burdened by the past like the camel, nor is it angry, in opposition, as the lion; it is free to hear and create.[10] Emerson's sublime sentences work to render readers momentarily infantile as well, engaging their full attention with riddling words, causing a silence – a simmering before the boil, the upwelling of speech.

The following two sentences reinforce the dichotomies established in the first four. 'Why should not we also enjoy an original relation to the universe? Why should not we have a poetry and philosophy of insight and not of tradition, and a religion by revelation to us, and not the history of theirs?' Through a compression of the figures of anaphora and parallelism, as well of two rhetorical questions, Emerson heightens his rhetoric, preparing his readers for the ensuing celebration of nature's energy. These two sentences 'rhyme' with and oppose the first two anaphoric, parallel sentences beginning with 'It...'. Those two sentences suggest static, dead building, while these two anaphoric parallel structures celebrate 'insight' and an 'original' relation to nature. 'Original' further reinforces the dynamism of nature, proper seeing, and proper building, for the word derives from the Latin *oriri*, to rise or spring.

Emerson's syntax here supports the passage's move from stillness to motion. The sentences leading up to the rhetorical questions share the syntactic pattern of 'subject–verb–object', reinforcing the monotony and stagnation of 'biographies, histories, and criticism'. The rhetorical questions not only invert this pattern but also engage readers to participate in the floods of life, for questions demand activity. Further, the second rhetorical question dissolves the opening sentences. It and the sentence following (yet another rhetorical question) are both long, flowing, complex constructions, markedly in contrast to the short, stiff, simple sentences that open the passage. The three questions literally pull readers away from stasis into inquiry, loosening their minds into floods of words. Indeed, these sentences and this entire passage make readers *ec*-static, moving them out of stillness.

The sentence beginning with 'Embosomed' is the core of the passage. Not only does it continue the series of rhetorical questions but also compresses several tropes and two allusions. 'Embosomed for a season in nature, whose floods of life stream around and through us, inviting us by the powers they supply, to action proportioned to nature, why should we grope among the dry bones of the past, or put the living generation into masquerade out of its faded wardrobe?' The word 'embosomed' condenses several senses. It metaphorically casts nature as a sheltering, maternal figure. Moreover, a bosom is often a metonymy for the center of emotion, the heart. Through prosopopoeia, Emerson intimates that one way to behold nature is as an infant embraces its mother. However, 'embosomed' also carries the connotation of 'enwombed', for 'bosom' derives from the Old English *bosm*, which means 'womb' as well as 'breast'. 'Season' further reinforces the imagery of birth, suggesting the rhythms of gestation, growth and decay, deriving from *serere*, to plant.[11]

The next clause supports this birth imagery. On one level, nature's 'floods of life' is a metaphor for the mother's milk of the nature in which we are embosomed or an amniotic fluid nourishing us in nature's womb. However, the verb 'stream' (the 'floods of life streaming around and through us') bursts the sheltering structure of the bosom or womb, transforming it into a vessel channeling the powerful flows of life. This complex metaphor compresses several paradoxical ideas: stillness and motion, safety and risk, stability and flux. The 'we' or 'us' in the sentence is troped from being a passive recipient of nature's nourishment to being charged with life and motion. 'We' become an active participant in its energy. The passage and 'we', the readers, are suddenly brought to life, floated away from the sepulchres of the dead toward the light of the sun.

This paradoxical interaction between motion and stillness characterizes Emerson's cosmology. The 'floods of life' are spirit, the force – be it electric or otherwise – that generates, shapes, and nourishes matter, that 'alters, moulds, and makes' nature, rendering it 'fluid' and 'volatile' (N 93) – indeed, Emerson learned from Faraday that 'water' is 'explosive' (TN 1: 278). 'We', like all matter, are nourished by spirit – even while we are stationary, we are still moving, conduits of its force. As Emerson explains later in *Nature*, 'spirit, that is, the Supreme Being, does not build up nature around us, but puts it forth through us, as the life of the tree puts forth new branches and leaves through the pores of the old. As a plant upon the earth, so man rests upon the bosom of God; he is nourished by unfailing fountains, and draws, at his need, inexhaustible power' (N 79–80).

Alan Hodder observes that 'floods of life' also carries a Biblical reference, Isaiah 44: 3, in which God says to the Israelites 'For I will pour water upon him that is thirsty, and floods upon the dry ground: I will pour my spirit upon thy seed, and my blessing upon thine offspring'. Moreover, Hodder notes, these 'floods' rehearse imagery connected with the Kingdom of God.[12] In equating God with nature, whose water flows through us, Emerson is again revising the Bible. God is not so much a savior and provider for a chosen people, but the force of life immanent in the universe that the scientist can reveal as well as the mystic.

After this clause on the 'floods', Emerson asks the third rhetorical question that reinforces the opposition between life and death. When we can partake of the energy of nature, why should we grope among the 'dry bones of the past'? 'Dry bones' is not only a metonymy for the sepulchres of the fathers, contrasted to the 'floods of life', but echoes and revises the Bible, the 'dry bones' sequence in Ezekiel 37: 1–6. In that prophetic book, God leads Ezekiel to a valley of dry bones, where he tells the prophet, 'Prophesy upon these bones, and say unto them, O ye dry bones, hear the word of the Lord. Thus saith the Lord God unto these bones; Behold, I will cause breath to enter into you, and ye shall live. And I will lay sinew upon you, and will bring up flesh upon you, and cover you with skin, and put breath in you, and ye shall live; and ye shall know that I am the Lord' (Ezek. 37: 4–6). As Ezekiel speaks these words, the bones come to life; they are covered with flesh and animated with breath, or spirit. God then commands Ezekiel to proclaim to the newly living host, which is the resuscitated House of Israel, that He will raise the children of Israel (who are in exile in Babylonia) from their graves and put his spirit into them.[13]

In rehearsing this famous moment in the prophetic tradition, Emerson relates his text to Ezekiel's in complex, provocative ways. Most obviously, he separates himself from Ezekiel. Unlike the Hebrew prophet, he will not grope among bones laboring to revive the dead. His *topos* will not be dry valleys of decay, but the present moment in fluid nature. But Emerson's relationship to Ezekiel is not one of simple contrast – Emerson is a new Ezekiel. Where Ezekiel's words create tissues – texts – for bones, Emerson's words must be proportioned to fit flowing, living nature; instead of reviving the dead, his words reveal life. Emerson revises the Hebrew prophet of Scripture by casting himself as a naturalist prophet of the living.

When Emerson questions why the 'living generation' should be put in a 'masquerade out of its faded wardrobe', he again metaphorizes the sepulchres of the fathers and also echoes the Bible once more. In choosing the word 'wardrobes', garments, in connection with revelation, Emerson alludes to the many mentions of 'garment' in Revelation. Of course, Emerson's faded wardrobes of a masquerade (which derives from a word meaning 'buffoon') are directly opposed to the white garments of the righteous chosen to dwell with God in the New Jerusalem. Of the several appearances of white garments in Revelation, the mention of them at 7: 13–14 is the most important in connection with Emerson. In this passage, God's chosen, whose garments have been washed and made white in the blood of the Lamb, are praised in a brief interlude between the opening of the sixth and seventh seals of the great scroll that reveals the apocalypse, the unveiling of God's final truth. Those who are washed in Jesus's blood stand at the hand of God ready to witness the opening of the seventh seal, at which time the apocalypse begins.

Appropriating this scriptural passage for his own purposes, Emerson suggests that those in faded masquerade, involved with the texts of the past, will experience no such revelation. However, those wearing the white linens woven from the 'wool' and 'flax' in the fields 'today' are prepared for apocalypse. Indeed, 'wool and flax' are used in the Bible to signal revelation of God. As Hodder remarks, 'wool and flax' appears several places in the Bible, most notably in Proverbs 31: 13, where it is connected to a virtuous wife: 'She seeketh wool, and flax, and worketh willingly with her hands.' Hodder goes on to note that 'wool and flax' is associated with several images throughout the Bible associated with marriage, appearing in this connection, for example, in Proverbs and Hosea (2: 5 and 2: 9). In both cases, 'wool and flax' stands for clothing 'which signifies the fullness of God's grace and betokens his constancy.'[14] More importantly, white garments appear in connection with marriage in Revelation, where the Lamb prepares to marry New Jerusalem, his bride who is 'arrayed in fine linen, clean and white'. As M. H. Abrams observes, this marriage symbolizes perfect union with God.[15]

Again, Emerson's relation to these Biblical passages is revisionary. He edits these Biblical textiles, the garments of the blessed, by suggesting that we should not wait to be clothed by God on Judgment Day, but that we should weave our own garments in the present, preparing for immediate vision, an apocalypse that flashes forth not because the garments are washed in the blood of Jesus, but because they are cleansed in the floods of nature. Those washed in these floods know readiness is all – in an instant nature might unveil. Just as the sun shines today, so the possibility of revelation is afoot. Wool and flax are not only the raw material for apocalyptic textiles, as it were, but also, metaphorically, the stuff of texts, of books. 'Textile' and 'text' both derive from the Latin *texere*, to weave or to construct. Emerson requires not only that we prepare for revelation today but also that we weave our own texts to figure this revelation. Instead of building sepulchres of the fathers we should weave new texts to pattern the energy of the sun. Indeed, speaking a vision is clothing it; later in *Nature*, as we have seen, Emerson writes that inspired thought spontaneously 'clothes' itself in imagery (N 39), figuring forth the original cause.

Emerson's apocalyptic theme is further reinforced by his invocation of the new world in Revelation. In Revelation 21: 1, a primary image of apocalypse appears: 'And I saw a new heaven and a new earth: for the first heaven and the first earth were passed away'.[16] Likewise, in Emerson's vision there are 'new lands, new men, new thoughts'. Again, Emerson edits the Bible; instead of offering a future vision of a heavenly city, Emerson asserts that the new heaven and earth are already here, if we can see them. For Emerson, if we scientifically observe nature with a religious impulse, then we will see the causes of nature clearly: 'the axis of vision' will be 'coincident with the axis of things' and all will be 'transparent', and not 'opake' (N 91).[17] Then we will see the sun; then the world is new.

The anaphora and parallelism in 'There is more wool and flax...' and 'There are new lands...' rhyme with the similar figures of speech in the two sentences beginning with 'It builds...'. and 'It writes...' and the two commencing with 'Why should...' The final instance of these figures of speech returns the passage to balance. The first set occurs in a static syntactic pattern denoting death and stillness; the second set is dynamic, its syntax embodying life and flux. The final set is presented in a pattern of 'expletive–copula–subject', returning the passage to stability after the loose constructions of the second set. While the third set mimics the stable patterns of the first set, it does not return the passage to stasis. Not only do the sentences semantically praise the burgeoning life of nature in the present, but the second sentence of the set is cast in the figure of asyndeton. Emerson omits the conjunctions between the series of clauses 'new lands, new men, new thoughts' to produce 'a hurried rhythm in [a] sentence', appropriate for stirring the emotions at the end of a discourse.[18] Though Emerson constructs stable, simple patterns to end his opening, they are energetic, nonetheless: matter is always energy. The final sentence appropriately counters asyndeton with polysyndeton, 'works and laws and worship'. Polysyndeton slows the rhythm of prose, placing special emphasis on each word separated by the conjunctions. Emerson thus highlights the need for us to build our own worlds, our own works, laws, and worship.

Emerson likewise deploys other sound effects to support these semantic and syntactic senses, to reinforce the passage's central opposition between 'insight' and 'tradition'. 'Tradition', a polysyllabic word of Latin origin, is aurally linked to other polysyllabic terms deriving from Greek and Latin. For example, the initial sentences metaphorically describing the traditions that hinder insight contain five words of this sort: 'Our age is *retrospective*. It builds the *sepulchres* of the fathers. It writes *histories*, *biographies*, and *criticism*.' These 'ornate' words are contrasted to those associated with 'insight', a word of Anglo-Saxon origin, apt for suggesting the possibility of revelation in the present, on American soil, and the impossibility of experiencing vision by studying the Greek and Latin traditions. One gains insight by sensing the 'floods' of 'life', Anglo-Saxon monosyllables; these floods reveal that 'There is more wool and flax in the fields. There are new lands, new men, new thoughts. Let us demand our own works and laws and worship.' 'Wool', 'flax', 'lands', 'men', 'thoughts', 'works', and 'laws' are all monosyllables of Anglo origin, as is the disyllable 'worship'. These sounds oppose simplicity and the concrete to the complexity and abstract quality of the Latin/ Greek words.

The sequence is an edification on how to build a world. It teaches that tropes should be as volatile and electric as nature. *Materia poetica* is not the past but the currents of electricity flowing in the present. One should compose in the light of the sun, not the torches of tradition. Aptly, the ideal building Emerson here proposes is not a static structure built for storage, but a conductor, an electric circuit that channels the vital flows of nature, a sublime pattern. This conductor, like Emerson's passage here, should bear multiple strands of mutually interacting meanings, attractive and repulsive interchanges of significance. If this passage constitutes directions on how to make a conductor, the next visionary sequence is on how to become a conductor, on how to become a pattern of the circulations of universal force.

CROSSING

Harold Bloom ambiguously hails the famous 'transparent eyeball' passage as the 'most notorious' in Emerson's work.[19] Certainly this passage has drawn more attention than any other in Emerson's oeuvre, earning more frequent and disparate interpretations than any other. Whatever the passage might be, it clearly epitomizes Emerson's compressed, polysemantic style. It crowds together numerous tropes and allusions to the Bible, fully embodying the traits John Burroughs finds in Emerson's best writing: 'It is abrupt, freaky, unexpected . . . darts this way and that, and connects the far and the near in every line . . . . [I]t is a leaping thread of light.'[20]

The sequence is Emerson's most visionary. He blends with the energy of God to command a full view of the processes of nature.

Crossing a bare common, in snow puddles, at twilight, under a clouded sky, without having in my thoughts any occurrence of special good fortune, I have enjoyed a perfect exhilaration. Almost I fear to think how glad I am. In the woods, too, a man casts off his years, as the snake his slough, and at what period soever of life is always a child. In the woods, is perpetual youth. Within these plantations of God, a decorum and a sanctity reign, a perennial festival is dressed, and the guest sees not how he should tire of them in a thousand years. In the woods, we return to reason and faith. There I feel that nothing can befal me in life, – no disgrace, no calamity, (leaving me my eyes,) which nature cannot repair. Standing on the bare ground, – my head bathed by the blithe air, and uplifted into infinite space, – all mean egotism vanishes. I become a transparent eye-ball. I am nothing. I see all. The currents of the Universal Being circulate through me; I am part or particle of God.   (N 12–13)[21]

B. L. Packer has rightly observed that in *Nature* the mind's alienation from nature is caused by 'an error in vision'. When the 'axis of vision' is 'coincident' with the 'axis of things', the world is transparent and one sees the cause, the spirit, the force, generating matter. This passage details such a moment: Emerson's speaker sees through the opacity of matter to the electric currents of universal being, becoming transparent himself. Using these same poles of opacity and transparency, Kenneth Burke has used this passage to exemplify Emerson's mode of crossing from matter to spirit, transcending the natural to the supernatural. Indeed, the passage is liminal: it crosses boundaries, moving between contradictory, polarized (positive and negative) elements, crossing from matter to the electric cause that emanates through it.[22]

'Crossing a bare common' immediately alerts us to the threshold quality of the passage. 'Crossing', first of all, is a pun. Not only is the 'Visionary' (the character in the essay, as distinguished from the historical Emerson) literally moving from one place to another, but he is also at a crossroads, a crux. 'Cross', deriving from the Latin *crux*, means not only a physical cross but also a fateful juncture. Among Christians, 'crossing' (making a cross sign in the air) is an act of blessing. Jesus died on the cross and so bearing a cross metaphorically suggests the proper Christian life (Matt. 10: 38). Thus 'crossing' indicates an act of great import involving the sacred.

The Visionary echoes and revises the Christian act of 'crossing' and 'bearing a cross', for he blesses nature in winter, not the altar of a church in spring; he is not burdened by life in an imperfect, fallen world, but enjoys instead 'perfect exhilaration'. Moreover, his act of crossing does not necessarily acknowledge the Judeo-Christian God, but rather moves across a threshold toward an idea of a God who circulates through nature as Universal Being. Emerson does not deny this world to find a greater one, as Jesus teaches, but affirms this world because there is nothing else we can know.

Moreover, 'crossing' constitutes a chiasmus, a rhetorical figure that means 'placing crosswise'. The figure describes 'any structure in which elements are repeated in reverse, so giving the pattern ABBA'.[23] Emerson's allusions in these sublime passages are chiasmi; he repeats the Bible in alluding to it while he reverses its meaning in revising it to fit his intuitions of nature. Likewise, his pun on 'crossing' is itself a chiasmus; it intersects a spiritual act and symbol in Christianity with the act of making way toward a vision in nature.[24] Several other puns throughout this passage also embody this chiasmic structure. Indeed, the entire structure of *Nature* could be characterized as chiasmic, for Emerson throughout the essay crosses nature and scripture, words and things, mind and matter. This crossing, of course, instances the oscillatory polarities of electromagnetic energy, for each pun is a spherule of force, a tension of positive and negative energy.

The entire first sentence figures liminality. As he crosses the common, the universal threshold between matter and the spirit, the Visionary registers several transitional events. He walks through 'snow puddles', a synecdoche for the state of both the speaker and nature. Like the Visionary – who is between fear and gladness, adulthood and childhood – and like the natural environment – which is in between day and night ('twilight') and gas and liquid ('under a clouded sky') – the snow puddles are liminal, ice on the verge of becoming water. This synecdoche is a complex trope, for it yokes together water and ice, fluidity and stasis. It moves not only to more remote images of solidity and liquidity. It also predicts the Visionary's impending transition from solid to liquid when he is transformed from a material person to an ethereal conduit through which Being flows. 'Twilight' and 'clouded sky' are also tropes, versions of the synecdochal 'snow puddles', parts standing for an entire liminal scene. Twilight is not only the threshold point between day and night, dark and light. It also metaphorically signals a move from the life of the sun to the moon's deathly glow to anticipate the Visionary's ironic annihilation into 'nothing' while he 'sees' all. Clouds are, again, both gas and liquid, moving toward liquid, but they also suggest 'gloom', reinforcing the irony of this ecstatic passage that celebrates transparency.

The first sentence, then, institutes the structure of the passage. It delineates the poles between which the Visionary moves and establishes chiasmic reversals of scripture and nature. Moreover, it sets a rhetorical precedent that will reach a vertiginous pitch at the core of the passage. Importantly, this opening sentence likewise establishes the electromagnetic constitution of the passage, its boundless semantic energy, its polarity, its mutual interaction.

Other figures charge Emerson's language. He revises the Biblical notion of innocence in comparing the return to innocence to a snake casting off its slough. 'In the woods, a man casts off his years, as the snake his slough, and at what period soever of life is always a child'. In Genesis 3: 1, the serpent is associated with subtlety and is the cause of the fall of man from innocence to experience, from perfection to imperfection. Emerson reverses this. The snake is part of nature and therefore *innocent*. Indeed, the sentence relates the snake, a traditional symbol of evil, and the child, often equated with innocence and knowledge of God in the Gospels (esp. Matt. 19: 13–14).

To eat from the tree of knowledge is to understand Being, not to offend God. As Emerson writes in a journal entry in 1840, 'I dreamed that I floated at will in the great Ether, and I saw this world floating also not far off, but diminished to the size of an apple. Then the angel took it in his hand & brought it to me and said "This must thou eat". And I ate the world' (JMN 7: 525). Among the many readings of this provocative dream, one is that Emerson revises Genesis in light of his celebration of nature, not scripture, as the locus for revelation. Emerson's Visionary would eat from the tree of knowledge of good and evil and report his findings.

Indeed, there is a parallel in Emerson between eating and prophecy.[25] In Revelation 10: 8–11, John is told by a voice from heaven to take a scroll from an angel and eat it: 'And I took the little scroll from the hand of the angel and ate it; it was sweet as honey in my mouth, but when I had eaten it my stomach was bitter. And I was told, "You must again prophesy about many peoples and nations and tongues and kings".' This passage alludes to a similar scene in Ezekiel where that prophet must also eat the words of God.

Emerson transumes these prophetic moments in claiming that the prophet is the scientist whose message is not bitter but joyous, whose knowledge is perfection, power. Indeed, the world is not fallen out of grace, but the site of grace: '[n]othing' can 'befal' the speaker, no 'disgrace', that nature itself cannot 'repair', or redeem.

Emerson supports this perfection through the figure of anaphora, as two other sentences beginning with 'In the woods' emphasize nature as the sacred. In the three phrases beginning with 'In the woods', he suggests that nature is a site not only of innocence, 'perpetual youth', but also of 'reason', the faculty of knowledge, and 'faith', a category of religion. For Emerson, though we have been cast from the garden of Eden into the forest, we retain our innocence, knowledge, faith. The syntactic rhymes of anaphora not only reinforce this idea, but plot a growing appreciation of nature. The second element of the anaphora designates the woods as a region not merely of childhood, but for 'perpetual', or eternal youth. The third element improves on this, proclaiming that the woods are not only a place of eternal innocence, but also of knowledge and faith. These repeated prepositional phrases signal an increase in verbal energy that will break into a rhetorical storm in the 'transparent eye-ball' sentence, which gathers each element of the anaphora into dynamic synthesis when the Visionary joins with God.

In the midst of this anaphora, Emerson structurally mimics his upsetting of traditional Christianity and prepares readers for the Visionary's becoming 'nothing' and seeing 'all' by employing the figure of hyperbaton, the inversion of normal syntax. In 'Almost I fear to think how glad I am', Emerson transposes the normal pattern of 'I almost fear...'. This reversal not only highlights the word 'almost', thus reinforcing the fact that the Visionary is at a threshold, but also corresponds to Emerson's reversals of darkness and light, imperfection and perfection, nothing and all. A second hyperbaton occurring in the phrase 'at what period soever of life', which reverses the normal order of 'at whatsoever period of life', further underpins these transpositions.

This great confidence in the grace of nature is questioned, however, in the ensuing parenthetical 'leaving me my eyes'. Emerson writes that '...nothing can befal me in life, – no disgrace, no calamity (leaving me my eyes,) which nature cannot repair'. The Visionary feels that nature can mend any disgrace or calamity as long as he has eyes. This aside reinforces the physical nature of vision. Unlike

John of Patmos, whose vision struck the inner eye of dream, this Visionary's revelation is dependent on physical sight. However, another reading of the parenthesis undercuts the necessity of physical sight. 'Leaving me my eyes' could indeed be a calamity that nature *can* repair. The disgrace or calamity could well be 'my eyes' 'leaving me', the loss of sight. In this case, nature *could* repair this problem, exhilarating even the blind man, restoring him to sight.

This parenthetical aside is another example of chiasmus, crossing both the necessity and superfluity of sight. As such, it is a proleptic version of the core of the passage in which the Visionary becomes the transparent eyeball, an electromagnetically polarized site that crosses nothing and all, full sight and the annihilation of self. This paradox points to a Blakean act of seeing, in which the Visionary sees not with the eye, but *through* it. Physical sight is necessary for closely observing nature, as the Visionary does, cataloging the details of the scene in minute detail, noticing the landscape, the weather, the time. This close observation leads to an insight of the invisible energy generating and animating the visible, an insight that makes sight superfluous. Insight is the goal of sight; sight, the catalyst of insight. Inductive observation leads to vision. Emerson marries Bacon and Plato, St John and Newton.

Emerson intensifies these crossings by again editing Revelation. In nature, a 'perennial festival is dressed'. This festival revises the marriage festival for the Lamb and New Jerusalem in Revelation 19: 9: 'And he said unto me, Write, Blessed are they which are called unto the marriage supper of the Lamb'. This festival symbolizes the marriage between God and His followers in heaven after the world-ending apocalypse.[26] For Emerson, the marriage festival of God and believer takes place not in heaven in the future, but in nature in the present.

The eye of the passage, its most shocking moment, begins with the participial phrase 'Standing on the bare ground...'. The phrase conceptually and syntactically rhymes with the liminal opening phrase of the passage, 'Crossing a bare common', signaling the Visionary's move from the liminal into the world of Universal Being. Between the time the Visionary crosses the common and finds himself standing on bare ground, he, like Dante's Pilgrim, has crossed Lethe and Eunoe and entered into earthly paradise, the realm where one is prepared for a vision of the absolute. The 'bare ground' is yet another in a series of puns: it is literally the winter earth, but also the absolute foundation, the basis underlying everything. Emerson has troped the 'bare common' into the site where the universal principle of life will emerge in a sublime moment. Moreover, 'ground' is a primary term used in speaking of electricity. It is a large conducting body, like the earth, whose potential or voltage is zero as well as an electric circuit connected to the earth and thus grounded, or rendered impotent. The ground, like the Visionary, is still, empty, waiting to be filled and charged by Being. The famous transparent eye-ball passage is as much about becoming empowered by the electrical energy coursing through the cosmos as it is about becoming one with spirit. This pun, then, contained in a participial phrase, will modify its potential subject by metaphorically 'grounding' it, emptying it of voltage.

But Emerson appears to provide no subject. 'Standing on the bare ground' should modify 'I', the Visionary, not 'egotism': 'Standing on bare ground, – my head bathed by the blithe air, and uplifted into infinite space, – all mean egotism vanishes.' It seems as if the Visionary has disappeared;[27] the 'I' in the opening sentence of the passage is lost. Emerson uses the figure of anacoluthon, a mode of expression in which the writer or speaker changes a construction mid-sentence, thus leaving its beginning uncompleted. Quite simply, Emerson employs a dangling modifier. This suggests that the Visionary has lost his particularity to become one with the universal electric principle, fading into the 'ground', his energy merging with the earth's, both circuits empty of energy.

Alternatively, one could read that 'Standing on the bare ground' modifies 'head'. 'Standing on bare ground, – my head bathed in the blithe air. .'. This would do away with anacoluthon and present a catachretic metaphor, in which a head 'stands'. In this interpretation, 'head' becomes a dense site, compressing metonymy, synecdoche, and metaphor. First, it is a metonymy for 'mind'. It is also a whole substituted for the part of the eye, as the head will be metaphorized into an eye in the next sentence. Still yet, if 'head' is interpreted as the subject of the sentence, then it is metaphorized into a circuit grounded in the earth.

Emerson's grammar is in conflict with itself. The readers are caught among several possibilities, each of which is equally valid. Emerson has placed his readers in a liminal state, casting them in the same role as the Visionary.

At this juncture in the passage, both the Visionary and sympathetic readers find themselves anxious, polarized, oscillating like electricity between opposing poles, gladness and fear. The Visionary is about to cross a threshold between what Angus Fletcher calls labyrinth and temple, the terms representing the dialectic between 'sacred stillness' and 'profane movement'. The transition between these antinomies is epitomized by 'Homer's Cave of the Nymphs, Vergil's twin Gates of Horn and Ivory, Dante's Limbo.'[28] The Visionary is 'in between', edging toward union with the sacred force of God. He will not, however, reach mere 'stillness' in the temple. Instead, he, as part or particle of a circulating God, will become an intersection of stillness – the stationary pattern of the 'eye-ball' – and motion – the currents of the God. The Visionary is a synthesis of the temple and labyrinth in his sublime moment, a chiasmus of spirit and matter, time and eternity: the labyrinth of the woods *is* the temple of God.

Attentive readers are likely to be tense as well. The slippages in language cause anxiety; the richness of signification is overtaxing. In the midst of Emerson's textual labyrinth, the temple seems far away. Yet, Emerson's own language, like the Visionary, is on the verge of transcendence, of joining conflicting meanings into a dynamic unity.

An echo of Jesus's baptism in Matthew 3: 16–17 in the phrase 'bathed in the blithe air, and uplifted into infinite space' confirms that the Visionary and the form of the passage are on the brink of transformation. The Biblical passage describes John's baptism of Jesus.

> And Jesus, when he was baptized, went up straightaway out of the water: and, lo, the heavens were opened unto him, and he saw the Spirit of God descending like a dove, and lighting upon him: And lo a voice from heaven, saying, This is my beloved Son, in whom I am well pleased.

Like Jesus, Emerson's Visionary is bathed in the joyous air, which is troped into 'the currents of Universal Being' in the next sentence, suggesting water, air, and electricity. Like Jesus, the Visionary looks to the heavens as he is 'uplifted into infinite space'. In the next sentences, he is 'blessed' by God, becoming 'part or particle' of Him, losing his self, seeing all. The Visionary is a new Jesus, blessed by the forces of the universe.

'Bathed in the blithe air' suggests not only baptism, but also the Pentecost. In Acts 2: 1–4, on the day of the Pentecost, the Holy Ghost rushes from the heavens in the form of a mighty wind, filling the followers of Jesus with spirit, turning their tongues to fire, inspiring them to speak strange languages. Their ecstatic speech is not drunkenness, Peter claims, but a consummation of God's power and glory that was forecast by the prophet Joel (2: 14–21). Emerson's Visionary undergoes his own Pentecost, being filled with the wind of the spirit, describing his vision in ecstatic speech. Indeed, *Nature's* sublime moments resemble the glossolalia of Jesus's early followers.

This transformation, simultaneously baptismal and Pentecostal, affecting both Visionary and readers, takes place in the next sentence, the 'transparent eye-ball': 'I become a transparent eye-ball. I am nothing. I see all. The currents of the Universal Being circulate through me; I am part or particle of God.'

The sentence edits several revelatory scenes in the Bible. 'Eye' is associated with the true sight of God's revelation, as it is when Job proclaims his intimate knowledge of God after he sees Him in the whirlwind: 'I have heard of thee by the hearing of the ear; but now mine eye seeth thee' (42: 5). Moreover, in Proverbs, the eye is linked to blessedness and generosity: 'He that hath a bountiful eye shall be blessed; for he giveth his bread to the poor' (22: 9). Emerson's earlier revisions of Genesis are further apparent in this sentence as well. When Adam and Eve eat from the tree of knowledge of good and evil, 'the eyes of them were both opened' (3: 7). While in Genesis knowledge and sight are related to imperfection and despair, the sight of Emerson's Visionary is one with perfection and joy. Perhaps the passage most directly connected to Emerson's sentence occurs in Jesus' words in Matthew 6: 22: 'The light of the body is the eye: if therefore thine eye be single, thy whole body shall be full of light.' Emerson literalizes this passage, troping his speaker's body into a single eye so full of light that it (ironically) sees all in the twilight. Still another passage that faintly reverberates when we hear 'transparent' is Revelation 21: 21 of the King James Bible. The street of the heavenly city is 'pure gold, as it were transparent glass'. Likewise, in the sublime moment for Emerson, when the axis of vision is coincident with the axis of things, the world is transparent, 'causes and spirits are seen through [things]' (N 62). During this revelation of nature's cause, both the beholder and nature become transparent: the Visionary sees through things because he is part of the energy generating them.

The sentence is epiphanic not only for the Visionary as it describes his move from the liminal to the sublime, but also for sympathetic readers, for it resolves semantic and syntactic indeterminacy into an aesthetic whole. The sentence is a warp onto which are woven three separate threads of imagery. The liminal tropes are now sublimated, for the Visionary has ironically moved from twilight to pure light, from crossing the threshold to the shore of vision, from the world of matter to spirit. The baptismal tropes are woven into the text as well; the Visionary has been transformed by the spirit into a condition of perfect knowledge of and oneness with God. Further, the tropes suggesting electricity have been transformed. The 'grounded', impotent Visionary has now become an open circuit through which the powerful charges of the universal being will flow. Here, the Visionary, ideal seer and sayer, is truly a conduit for the force of life. For a moment, all the disparate currents of the cosmos and of words in conflict are harmonized, concentrated in the point of the Visionary's eye.

Kenneth Burke has elaborated on Emerson's word play on 'eye', 'I' and the affirmative 'ay'.[29] The sentence sets off a series of paranomastic puns, where for every 'I', 'eye' or 'ay' can be substituted. 'Transparent eye-ball', like 'head' earlier, also is a dense region of three overlapping tropes. It could be a synecdoche of part for whole, if the eyeball stands for the head, the perceiving mind. Likewise, it is perhaps a metonymy, in which cause is substituted for effect, if the instrument of vision, the eye, stands for the moment of vision. Further, it is, of course, catachresis: to visualize a man as an eyeball strains the faculties. Likewise, the figures of irony, hyperbole, and oxymoron are condensed in the 'eye-ball', for it is ironic to see all at twilight, hyperbolic for a man to turn into an eye, and oxymoronic to be nothing while seeing all. Emerson again utilizes the figure of asyndeton, the omission of conjunctions between a series of clauses, appropriate for stirring emotions:[30] 'I become a transparent eye-ball. I am nothing. I see all.' Longinus includes asyndeton in a list of figures that loosen the links that stifle the energy of language and therefore emit energy and passion at great speed.[31] Longinus's language could well detail the Visionary and the passage, both ecstatic with significance.

Emerson employs paronomasia to support his semantic and syntactic meanings. The core of the passage is worth quoting again.

> Standing on the bare ground, – my head bathed by the blithe air, and uplifted into infinite space, – all mean egotism vanishes. I become a transparent eye-ball. I am nothing. I see all. The currents of Universal Being circulate through me; I am part or particle of God.

Appropriately the primary recurring sounds are 'b' and 'i' sounds, as the passage is about Emerson's 'I' and 'eye' becoming one with 'Being'. 'Bathed' and '*blithe*' alliterate with '*bare*', but also support each other's connotations. 'Bathed' connotes baptism, and is thus connected with the blitheness of conversion, of becoming one with the unifying force. 'Bl*i*the' contains the long 'i' sound that echoes 'eye' and 'I'. The 'I' is blithe. Moreover, it is 'upl*i*fted' into the '*infinite*'. Both of these words contain short and long 'i' sounds, reinforcing the echoes. This is the sentence in which the 'I' falls out as egotism vanishes. Emerson has spread the 'I' throughout this sentence, mixing it with the 'b'. This mixing prepares us for and reinforces the ultimate union with the 'I/eye' and 'being'. The next sentence supports this mixing with further 'b' and long 'i' sounds in 'I', 'become', and in the all important union of the two in 'eye/I-ball'. These subtle uses of paronomasia – repeatedly joining 'I' and 'be' – constantly whisper the grand theme of the passage: the 'I/eye' is one with 'Universal Being'.

The Visionary has crossed from matter to spirit, becoming pure energy, Faraday's grain of water containing electrical relations equivalent to a flash of lightning. This charged passage itself, like the Visionary, has crossed from material to the energy animating it; it is an atom, its tropes like electrons turning around a highly charged nucleus. The passage and the Visionary are transparent eye-balls, structures through which the energy of 'the Universal Being' is revealed. They goad readers into their own crossings: from word to energy, from reading to creating, bookworm to silkworm.

Thus far, Emerson's visionary sites have instructed readers in building patterns to channel electricity and in merging with universal electric currents. In yet another similar sequence, he schools readers in the art of oscillating like the polarized spherule of force. He instructs in the practice of breathing, gathering attraction and repulsion, inhalation and exhalation while partaking bodily of spirit, wind, electric current.

BREATHING

In this third visionary moment in *Nature*, nature's beholder and Emerson's language merge with electrical spirit by *conspiring* with it. While this sequence has not attracted nearly the attention of the essay's opening or the 'eye-ball', it is nonetheless, though more subtly, charged. Alluding primarily to Genesis, the passage is appropriately a morning piece, the Visionary a new Adam partaking of God's breath.

> I have seen the spectacle of morning from a hillside over against my house, from day-break to sun-rise, with emotions an angel might share. The long slender bars of cloud float like fishes in the sea of crimson light. From the earth, as a shore, I look out into that silent sea. I seem to partake its rapid transformations: the active enchantment reaches my dust, and I dilate and conspire with the morning wind.   (N 21)

Emerson indirectly links this passage to the transparent eye-ball one by calling morning a 'spectacle', recalling the imagery of sight in the earlier passage. Like the eye-ball, both the Visionary and nature here are transparent patterns generated and shaped by rapid transformations of spirit. Like an angel in heaven admiring and participating in God's power, the Visionary not only looks at the bright atmosphere, but partakes of it, shaping it through his own rhythmic breathing as he dilates and conspires. As with the earlier passages, water imagery is present. The 'sea of crimson light' corresponds to the 'floods of life' and the 'currents of Universal being'. It betokens life, baptism, purity, redemption, spirit.

This passage, like its predecessors, condenses several tropes and figures. Most obviously, the sky metaphorically becomes an ocean – 'silent sea' – and the clouds, fishes, as the earth becomes their shore. This basic metaphor is then converted into no less than three new ones. The 'sea', already a trope for the sky, is troped into 'crimson light', suggesting that the air of the sky, the water of the sea, and the light correspond. Then, this sea of light is further metaphorized into a shaping force, a transformer, as the Visionary 'partakes' of its rapid 'transformations'. Like a conductor of electricity, the air channels the charges of the atmosphere to the circuits of the Visionary. The 'transformations' are 'enchanting', their activity reaching the Visionary's dust. The metaphor of enchantment activates the figure of paradox, converting the 'silent sea' into a *singing* sea, for 'enchantment' derives from *incantare*, 'to sing against'. Finally, the ocean is turned back into the morning wind, ending its protean journey through this maze of tropes back where it began.

This 'morning wind' is a metaleptic allusion. Placing his Visionary in conspiracy with the morning wind, Emerson echoes Genesis

2: 6–7, in which God creates Adam: 'But there went up a mist from the earth, and watered the whole face of the ground. And the Lord God formed man of the dust of the ground, and breathed into his nostrils the breath of life; and man became a living soul'. Emerson here rehearses this primal creation scene by fashioning the Visionary as a new Adam inflated by the breath not of the Judeo-Christian God but by nature: '[T]he active enchantment reaches my dust'. Also, Emerson's Visionary, unlike Adam, remains angelic and partakes of God's creative breath even after his eyes are opened to the *spectacle* of morning, to knowledge of nature. Moreover, this wind is related to water and light; as such, it echoes the several Biblical passages relating God to floods of life and light. Further, as in the eye-ball passage, Emerson alludes to Jesus's baptism. The Visionary is washed in creative waters, imbibing their primal power. This Visionary is simultaneously a revised God at the creation of his world, Adam at his own creation, and Jesus at his baptism.

Like the morning wind, the Visionary himself turns through several tropes. First, he is equated with the shore: 'From the earth, as a shore, I look out into that silent sea.' Though 'shore' ostensibly points to earth, grammatically, it can also refer to the 'I'. This double meaning not only indirectly equates the Visionary with the earth, but also connotes that he is a mixture of water and matter. As seen in the analyses of the first two visionary passages, water corresponds to spirit: in the first passage, nature is animated by 'floods of life'; in the second, by 'currents of Universal Being'. The Visionary in this passage, then, is a mixture of spirit and matter, a pattern of energy like all things in nature. Moreover, a shore is both shaped by and shapes the water running beside it, just as matter is a pattern that is figured by and figures the energy that generates it. This correspondence between human and nature is reinforced when the speaker himself is metonymically turned into 'dust'.

'Dust' is the spectacle of this passage, its center. As the Visionary's 'dust' is acted on by the protean sky, it expands and breathes with the 'active enchantment' of the sky as a 'silent sea'. This interaction results in a catachretic metaphor in which the Visionary's dust expands in water (of the 'silent sea') in which it should dissolve. He, like an electric spherule, is polar, simultaneously expanding and dissolving. This catachretic paradox echoes the paradox between a silent and singing sea and confirms the paradox of the universe, which is matter and spirit, positive and negative.

Sympathetic readers share in this journey, taught by Emerson's sound effects to breathe with the wind, to oscillate like electricity. The sound effects of the passage literally encourage readers to mimic the actions of the conspiring speaker: they inspire breath. In the first two sentences, there are frequent voiceless spirants, consonant sounds produced by the breath flowing from the mouth unimpeded by vocal cords. These sounds are thus entirely dependent on the force of the breath for sound. In the first sentence, the voiceless spirant 's' occurs in 'seen', 'spectacle', 'house', 'sun-rise', 'emotions', followed by 'slender', 'bars', 'fishes', 'sea', and 'crimson' in the second. Further, in the second sentence 'f', another voiceless spirant, stands out in its alliterative position in 'float' and 'fishes'. In the third sentence, other instances of 's' and 'f' occur, but also 'th' and 'sh', other voiceless spirants: 'From', 'earth', 'shore', 'silent sea'. One must breathe more forcefully to produce these sounds than in making others. In the next sentence, the consonants quicken this breathing, for there are several 't' sounds, voiceless stops. These sounds are generated by the breath flowing from the lungs unimpeded by the vocal cords but forcefully stopped and then suddenly released in an explosive sound. These 't' sounds are interspersed with several voiceless spirant 's' sounds to produce the effect of rapid breathing: 'to', 'partake', 'its', 'transformations', 'active', 'enchantment', 'reaches', 'dust', 'dilate', 'conspire'.

Emerson wishes his readers to perform the script of nature, to oscillate in electric currents. His words are not only polarized – tense with competing meanings – but send polar currents into the world. Emerson's writing is truly electric, literally sending a charge.

After being struck by these sequences so early in the essay – all occur within the first three chapters – how are we to proceed through the rest of the *Nature*? The pace has been exhausting, like beholding one immense natural scene after another. Perhaps we crave calmer vistas. Yet, after having been smitten by three consecutive theoptic, sublime moments, certainly our way of seeing will be altered – it will be more attuned to forces, sensing that even the most static, serene scenes are driven by the same energy, at lower potencies, as the disruptive ones. What of the rest of *Nature*, including its more lucid, discursive passages? Are they equally as charged? Are they centripetal counters to the centrifugal force of the visionary moments?

6
Scientific Edification

The hermetic unity that Faraday had revealed in the spark did not put an end to Emerson's inquiry. Instead, it galvanized it, rendering the riddle of the Sphinx all the more tantalizing by partially lighting it. The holistic force glimpsed by Emerson in electromagnetics was not a comfortable unity, reducing the many to a static principle, questions to rigid answers. It was sublime, the ineffable 'unity' of infinity. It overflowed boundaries, as immense and enigmatic as the solar system, more likely to inspire quivering wonder than crystalline equation. Emerson's sense that spirit is electric far from ended his religious and scientific quest. It goaded him into richer forays, more exuberant approximations. For Emerson the poet, the claim that spirit is electric, wonderful and true though the utterance was, did not entirely suffice: he needed a theory of relation – how does the one relate to the many, to the human?

This question is always the portal to the sublime, leading to a region where the agitation of paradox keeps philosophy, science, religion fresh, alive: where the particle contains the cosmos, the cosmos is filled by the particle, the near is the far, the familiar, unfamiliar. This question prompted Emerson to declare in the years following *Nature* that while a 'principle [like electricity] must be assumed' that 'inhabits and makes' organisms, it remains 'mysterious', just beyond the equations of physiology, chemistry, physics (CW 1: 125). Though we learn from science the nature of this principle, to sense fully its relation to us, to apprehend it, we must 'feel it, love it, [we] must behold it in a spirit as grand as that by which it exists, ere [we] canst know the law. Known it will not be, but gladly beloved and enjoyed' (1: 125). The scientist can say: spirit is electricity. Only the devout meditant can intone: *I am electricity*.

Emerson the Romantic, aspiring to be Plato and Bacon, teaches in *Nature*, through his electromagnetic style, that proper scientific investigation is edification: hermeneutics is meditation. Emerson in *Nature* metaleptically unveils a turbulent, infinite universe; his prose shocks as much as it attracts, dissolves more than resolves. He defamiliarizes his readers in order to stimulate them to find their relation to the primordial.

It is precisely this paradox – defamiliarization and extreme familiarity – that Emerson himself undergoes in his grandest epiphany, the 'eye-ball' sequence, after which he spends the rest of his days and words essaying to grant his audience similar ecstasies.

Right after the the the transparent eye-ball experience, Emerson meditates on the relationship between the familiar and the unfamiliar, the old and the new to extract a moral from his great vision:

> The greatest delight which the fields and woods minister, is the suggestion of an occult relation between man and vegetable. I am not alone and unacknowledged. They nod to me and I to them. The waving of the boughs in the storm, is new to me and old. It takes me by surprise, and yet is not unknown.   (N 13–14).

After becoming a conduit of nature's force, he understands that this link to nature is always present, that though this force is *other* it is also the *same*. Paradoxically, the extreme unfamiliarity of turning into a transparent eye-ball has shown him that he is in fact a familiar of nature, sharing in its currents of being. Emerson had to be jolted, as it were, from the familiar in order to apprehend what is most primordial – the connection among human, nature, and spirit. Following this insight, he views all of nature as surprising *and* familiar – as a site of the near as well as the far.

Emerson has undergone, and through his style wishes readers to apprehend, what Freud and Heidegger, in their respective modes, would call an 'uncanny' experience. In his 1919 paper 'Das Unheimliche' – 'the uncanny' – Freud defines the uncanny as the anxiety associated with an experience of the return of the repressed. The word, he finds, bears antithetical meanings – pointing to the familiar and the unfamiliar.[1] This duplicity is appropriate, for the term details the contradictory feelings that occur when a repression rises from the unconscious to the light of awareness: on the one hand, the repressed feeling is unfamiliar, having been long hidden; on the other, it is familiar, indeed, a primal and primordial instinct alienated only through the act of repression. The uncanny occurs when the primal, in suddenly welling up from the depths of the unconscious, seems strange. Likewise, Heidegger in *Being and Time* (1927) links the uncanny to the anxiety of being defamiliarized by the most primordial. For him, the uncanny arises when the familiar, everyday, habitual world slips away, and one consequently undergoes the insecurity of facing his existence alone, an anxiety that is preparatory for the most primal experience of all: sensing Being, the source from which the world arises.[2]

For Freud and Heidegger both, the uncanny involves a back and forth play between the strange and the intimate. Suddenly, one is jolted from the customary to a strange energy that is really a primal source; after this experience, what was once customary now seems strange, what was once strange is now the most familiar.

This complex interplay is elicited by metalepsis, a vehicle of the linguistic sublime. In his meditations on revisionary troping, including that of Emerson, Harold Bloom has drawn generously from Freud's essay 'The Uncanny', relating the Freudian uncanny to the sublime of a transumptive style. Bloom reads Freud's 'return of the repressed' as a return of 'anterior powers', instanced by the influence of poetic predecessors.[3] The Bloomian sublime, the act of transcending the influence of poetic fathers, is uncanny. It involves the simultaneous repression and inscription of past texts (transumption), both a veiling and disclosure of the repressed fathers. Diachronic metalepsis, which occurs when a poet makes what is 'not his' seem as if it were 'his' through the mode of elusive, revisionary allusion, is clearly the vehicle of this sublime revision, an uncanny interplay between different and same, near and far, unfamiliar and familiar.

Angus Fletcher and John Hollander forge similar links. Elaborating on the work of Paul Goodman, Fletcher notes that the feeling of being overtaxed with a metaleptic style emerges 'in works of "the uncanny"'.[4] These words forecast later ones by Fletcher and Hollander, in which they remark that the effect of diachronic metalepsis is 'often uncanny, since the poet has now made "his" what is simultaneously "not his", allowing for what one might call "textual alienation"'.[5]

These critics primarily emphasize diachronic metalepsis and the Freudian uncanny, a return of a forgotten past by way of elusive allusion. In Emerson's case, this tells only half of the story. In looking backward, returning to 'repressed' religious influences, Emerson simultaneously looks forward, to the vigorous nature in front of him, attempting to channel its force with synchronic metalepsis. Here Heidegger's uncanny complements Freud's. In maintaining that the uncanny is the region in which Being arises, Heidegger points to the sublime moment, in which anxiety is preparation for insight into the whole. Heidegger's Being, like Emerson's spirit, is always beyond the grasp of representation, a mysterious force that reveals as much as it conceals. Attempts to inscribe it must be enigmatic, dense, agitated – synchronically metaleptic.

The eye-ball passage blends the uncanny of repression – through its reinscriptions of scripture – and the uncanny of Being – through its patternings of spirit – into a sublime sequence. Emerson's Visionary is defamiliarized into the primal, an experience that blurs the categories of strange and intimate. As Emerson's next paragraph after the 'eye-ball' sequence suggests, he sees nature anew in the afterglow of his vision, keenly aware of an 'occult relation' between him and nature, finding it polar, both new and old. The uncanny is yet another figure of polarity, the psychological equivalent of an electromagnetic cosmos. It is the polarized psychological state inspired by the polarized solar system.

The remainder of *Nature*, moving in the blurred clarity of the uncanny, meditates, from a number of angles, on how electromagnetic nature is near and far, how it polarizes consciousness. In the first chapter, 'Nature', for instance, Emerson claims that what seems most ordinary, nature and its light, the sun, are beyond vision: 'To speak truly, few adult persons can see nature. Most persons do not see the sun' (N 11). Only the childlike seer, with cleansed, unbiased eyes, apprehends the sun, makes it his familiar. In the 'Beauty' chapter, Emerson gazes at the familiar and sees the exotic: 'The dawn is my Assyria; the sun-set and moon-rise my Paphos, and unimaginable realms of faerie; broad noon shall be my England of the senses and the understanding; the night shall be my Germany of mystic philosophy and dreams' (22). In the 'Language' section, he finds the unfamiliar, an insect, familiar:

> The instincts of the ant are very unimportant considered as the ant's; but the moment a ray of relation is seen to extend from it to man, and the little drudge is seen to be a monitor, a little body with a mighty heart, then all its habits, even that said to be recently observed, that it never sleeps, become sublime.   (36)

Emerson provides somewhat comic directions for defamiliarization in the 'Idealism' chapter: 'Turn the eyes upside down, by looking at the landscape though your legs, and how agreeable is the picture, though you have seen it any time these twenty years' (64). More seriously, the office of the poet is to defamiliarize: to 'un[fix] land

and sea [and make] them revolve around the axis of his primary thought and dis[pose] them anew' (64–5).

These are all accounts of Emerson's effort to surprise himself into the uncanny, prelude to the sublime. Once one has experienced a theoptic moment, one spends the rest of one's days viewing nature as a region for vision – one's seeing is altered. The sun, the ant, the dawn are no longer mere occurrences that one observes, but potential habitats of vision, if one can see through the visible to the electric invisible haunting them.

Readers of *Nature*, if they are sufficiently shocked by Emerson's visionary sequences, will likely behave similarly to Emerson in his own essay. They will be prone to performing acts of extreme attention on the remainder of *Nature*'s verbal landscape, scrutinizing seemingly ordinary passages with diligence, searching for the extraordinary, yet primordial forces sustaining them. Those overtaxed by the centrifugal force of Emerson's metaleptic bursts will peruse more centripetal passages with care, knowing that the sublime is afoot in the small eddy as well as the immense whirlpool.

If we attend to words as Emerson teaches, if we attempt to redeem them, convert them into seeds of thought, then we find that the remainder of *Nature* – even those parts which seem familiar, static, discursive – is likewise a polarized field of force, yet containing lower potencies of voltage, forces more centripetal. The overcharged vectors analyzed earlier work to shock readers into a heightened awareness of other Emersonian sequences. Subjected to close reading, even ostensibly stable sentences and structures prove unsettling. Even Emerson's most quotidian passages become windows to nature's turbulent 'spherules of force', even sentences whose sole purpose is ostensibly to clarify terms. *Nature* is never safe. Every word is potentially a grain containing sublime energy. Each hermeneutic investigation turns into an edifying meditation.

DENSITY

Before turning to the remainder of *Nature*, we should consider a further virtue of Emerson's uncanny essay: its 'density'. This is a term used by Richard Poirier, in contrast to 'difficulty', to describe writing, like that of Emerson, Wordsworth, and Shakespeare, 'which gives, or so it likes to pretend, a fairly direct access to pleasure, but which becomes, on longer acquaintance, rather strange and imponderable'. A dense style, like that of Emerson or Frost, is a deceptively easy one, whose density often goes unnoticed. A difficult style, on the other hand, like that of Joyce in *Ulysses* or of Pound in the *Cantos*, is on first encounter 'bristly', 'resistant', but likely to be mastered, lacking the depth of the 'dense' text, when perused with the aid of notes and other scholarly machinery. A difficult style is characterized by the 'extruding allusiveness of modernism', while a dense one is accompanied by 'the covert allusiveness of troping'.[6]

This sort of troping, Poirier observes, 'gives evidence of the human involvement in the shaping of language, and it prevents language from imposing itself upon us with the force and indifference of a technology. It frees us from predetermined meanings. Troping is the turn of a word in directions or detours it seemed destined to avoid'. For instance, Poirier points out, Emerson in *Nature* claims that the landscape comprised of several farms is not really owned by the farmers: 'There is a property in the horizon which no man has but he whose eye can integrate all the parts, that is, the poet' (N 11). The poet who details the land in tropes of his own making is the true owner; he turns, through his troping, land away from mere property to be exploited to a site of beauty, edification, the sublime, the uncanny.[7] Throughout *Nature*, Emerson is this ideal poet. He turns words away from the meanings attributed to them by a dead past and makes them live in the present. For example, he redeems 'spirit', 'vision', 'nature' from religion and reclaims them for his new hermetic science. He saves language from the property deeds of past owners, freeing it to be reappropriated by present readers.

New tropes must be constantly fashioned to keep language alive; Emerson details this exigency in his journal:

> The metamorphosis of Nature shows itself in nothing more than this, that there is no word in our language that cannot become typical of Nature by giving it emphasis. The world is a Dancer; it is a Rosary; it is a Torrent; it is a Boat; a Mist; a Spider's Snare; it is what you will; and the metaphor will hold, and it will give the imagination keen pleasure. Swifter than light the world converts itself into that thing you name, and all things find their right place under this new and capricious classification.   (JMN 6: 18)

Emerson's tropes battle against cliché, stasis, the 'sepulchres of the fathers' in order the keep up with the powerful flows of nature. His writing practice is grounded precisely on a resignation of prefabricated form – 'preparation' – in favor of spontaneity – or 'casting': 'It is one of the laws of composition that let the preparation be how elaborate, how extended soever, the moment of casting is yet not less critical, not the less all important moment on which the whole success depends' (JMN 5: 14). The transcriber of nature must be willing to let his words go where nature moves them: 'Every writer is a skater, and must go partly where he would, and partly where the skates carry him; or a sailor, who can only land where sails can be blown' (CEC 521).

Mimicking nature in tropes, Emerson's *Nature*, as shown earlier, works to inspire readers to do the same, to struggle against cliché, habit, stasis. His dense style, generated by engaging tropes, seemingly familiar at first, attracts readers into its rhythm, its energy. Yet soon after, his essay shocks them with the vigor of its turning. *Nature* invites readers into a comfortable house that unexpectedly contains an inscrutable God. It affects readers like a benevolent revival preacher whose words secretly pierce the soul, irritating it into conversion. His style, at first glance appealing, full of 'quotable quotes', likable, pulls readers into its optimistic world, where they suddenly find themselves uncomfortable, in a polarized, paradoxical, electrical world. This process – overt in the highly charged metaleptic sequences, less so in passages of lower voltage – yields a composition by fields of varying densities, always too dynamic to comfort readers with static definitions, univocal metaphors, or easy 'truth'. Instead, Emerson's unsettling style agitates readers into fashioning their own tropes, into participating in the redemption of language from the past, authority, technology. Emerson's dense prose encourages readers to *abandon* themselves to the turns of active thought, opening themselves to meditation.[8]

Having undergone moments of extreme density in attending to metaleptic sites, we now turn to passages of less density. We shall find that Emerson's entire verbal landscape is an invitation to meditation.

LEXICON

What we might call the 'glossary' section of *Nature*, apparently meant to define terms, does not provide security. Rather, it is uncanny, familiar and unfamiliar, polarized.

In the 'Introduction', Emerson refers to 'nature', the subject of the essay, several times before offering definitions of the term. The word first appears in the fourth sentence of the essay: 'The foregoing generations beheld God and nature face to face...' (N 5). Here nature is personified, a visage. The word appears again a few sentences later in the clause 'Embosomed for a season in nature, whose floods of life stream around and through us...' (5). Again, nature is rendered by prosopopoeia, compared to a person with a sheltering bosom, but then is suddenly turned into a liquid flood that flows powerfully. 'Nature' soon after appears in a sentence that claims that nature, like man, is a hieroglyph that 'describes its own design' (6). Nature as liquid is suddenly turned into sacred writing. The next prominent uses of the word occur in the final paragraph of the introduction. In this paragraph, 'nature' is scripted in a number of forms; 'Nature', 'nature', 'NATURE', and *'Nature'*. What are the differences among each form of the word? The universe is comprised of 'Nature' and 'Soul'. All that is distinguished from the human as the 'NOT ME', among which is 'nature', is 'NATURE'. The word entails both a common and philosophical import. 'NATURE', one can surmise, is the philosophical term, while *'Nature'*, 'essences unchanged by man', is the common one. What is the difference between the common and philosophical sense of the word? What does 'nature' with a small 'n' designate? How do these definitions of nature interweave with nature as a face, a bosom, a river, sacred writing?

'Nature' becomes more vertiginous as the essay continues. In the first chapter, Emerson claims that 'Nature never wears a mean appearance.... Nature never became a toy to the wise spirit' (N 10). Here he suggests that nature exhibits inherently noble and beautiful qualities. However, later, Emerson favorably quotes a sentence from Guillaume Oegger stating that nature is but the *'scoriae'* – dross, refuse – of the thoughts of God (44). Likewise, still later, he extols religion and ethics for 'put[ting] nature under foot' (72). Is nature mere refuse or a servant to man? Or is it beautiful, integral for his happiness and wisdom?

The very subject of the essay, 'nature', a term one would expect to be securely defined, is polar, paradoxical, near and far. If the 'eyeball' passage is a whirlpool, each mention of 'nature' is an eddy – dynamic, spiraling, gathering opposites, though of less force, more centripetally balanced. Even in more discursive sections, Emerson continues to stimulate readers into thought, forcing them to redeem 'nature' by attaching it to a meaning, finding for it a trope.

Emerson's early definition for 'man' likewise dissolves into an intensity. In the second paragraph, Emerson writes: 'Every man's condition is a solution in hieroglyphic to those inquiries he would put. He acts it as life, before he apprehends it as truth. In like manner, nature is already, in its forms and tendencies, describing its own design' (N 6). One's condition is, like nature, a hieroglyph, a form of writing, a 'solution' in writing. A 'solution' in this context is an answer, arising in the form of a man's condition, to any question he might ask. Yet, a solution is not only an answer. It is also a mixture of two or more substances, and solving is the action of separating or loosening, as in the sense of solving a problem or of dissolving something. A solution, then, can dissolve as much as resolve. Does the solution to the inquiries man would put comfort or unsettle? clarify or loosen? Is man's condition rendered in a transparent book, a univocal hieroglyph? Or is it rather a polyvocal, loose text, an enigma?

The passage goes on to state that nature corresponds to the human condition; it too acts out its condition while at the same time embodying a solution. In its forms and tendencies, it describes, or writes down, its own design, or pattern. But the prefix 'de' means the reverse of, or to remove from, as in to '*de*-throne'. To *de*-scribe then, also means 'not to write', or to remove from writing, just as de-sign also implies the undercutting or removal of a sign. The prefix 'de' also derives from the Latin 'from', or 'out of'. The signs and scripts of nature are constantly moving outside of themselves. *Nature*, then, writes a pattern in the form of a hieroglyph while simultaneously erasing it, and pens a description that is in transit, metamorphosing, constantly moving out of itself.

The semantic coherence of Emerson's definitions of 'nature' and 'man' loosens into intensities, energies, fields. Emerson's definitions for 'words' in the 'Language' section likewise dissolve. He first of all designates words as 'signs of natural facts' (N 32). As shown earlier, univocal 'signs', tools of Locke, are opposed to polyvocal 'symbols', vehicles of Coleridge. Yet Emerson soon after refers to words as 'symbols' (36–7). The etymology of 'sign' betrays its static nature, as it derives from *signum*, a visible impression or stamp. 'Symbol', however, is dynamic and flexible, deriving as it does from *symballein*, to throw together. The sign is fixed; the symbol metamorphoses.

Again, semantics become energies; discrete meanings, blurred into fields.

Emerson provides other definitions of words based on the root *ballein*, to throw: he calls them 'emblems' (N 41) and 'parables' (42). 'Emblem' derives from the Greek for 'to throw in'; parable, 'to throw beside'. The origin of these words reveals their common source in natural action and that words throw something. Do they throw meaning, or their readers, or both? Do they throw in the same direction? They throw 'together', 'in', and 'beside'. Emerson's words indeed hurl readers in different directions, keeping them guessing.

In addition to the terms listed above, Emerson refers to words that depend on nature as 'types', 'allegories', 'images', 'proverbs', and 'fables' (N 33–45). Schooled in Biblical hermeneutics, Emerson would have been well aware that 'allegory' and 'type' were terms belonging to opposing camps of Biblical interpretation in the centuries before Emerson's. Catholic theologians favored the fourfold 'allegorical' hermeneutic while the Protestant thinkers employed a more historically grounded 'typological' method of interpretation. Emerson blurs these two words not only with one another, but also with 'symbol', which was defined by Goethe and Coleridge, as Emerson knew, in opposition to allegory. It is impossible to reconcile all of these terms into a clear, univocal definition.

Yet another word for 'words' is 'metaphor': 'The world is emblematic. Parts of speech are metaphors because the whole of nature is a metaphor of the human mind' (N 41). 'Metaphor' derives from the Greek meaning 'to carry over', 'to transfer' but also to change or alter actively, as in 'to goad a horse'. Emerson's definitions for words indeed work to goad readers, transferring them from security to risk, from stasis to force.

CLASSIFICATION

Like Melville's classifications of whales in *Moby-Dick*, Emerson's definitions do not reinforce order but call it into question, suggesting that an electrical cosmos cannot be corralled in rigid categories. The overall structures of Emerson's essay, his organizations and classifications, likewise unsettle more than stabilize. Early in *Nature*, Emerson asks the primary question of his essay: 'Let us inquire, to what end is nature?' (N 6). Not surprisingly, he puns on 'nature', as it means both the natural world and his essay. He reasks this question in each of his chapters. As he writes at the beginning of 'Commodity', 'Whoever considers the final cause [end] of the world [nature] will discern a multitude of uses that enter as parts into the result. They all admit of being thrown into the following classes: Commodity; Beauty, Language; and Discipline' (N 15). In each of these section he considers the question of nature's end and appears to provide an answer. However, he then undercuts the answer in the following section. In 'Commodity', he asserts that 'All the parts [of nature] incessantly work into each other's hands for the profit of man' (16). Then, at the beginning of 'Beauty', the next chapter, he questions this claim by proclaiming that 'A nobler want of man is served by nature, namely, the love of beauty' (19). Right after he ends the 'Discipline' chapter, he writes 'To this one end of Discipline, all parts of nature conspire' (59), as if he has answered the question once and for all. Indeed, 'Discipline' was the final category in the list of ends he announced he would consider. However, he disrupts his early plan of considering the question in four chapters by meditating on it in three more, 'Idealism', 'Spirit', and 'Prospects'. A few paragraphs after his clear assertion that nature's end is discipline, he again revises by claiming that 'Nature is made to conspire with spirit to emancipate us' (63), a statement which seems to work against discipline and toward freedom.

When Emerson again ponders the question in the penultimate chapter 'Spirit', he suggests that the end of nature, both the essay and the natural world, is, paradoxically, endless. 'Uses that are exhausted or that may be, and facts that end in the statement, cannot be all that is true of this brave lodging wherein man is harbored, and wherein all his faculties find appropriate and endless exercise' (N 76). Questioning of nature is an 'endless exercise', yielding an 'infinite scope'. Indeed, in the final paragraph of the essay, Emerson observes that questions about ends are endless: 'So shall we come to look at the world with new eyes. It shall answer the *endless* inquiry of the intellect' (93) (italics mine).

Nature, though resembling a linear philosophical treatise, with defined terms, sections and subsections, is full of contradictions. After the introduction, the essay is divided into eight chapters. Most of the sections are further divided into three or four numbered subsections. This organization gives the appearance of order, a familiarizing map by which to negotiate the essay. However, Emerson's structures are disrupted by the centrifugal forces of nature. For example, in the introduction to the essay, Emerson defines nature. It is distinguished from the 'ME' of the soul as the 'NOT ME' (N 7). Later, though, the essay suggests that 'Nature is so pervaded with human life, that there is something of humanity in all..'. (78). And still later, Emerson claims that humans created nature: 'Out from him sprang the sun and moon; from man, the sun; from woman, the moon' (88). In fact, Emerson contradicts himself in the same paragraph. He concludes his section 'Beauty' by writing, 'The world thus exists to the soul to satisfy the desire of beauty. This element I call an ultimate end' (30). But three sentences later, he writes, 'But beauty in nature is not ultimate.... not as yet the last or highest expression of the final cause of Nature' (31).

AUTHORITY

Who is the author of *Nature*? Who the demiurge fashioning this giddy cosmos? Surely not a unitary, *unitarian*, univocal *persona*. Indeed, B. L. Packer has detected 'layers of purpose' in the essay similar to those in complex Old Testament narratives composed by several different stylists, believing the essay to be written by three different, conflicting figures: the 'supernatural rationalist', the 'antinomian', and the 'redactor'.[9] Alan Hodder likewise exposes several conflicting voices in the essay, likening Emerson's style to the 'voice of many waters' in the revelations of John and Jeremiah. He finds that Emerson interweaves several oratorical styles – dispositional, epideictic, hortatory, philosophic, propositional, pulpit, oracular, and wisdom.[10]

We have become acquainted with Emerson the 'Visionary', a *persona* blossoming into its full power as the 'Orphic Poet' whose vatic intonings close the essay: 'The kingdom of man over nature, which cometh not with observation, – a dominion such as now is beyond his dream of God, – he shall enter without more wonder than the blind man feels who is gradually restored to perfect sight' (N 95). The Visionary grounds his oracles on the conviction that 'seeing', as opposed to mere empirical observation, can be 'perfect', unlimited, clear; that one can gain 'insight' into an 'original relation to the universe'; that one can become entirely eye and see 'all'.

Nature is if anything a meditation on the faculty of vision, making repeated distinctions between *mere* sight – empirical registration – and *in*sight – intuitive apprehension. Most are ruled by 'superficial seeing' and indeed cannot even see nature, allowing it to illuminate only the physical eye; however, the child opens his eye and suffers nature to enter into his heart – he is the 'lover of nature' 'whose inward and outward sense are still truly adjusted to each other; who has retained the spirit of infancy even into the era of manhood. His intercourse with heaven and earth becomes part of his daily food' (11). It is this childlike man who becomes the transparent eye-ball, able to see all, both visible and invisible, the whole coursing through the parts. While '[e]mpirical science is apt to cloud the sight', a 'dream', an intuition, 'may let us deeper into the secret of nature than a hundred concerted experiments' (82). The man who finds harmony with nature, sensing his intercourse with its flows – his eyes will be cleansed, purged, initiated into an understanding of its book (44). This man is intellectual, searching out the 'absolute order of things as they stand in the mind of God, and without the colors of affection' (28). Taken together, these passages suggest that one can attain perfect, unclouded, unbound, purely objective sight, a full apprehension of the parts and whole of nature.

Yet, the Visionary has an *alter ego*, the Perspectivist, who can even occupy the same space as his twin. The Visionary suggests that one can be nourished by intercourse with nature if his 'inward sense' is adjusted to his 'outward' one. While this suggests that one can attain perfect sight of nature, it also intimates that sight is always dependent on the inward sense, that seeing is bound by perspective and therefore limited. This latter idea, ironically, follows on the heels of the eye-ball passage:

> [N]ature is not always tricked in holiday attire, but the same scene which yesterday breathed perfume and glittered as for the frolic of the nymphs, is overspread with melancholy today. Nature always wears the colors of spirit. To a man labouring under calamity, the heat of his own fire hath sadness in it. (N 14).

Mood controls seeing, it seems: to a happy, childlike, gamesome man, nature will appear gay; to a dour one, saturnine.

One is not only bound by disposition, however, but also by physiology: the eye itself possess a 'plastic', or shaping 'power'.

> The eye is the best of artists. By the mutual action of its structure and of the laws of light, perspective is produced, which integrates every mass of objects, of what character soever, into a well colored

and shaded globe, so that where the particular objects are mean and unaffecting, the landscape which they compose, is round and symmetrical.　　　　　(19).

The mind and the eye shape and dictate what we see, altering the visible to fit both the tenor of mood and the orb of the eye. How is it possible to attain perfect vision unbound by perspective? How possible to see 'all'? It isn't. As Emerson suggests near the end of his essay, 'The ruin or the blank, that we see when we look at nature, is in our own eye. The axis of vision is not coincident with the axis of things, and so they appear not transparent but opake' (91).

Transparency and opacity, respectively the goal of the Visionary and the doom of the Perspectivist, appear both to be fictions, subjective constructs through which the world enters the mind in varying degrees of clarity. We choose what we wish to see – both an exhilarating and deflating proposition: 'What we are, that only can we see.' Therefore, we can build our own world, conforming life to idea; then, a revolution will occur in sight: disagreeable appearances will vanish, like swine, spiders, snakes, pests, mad-houses, prisons, enemies, the filths of nature; and beautiful ones will take their place – beautiful faces, warm hearts, wise discourse, heroic acts (94–5). While seeing is creative, it is bound: the all of the Visionary is but a fiction, a beautiful cosmos created – not discovered – by sight.

EPISTEMOLOGY

Seeing is of course knowing. If we cannot answer the questions 'who is seeing?' and 'what is he (whoever he is) seeing?' then how can we answer the question 'what does he know?' With his characteristic optimism, Emerson opens his essay by supposing that nature is thoroughly scrutable: 'Undoubtedly we have no questions to ask which are unanswerable. We must trust the perfection of the creation so far, as to believe that whatever curiosity the order of things has awakened in our mind, the order of things can satisfy' (N 6). This seemingly credulous expectation is met by the scientist, whose aim is 'to find a theory of nature'. Later, Emerson praises the recent efforts of scientists, perhaps with Davy and Faraday in mind: 'How calmly and genially the mind apprehends one after another the laws of physics!' (49). Certainly, as this study has shown, Emerson had every reason to believe that science was well on its way to answering all questions, expelling all mysteries, explaining riddles. Each age has sent its prophet to the 'Sphinx at the road-side', and it would seem that Emerson's prophet, the 'Visionary', had solved, with the help of science, its tantalizing query.

Yet, again, the seed of discord is planted on seemingly safe ground. What is a theory of knowledge but an epistemology grounded on sight. 'Theory' derives from the Greek *theasthai*, to observe, suggesting that 'Visionary's' perfect knowledge should come from sight, a problematic issue, as we have seen. Moreover, it is curious that Emerson would follow his optimistic wishes on the ability of science to explain all phenomena with this almost surrealistic sentence on the eternally cryptic: 'Now many [phenomena] are thought not only unexplained but inexplicable: as language, sleep, dreams, beasts, sex' (N 7). We would expect Emerson to explain these phenomena in his essay, which indeed he begins to do, trying fully to account for language in the famous chapter of that name. Yet, not only does he *not* go on to explain, say, sleep and sex; he ends his essay by posing the questions: 'What is woman?' and 'What is sleep?' Do these queries suggest that these issues must remain unexplainable? As for beasts, Emerson concludes not that we can know them but that they will disappear if we see correctly: remember, perfect seeing vanquishes swine, spiders, snakes, and pests. Dreaming also remains unexplained.

Perhaps much of nature remains inscrutable. Indeed, to open the 'Idealism' chapter, Emerson asks if we can know nature at all or if our perceptions are only of our own mind – in other words, he raises the problem of solipsism. He does not grapple with it long, however. He quickly asserts that he cannot test the accuracy of his senses, cannot find out if his impressions correspond to external objects. He remains untroubled by this dilemma: 'Whether nature enjoy a substantial existence without, or is only in the apocalypse of the mind, it is alike useful and alike venerable to me. Be it what it may, it is ideal to me, so long as I cannot try the accuracy of my senses' (N 60). As with seeing, Emerson *chooses*, based on his disposition, the theory of nature most amenable to him. He leaves us wondering if knowledge of nature is possible at all, or if we are trapped in the labyrinth of our own sensations. Emerson selects the ideal theory, the notion that matter is a pattern of spirit and reflects laws in the mind, not because he can offer any philosophical proof for it, but because 'it presents the world in precisely that view which is most desirable to the mind' (74).

FREEDOM AND FATE

If Emerson's *persona* in *Nature* does indeed create what he sees and thinks, how unfettered is his creation? To invoke the polarities of a famous book on Emerson by Stephen Whicher, is he free or fated? This question, along with those of identity, perception, and knowledge, is considered throughout *Nature*. Mostly, Emerson maintains that the man of Reason is a free agent, with nature conforming to his wishes: 'Sensible objects conform to the premonitions of Reason and reflect the conscience' (N 51). When man's intellect apprehends the laws of physics, the 'beauty of nature shines on his breast', tacitly acknowledging that he is 'greater', the 'universe less, because Time and Space relations vanish as laws are known' (49–50). The Reason is able to uproot and rearrange 'land and sea', making them revolve around his thought because '[n]ature is made to conspire with spirit to emancipate us' (63). While the Understanding of the merely sensual man may be bound to its perceptions, the 'higher agency' of Reason frees the poetic thinker from limit, permitting him to create without bound.

Yet, curiously, in the 'Language' section, Emerson declares that Reason, the faculty of freedom, is a 'universal soul within or behind ... individual life': '[I]t is not mine or thine or his, but we are its; we are its property and men.' We are driven by an agency not our own. Call it spirit: as Emerson proclaims elsewhere, '[S]pirit, the Supreme Being, does not build up nature around us, but puts it forth through us, as the life of the tree puts forth new branches and leaves through the pores of the old' (N 79–80). If we, like trees, are shaped from within by an organizing force, how free are we? Is the man of Reason no more unfettered than the man of Understanding? Both are the property of external forces: the man of Reason, of spirit; the man of Understanding, of material. Both are controlled by the world, which cannot be 'subjected to the human will', whose 'serene order is inviolable by us' (80).

Not only is Emerson's *persona* limited by the controlling force of Reason and the world that bears its laws, but also by his expression. The vehicle of the Reason's intuitions, the 'Language' chapter asserts, is nature. The famous tripartite formula outlines the relationship between thought and word: 'Words are signs of natural facts'; 'Particular natural facts are symbols of particular spiritual facts'; 'Nature is the symbol of spirit.' Elaborating, Emerson claims that words grow out of and are dependent on nature: 'Every word which is used to express a moral or intellectual fact, if traced to its root, is found to be borrowed from some material appearance.' For instance, *'right'* originally meant *'straight'*, and *'spirit'*, *'wind'* (N 32–3). Words, then, are emblematic of nature; nature, too, is emblematic, of spirit. While each thing in nature 'corresponds' to a 'state of the mind', a realm of spirit, the mind, if it wishes to articulate its thoughts, must present some thing 'as its picture'. Language is 'dependent' on nature, requiring the visible objects and processes of nature to make invisible thoughts and feelings manifest to ourselves and others. If thought is dependent on language and language dependent on nature, then thought is certainly bound by the natural environment surrounding it.

PROSPECTS

Kenneth Burke once called *Nature* a 'happiness pill', boiling down to a catchy phrase what readers have found in the essay from the beginning: unabashed optimism.[11] This alleged optimism has perhaps been responsible not only for the essay's continuing popularity but also for the negative criticisms it has received, especially from twentieth-century critics who favor Melville's and Hawthorne's tragic visions to Emerson's seemingly more comic one. To be sure, Emerson's first book does look to the future with hope. He begins the essay by condemning his age for being 'retrospective', and ends it memorably with 'Prospects', a vision of a world without pain or evil.

Clearly, *Nature* is far from this simple. Time and time again, Emerson has dissolved his seemingly comforting solutions; he has shown that philosophical 'truths', like electromagnetic, polarized nature itself, are *'one thing and the other*, at the same moment'. Not only does he oppose the Perspectivist to the Visionary, the Skeptic to the Believer, the Free Man to the Fated One: he also opposes the Elegist to the Optimist. The essay is as much about, in the words of Yeats, '[w]hatever is begotten, born, and dies' as it is about '[w]hat is past, passing, or to come' – a meditation on the *ubi sunt* theme as much as a prelapsarian vision. Ecstasy is often followed by loss. A few sentences after the rapture of the eye-ball epiphany, Emerson reports the world's despair and loss: a man 'labouring under calamity' will find a kind of sadness in his fire; likewise, '[T]here is a kind of contempt of the landscape felt by him who has just lost by death a dear friend. The sky is less grand as it shuts down over less worth in the population' (N 14). Why would Emerson end his first chapter, right after his vision in which he feels 'no calamity', with this description of loss, acute enough to foreshadow his grandly elegiac 'Experience' of 1844? He certainly had reason enough to ponder nothing but death: in 1831, he lost his young, passionately beloved wife Ellen Tucker to tuberculosis; in 1834, his dear brother Edward, always in poor health, succumbed in Puerto Rico; these were followed in 1836, while Emerson was composing *Nature*, with the loss of Charles, Emerson's favorite brother, likewise to tuberculosis. Could this elegiac sense make the ecstasy of the writer of *Nature* all the more powerful? Surely, the optimism in *Nature* is not superficial, but hard-earned, perhaps a result of wisdom, coming from a man who has lost three dear friends in five years, one who is more likely to see sadness in his fire and an unworthy population, than beauty in man and nature.

Other elegiac notes are struck in the essay, almost always directly following rapture. In the 'Commodity' chapter, Emerson optimist- ically declares that nature is the servant to man: all parts work for the 'profit of man', sustained by the 'endless circulations of the divine charity' that nourish him. Man, then, is a king, catered to by '[b]easts, fire, water, stones, and corn', all of nature. Yet, curiously, Emerson ends this chapter by demoting man from his royal status, suggesting that he is part of the cycle that caters to him, a member of the biological community who lives to die: 'A man is fed, not that he may be fed, but that he may work' (N 16–18). The food offered to man by nature is energy needed to sustain life to work for more energy. Man, like the corn, the animals, must work – expend energy – to keep inevitable death at bay for as long as possible. He is no more kingly than the corn or cow he eats: he is part of those dying generations.

Moreover, at the end of the 'Discipline' section, after he has spent numerous paragraphs admiring the beautiful unities of nature and their salubrious influence on man, he abruptly changes his tone. The intimate friends of our adolescent and adult lives exert, like nature, a powerful influence on our education – '[w]e cannot chuse but love them', for they are sent by God to be an ideal toward which we reach to improve ourselves. Yet, when this friend has 'become an object of thought, and, whilst his character retains all its uncon- scious effect, is converted in the mind into solid and sweet wisdom, – it is a sign to us that his office is closing, and he is commonly withdrawn from our sight for a short time' (58). Wisdom, education, do not occur without great loss. When we gain wisdom from a friend, we know he will soon be absent from us. Does Emerson here have his dead loved ones in mind? Certainly, this is a stark declaration of the ephemerality, curiously coming on the heels of ethereal speculations on the eternal Unity.

Emerson similarly contrasts loss with gain at the end of the 'Spirit' chapter. After cheerfully announcing that 'As a plant upon the earth, so a man rests upon the bosom of God; he is nourished by unfailing fountains, and draws, at his need, inexhaustible power', he counters in the next paragraph by indicating the degeneracy of man, which results in serious alienation and loss:

> We are as much strangers in nature, as we are aliens from God. We do not understand the notes of birds. The fox and the deer run away from us; the bear and tiger rend us. We do not know the uses of more than a few plants, such as corn and the apple, the potato and the vine.

Indeed, laboring humans can mar a noble landscape: 'Yet this may show us what discord is between man and nature, for you cannot freely admire a noble landscape, if laborers are digging hard by. The poet finds something ridiculous in his delight, until he is out of the sight of men' (81). Alien, laboring, ridiculous: can this man be reason for optimism?

Even in the final assurance of the potential for perfection, the grand prospect of a wonderful world, the sheer quantity of disagreeable appearances listed suggest that no mere act of seeing can make them disappear: can conforming life to the 'pure idea' in the mind effect the disappearance of, to cite the list one more time, swine, spiders, snakes, pests, mad-houses, prisons, enemies, the sorders and filths of nature (N 94–5)? Why is Emerson's list so long? Is he emphasizing the impossibility of ever vanquishing such blights? What are we to think?

EDIFICATION

What are we to think? Of course this is the question posed, tentatively answered, and posed again throughout the essay. What does Emerson think about nature, language, logic, identity, agency, knowledge, prospects? Can he stop thinking of them? Or is the goal to think about them properly, not expecting a conclusive answer, but joying in the process of thinking. *Nature* suggests the latter possibility, for it refuses to be authoritative on these questions of major philosophical import while it inspires readers to behave as if they were authoritative thinkers on their own. Because of this simultaneous relinquishment and unleashing of authority, Harold Bloom has correctly suggested that Emerson beats the deconstructionists at their own game; his tropes have always already 'burn[ed] away context', deconstructing by themselves in order to inspire constructions from readers.[12] As Stanley Cavell has claimed, Emerson's project is one 'of building, of edification'.[13] His essay is an edifice that edifies as its foundations crumble.

Richard Rorty, to invoke another authority in the Emersonian line, develops this pun on edification – as building and education, *Bildung* – to apply to all fruitful philosophy. Philosophy, Rorty believes, should not be a quest for static answers but a process, a conversation keeping inquiry alive. The aim of philosophy, particularly that of Rorty's triumvirate of edifying thinkers, Heidegger, Wittgenstein, and Dewey, 'is to edify – to help...readers as a whole, break free from outworn vocabularies and attitudes, rather than to provide "grounding" for the institutions and customs of the present.' The process of edification, Rorty explains, following Heidegger's disciple Hans-Georg Gadamer:

> consist[s] in the 'poetic activity' of thinking up such new aims, new words, or new disciplines, followed by...the attempt to reinterpret our familiar surroundings in the unfamiliar terms of our new inventions.... For edifying discourse is supposed to be abnormal, to take us out of our old selves by the power of strangeness, to aid us in becoming new beings.[14]

This edification aptly describes the effect of Emerson's style, which shocks out of the old into the new, encouraging constant renewal, of language and thought. The way to keep philosophy vital for Rorty and Emerson is to disrupt the normal with the strange, to construct and deconstruct. Emerson's writing, a prediction, Cavell has shown, of Rorty's edifying thinkers, instances the vital theory that 'keeping a conversation going [is] a sufficient aim of philosophy'.[15] Fulfilling this requirement, Emerson's essay works to edify readers. It attempts to cast them as 'generators of new descriptions rather than beings one hopes to describe accurately',[16] to turn them into conversationalists, thinkers, trope-makers.

Emerson appropriately defines, in 'The American Scholar', the task of the scholar as edification; he is to build up and enlighten, 'to cheer, to raise, and to guide men by showing them facts amidst appearances' (CW 1: 62). The vehicle for his edifying discourse is of course his writing. As the opening paragraph in *Nature* suggests, sepulchres, dark glass, biographies, histories, criticism are incapable of conveying nature's flows while living texts, woven from wool and flax in the fields today, as it were, are capable of clothing the sun shining in the present.

Emerson elaborates in his journal on writing and building: 'I am a reader & writer', he writes, '[who] please[s] myself with parallelism & relation of thoughts, see[s] how they classify themselves on the more fundamental & the resultant & then again the new & newer result' (JMN 9: 231). This endless classification requires a flexible building, one capable of constantly assimilating the new: 'I go out', Emerson continues in the same passage, '& see the mason & carpenters busy building a house, and I discover with joy the parallelism between their work & my construction, and come home glad to know that I too am a housebuilder' (231). It is clear to him that his building cannot be static, as he parallels it further on with hunting: 'The next day I go abroad & meet hunters, and, as I return, accidentally discover the strict relation between my pursuit of truth & and their of forest game' (231). His buildings are works in progress, continually hunting, moving, questing.

Nature is Emerson's first effort as masterbuilder. It fulfills the dream of one of Emerson's very late essays, the ideal of a *gai science*, the ideal Nietzsche borrowed from Emerson: 'Poetry is the *gai science*. The trait and test of the poet is that he builds, adds, and affirms. The critic destroys: the poet says nothing but what helps somebody' (W 8: 37). As opposed to the buildings of the critic, which can be, as we have seen, sepulchres, the edifications of the poet, the master builder, are dynamic, constantly in the process of being built. In this poetic tradition, *Nature* is a *Bildungsreise* without conclusion, a perpetual apprenticeship, never offering a diploma.

Emerson's dissolving constructions keep his text from resting – it remains uncertain, risky. This insecurity is not meant to evoke despair but the exhilaration of perpetually charting the world afresh. What Nietzsche says of his own *Gay Science* (1882) in his *Ecce Homo* (1888) is also true of *Nature*: it is a 'Yes-saying book',[17] a text that embraces danger and insecurity as the muses of thought. *Nature* is attuned to Nietzsche's imperatives in *Gay Science*: '[T]he secret of the greatest fruitfulness and the greatest enjoyment of existence is: to *live dangerously*! Build your cities under Vesuvius! Send your ships into unchartered seas! Live at war with your peers and yourselves.' The risky writer, like Emerson, builds to unbuild, sails to become lost, lives for tension and strife. And these are the activities he would inspire in his readers, awakening them to 'the sense of comparison, of contradiction, of joy in the new, the daring, the untried'.[18]

This danger, for Emerson and Nietzsche both, does not lead to terror or morbidity; rather it is galvanizing wisdom, the impulse to happiness, to play: as Emerson urges in 'Considerations by the Way' (1860), 'Be merry *and* wise' (W 6: 265). Drawing from Emerson, Nietzsche continually emphasizes 'play' as the key to the gay science, Dionysian philosophy. It is the core idea of *Thus Spoke Zarathustra* (1883–92), Nietzsche's own *Nature*. As Nietzsche explains in *Ecce Homo*:

> Another ideal runs ahead of us, a strange, tempting, dangerous ideal to which we should not wish to persuade anybody because we do not readily concede *the right to it* to anyone: the ideal of a spirit who plays naively – that is, not deliberately but from over-flowing power and abundance – with all that was hitherto called holy, good, untouchable, divine.

This spirit of play dissolves static, totalizing forms that stifle healthy, dynamic thinking; it forces the thinker to create, leaving him with nothing to imitate. Play, in taking no static idea or structure too seriously, must take the dynamic *process* of thinking very seriously. As Nietzsche proclaims, it is perhaps only with the playful thinker that '*great seriousness* really begins, that the real question mark is posed for the first time.' Nietzsche admits, 'I do not know any other way of associating with great tasks than *play*: as a sign of greatness, this is an essential presupposition.'[19]

Embodying this spirit of play, *Nature* is more a litany of questions than a development of answers; its *raison d'être* seems to be the avoidance of final, static answers. Instead, it prompts a back and forth dance between question and answer that James S. Hans locates in play in his Nietzsche-inspired book on the subject. As Hans observes, play is a dynamic movement between questions that cannot be answered once and for all and tentative answers that offer temporary insights into the question. Obviously, play is a process that does not end in a static conclusion but continues endlessly as the thinker plays out the possibilities, the strengths, and the weaknesses of various answers and reasks his questions from different perspectives as he learns more. True play, Hans claims, is ecstatic, a constant moving out of stillness, as the thinker 'forget[s]' himself in the process of asking his questions of the world. Play is 'an ecstatic self-forgetfulness' that is also 'a self-remembering': as the philosopher plays, he forgets that he is an isolated subject over against an alien, objective universe, and remembers that he is part of a larger whole in which he can lose himself.[20]

All of this is to say that *Nature* (embodying yet another polarity) is simultaneously silly and serious. (Emerson once said that his strong strain of 'silliness' kept him from the morbidity that beset his brothers Charles and Edward.) It refuses to take seriously the static forms of traditional thought while at the same time it emphasizes the dire importance of creative, self-reliant thinking. In this playful refusal of one form of seriousness and playful affirmation of another, *Nature* is what Nietzsche would call Dionysian, animated by 'the most comprehensive soul, which can run and stray and from fartherest within itself; the most necessary soul that plunges joyously into chance'. While Emerson can face insecurity, agitation, flux – a heavy fate – he can also, like the Dionysian Zarathustra, 'be the lightest and most transcendent'.[21] All our buildings fall, victims of the power of nature, the force of thought; yet, the same energy will forever build new edifices.

Conclusion: Innocence and Experience

In January of 1842, Emerson, already battered by tragedy with the losses of Ellen, Edward, Charles, lost his first and dearest child Waldo to scarlet fever. He found this death devastating, writing a day after that 'Sorrow makes us all children again...The wisest knows nothing' (JMN 8: 165). Emerson tried to grieve the demise of his beloved boy, attempted to philosophize this crushing blow, in what many consider to be his most profound essay, the 'Experience' of 1844. He found, however, that thought is impotent, that the tragic vision is hollow. Wisdom is not bred of suffering; countering Aeschylus, Emerson sadly claims that we suffer and we do not learn:

> In the death of my son, now more than two years ago, I seem to have lost a beautiful estate, – no more. I cannot get it nearer to me.... So it is with this calamity; it does not touch me;... I grieve that grief can teach me nothing, nor carry me one step into real nature. (CW 3: 29).

If such intense grief does not produce insight, then what does? Nothing, it seems, and this is the 'most unhandsome part of our condition': '[T]his evanescence and lubricity of all objects, which lets them slip through our fingers when we clutch the hardest' (29).

Desiccated by such loss – of son, of knowledge, of contact – Emerson in 'Experience' struggles with extreme despair. 'Experience' is his 'Song of Experience', his Dantesque *Inferno*. It is an essay whose opening shows us a man in the middle of life's way trapped in a hopelessly dark world:

> Where do we find ourselves? In a series of which we do not know the extremes, and believe that it has none. We wake and find ourselves on a stair; there are stairs below us, which we seem to

have ascended; there are stairs above us, many a one, which go upward and out of sight . . . . All things swim and glitter.

(CW 3: 27)

Unlike Melville's Ishmael, Emerson finds no lifebuoy to lift him out of these murky waters; no Dante, he encounters no Virgil. He remains ensnared by the illusions produced by his temperament, his moods: 'Dream delivers us to dream, and there is no end to illusion. Life is a train of moods on a string of beads, and, as we pass through them, they prove to be many-colored lenses which paint the world their own hue, and each shows only what lies in its focus' (30). We are doomed to surfaces, perceiving never reality but only sheens and glimmers produced by the afterglow of a perpetually lingering dream.

Apocalypse is not afoot; indomitable light does not pierce these hallucinations. How to get on with living? Accept, Emerson says, and act. If life gives you only surfaces, then 'the true art of life is to skate well on them' (CW 3: 35). If life is to have value, we must *choose* to believe that it is sturdy, vigorous, and behave *as if* it is: '*the universal impulse to believe* . . . is the principal fact in the history of the globe' (42–3). To overcome skepticism, grief, despair, is to take the world as it is, not fretting away the hours in fruitless dialectics: 'To finish the moment, to find the journey's end in every step of the road, to live the greatest number of good hours, is wisdom' (35). Wisdom is not suffering, but overcoming suffering by choosing to trust ourselves, our perceptions, our actions: 'We must hold hard to this poverty, however scandalous, and by more vigorous self-recoveries, after the sallies of action, possess our axis more firmly' (46). The 'true romance,' the region for idealism, healing, hope, is not in contemplation, in frittering away the mind in idle speculation on ontology, epistemology, freedom and fate. Rather, it is in 'the transformation of genius into practical power' (49), in, to return to *Nature,* building one's own world.

'Experience' is Emerson's Romantic crisis ode, forged in the strain of Wordsworth's 'Ode: Intimations of Immortality' (1804) and Coleridge's 'Dejection: An Ode' (1802). All three movements seriously question ability to know and capacity to create, each wondering what to make of a diminished thing, what gain can be harvested from loss, what hope from despair. None of these pieces returns to the prelapsarian innocence whose loss it laments but meditates on how to survive in an irrevocably fallen world. Certainly,

Wordsworth in his ode yearns for this lost world of perfect visionary knowledge: 'Whither is fled the visionary gleam?/Where is it now, the glory and the dream?' However, knowing this question cannot be answered, he chooses, after much heart-wrenching reflection, to 'grieve not', but 'rather find/Strength in what remains behind'.[1] Likewise, Coleridge in his ode laments his loss of creativity, linked to his solipsism: 'O Lady! we receive but what we give/And in our life alone does Nature live.' Though his statement does away with perfect vision of the world, it nonetheless provides hope. While we can indeed weave for the world a funeral shroud, we can also choose to knit for it a wedding garment and enter into a romance with it.[2]

These three great movements, reaching forward to Stevens's nourishing supreme fictions in the midst of the modern wasteland, are fully engaged in pains besetting us all. These two poems and Emerson's 1844 essay do not offer idealistic solace, but instead delve to the heart of the wound to unearth a barely visible, beautifully impossible hope of restoration.

Compared to the profundities of 'Experience', Emerson's *Nature* has often been criticized as a 'Song of Innocence', a 'happiness pill', overly optimistic for what is not and never will be. While 'Experience' bleeds on the thorns of life, *Nature* merely pines for what is not, the familiar reading goes. Yet, as we have seen, Emerson in *Nature* is aware of the perpetual and slippery forces of nature. Indeed, reading *Nature* is an *experience* of swimming, glimmering, sliding, the evanescent, lubricity. Like 'Experience', the earlier essay is not out to answer questions, to resolve the 'what' and the 'why', but to engage the 'how', to inspire us to live vitally and think dynamically.

The 'electric' *Nature* is far from an undergraduate exercise preparing Emerson for his postgraduate masterpieces. It is a *magnum opus* in its own right, equal in power to the later pieces, grappling vigorously and creatively with the same intractable issues as 'Experience' or even the wizened 'Fate' of 1860: freedom and fate, subject and object, power and form. Not only that: it is also mature in its sense of the painful vicissitudes of life, and for good reason – the young Emerson had not only lost two brothers and a young wife, but had suffered very poor health in the years following graduation from Harvard, always in fear of losing sight and ability to walk. If suffering *did* inspire wisdom, Emerson would have been a sage.

But the wisdom of *Nature*, as of 'Experience', is that one does not need to give into the despair of skepticism in order to be wise.

Contrary to Melville's Ishmael, who believes the wise are men of woe, and to his Pierre, whose life is consumed in cynicism, Emerson believes that skepticism is a goad to joyful wisdom, to gay science. As he writes in 'Experience', '[S]kepticisms are not gratuitous or lawless, but are limitations of the affirmative statement, and the new philosophy must take them in, and make affirmations outside of them, just as much as it must include the oldest beliefs' (CW 3: 43). Skepticism is a key ingredient of active thinking, like electricity and metaleptic tropes. Affirmation and skepticism, like positive and negative charges, are polarities in a continuously creative dance, and it is this dance into which *Nature* gracefully enters, taxing us with skepticism so that we may learn to affirm anew.

And this is innocence. Not the naive innocence of Blake's childish speaker in the 'The Lamb', not the innocence of ignorance, but that of entering into the back and forth play of skepticism and affirmation, of loss and gain. It is this powerful, *knowing* innocence that the fallen Adam and Eve might retain, as Milton suggests in *Paradise Lost* when the angel Michael tells the fallen, experienced Adam that if one knows evil and still chooses to practice good, then one can possess '[a] Paradise within... happier far' than the Edenesque one in which neither good nor evil is known. This innocence is the 'abundant recompense' of the Wordsworth of 'Tintern Abbey', for whom the passing 'dizzy raptures' of youth and the 'sad music of humanity' are not losses but prologues to the 'sense sublime'. It is the hard-earned innocence of Nietzsche's 'tragic gaiety', which looks on life and all its suffering and chooses nonetheless to dance in Dionysian fervor. It is the experienced innocence of Yeats's Chinese masters in 'Lapis Lazuli', who know that 'All things fall and are built again / And those who build them again are gay.'

This is to say: we cannot know what innocence is until we have lost it. Then, its returns are sublime, healing, the 'spots of time,' the theoptic moments, that turn our earthly sojourn into a pilgrimage, our thought into edification. Fallen time, with all its illusions, fractions, deaths, becomes the field of significant toil, our cultivation and culture, the region in which spirit – life, electricity – makes its turns. This affirmation of skepticism, this tireless yea-saying in a world of negation, is perhaps the fiery coal of Romanticism. It is certainly the glowing core of Emerson's Romantic electricity. It sparks his *Nature*, galvanizes his 'Experience', and flows through a renaissance in the America of his century, still coursing through the tropes of our own.

Notes

INTRODUCTION: POETRY REALIZED IN NATURE

1. Robert D. Richardson, Jr, *Emerson: The Mind on Fire* (Berkeley University of California Press, 1995), 125.
2. For Coleridge's relationship to science, see Marilyn Gaull, 'Coleridge and the Kingdoms of the Worlds', *Wordsworth Circle*, 22:1 (Winter 1991): 47–52; Trevor H. Levere, *Poetry Realized in Nature: Samuel Taylor Coleridge and Early Nineteenth-Century Science* (Cambridge: Cambridge University Press, 1981); Kathleen Coburn, 'Coleridge: A Bridge between Science and Poetry', *Coleridge's Variety*, ed. John Beer (1974); Timothy Corrigan, '*Biographia Literaria* and the Language of Science', *Journal of the History of Ideas*, 41 (1980): 399–420; Ian Wylie, *Young Coleridge and the Philosophy of Nature* (Oxford: Oxford University Press, 1989); H.W. Piper, *The Active Universe: Pantheism and the Concept of Imagination in the English Romantic Poets* (London: Athlone Press, 1962).
3. James Marsh, 'Preliminary Discourse', quoted in Richardson, *Emerson*, 93.
4. For a brilliant discussion of the significance of the experience in the Jardin des Plantes for Emerson, see Lee Rust Brown, *The Emerson Museum: Practical Romanticism and the Pursuit of the Whole* (Cambridge, Mass. and London: Harvard University Press, 1997), 59–168.
5. Quoted in Douglas Miller, 'Introduction', in Johann Wolfgang Goethe, *Scientific Studies, Goethe: The Collected Works*, vol. 12 (Princeton, NJ: Princeton University Press, 1988), xxi.
6. John Keats, *Selected Poems and Letters of John Keats*, ed. Douglas Bush (Boston: Houghton Mifflin, 1959), 226.
7. William Wordsworth, *Selected Poems and Prose of William Wordsworth*, ed. Jack Stillinger (Boston: Houghton Mifflin, 1965), 107.
8. For Goethe's critiques of Newton, see the 'Preface' to his *Theory of Color*, in *Scientific Studies, Goethe: The Collected Works*, vol. 12, 158–162; Dennis L. Sepper, *Goethe Contra Newton: Polemics and the Project for a New Science of Color* (Cambridge, Mass.: Cambridge University Press, 1988); Frederick Burwick, *The Damnation of Newton: Goethe's Color Theory and Romantic Perception* (Berlin and New York: Walter de Gruyer, 1986). For Coleridge's problem with Newton, see Levere, *Poetry Realized in Nature*, 58–62.
9. Alfred North Whitehead, *Science and the Modern World* (New York: Mentor, 1925), 72–89.
10. Marilyn Gaull, 'Coleridge and the Kingdoms of the World', 49.

11. Gillian Beer, *Darwin's Plots: Evolutionary Narrative in Darwin, George Eliot and Nineteenth-Century Fiction* (London: Routledge & Kegan Paul, 1983), 149–67.
12. For other studies of Romantic literature and science, see Marilyn Gaull, *English Romanticism: The Human Context* (New York: Norton, 1988), 351–76; Andrew Cunningham and Nicholas Jardine, eds, *Romanticism and the Sciences* (Cambridge: Cambridge University Press, 1990); Levere, *Poetry Realized in Nature*; Piper, *The Active Universe*; Karl Kroeber, *Ecological Literary Criticism and the Biology of Mind* (New York: Columbia University Press, 1994); John Wyatt, *Wordsworth and the Geologists* (Cambridge: Cambridge University Press, 1995). For other work on Victorian literature and science, see George Levine, *Darwin and the Novelists: Patterns of Science in Victorian Fiction* (Cambridge, Mass.: Harvard University Press, 1988).
13. Laura Dassow Walls, *Seeing New Worlds: Henry David Thoreau and Nineteenth-Century Natural Science* (Madison: University of Wisconsin Press, 1995).
14. Brown, *The Emerson Museum*.
15. For a discussion of Emerson's relationship to Wordsworth and Coleridge, see Robert Weisbuch, *Atlantic Double-Cross: American Literature and British Influence in the Age of Emerson* (Chicago and London: University of Chicago Press, 1986), 3–35.
16. Only a handful of studies have developed Emerson's relationship to science during the years between 1832 and 1836, none focusing on his engagement with electricity. For example, see Gay Wilson Allen, 'A New Look at Emerson and Science', *Literature and Ideas in America*, ed. Robert Falk (Athens: Ohio University Press, 1975), 58–78; David Robinson, 'Fields of Investigation: Emerson and Natural History', in *American Literature and Science*, ed. Robert J. Scholnick (Lexington: University Press of Kentucky, 1992), 94–109; Leon Chai, *The Romantic Foundations of the American Renaissance* (Ithaca, NY and London: Cornell University Press, 1987), 141–55; Walls, *Seeing New Worlds*, 53–84; Richardson, *Emerson*, 122–4. 170–4; and Brown, *The Emerson Museum*.
17. See Ezra Pound, 'I Gather the Limbs of Osiris', *Selected Prose, 1909–1965*, ed. William Cookson (New York: New Directions, 1973), 34. For a discussion of how Pound carries on Emerson's poetic legacy, see Hugh Kenner, *The Pound Era* (Berkeley and Los Angeles: University of California Press, 1971), 157–8.
18. For discussions of the recent 'de-transcendentalizing' of Emerson, see Lawrence Buell, 'The Emerson Industry in the 1980's: A Survey of Trends and Achievements', *ESQ*, 30:2 (1984): 117–36; Michael Lopez, 'De-Transcendentalizing Emerson', *ESQ* 34:1–2 (1988): 77–139; Lopez, *Emerson and Power: Creative Antagonism in the Nineteenth-Century* (Dekalb: Northern Illinois University Press, 1996), 19–52, 165–89.
19. For recent compelling revisions of Emerson that attend to his dynamic style and thought, see Brown, *The Emerson Museum*; Lopez, *Emerson and Power*; Stanley Cavell, *Philosophical Passages: Wittgenstein, Emerson, Austin, Derrida* (Oxford, UK and Cambridge, Mass.: Blackwell, 1995), 12–41; George Kateb, *Emerson and Self-Reliance* (Thousand

182 *Notes*

Oaks, London, and New Delhi: Sage Publications, 1995); Richardson, *Emerson: The Mind on Fire;* David Jacobson, *Emerson's Pragmatic Vision: The Dance of the Eye* (University Park, Pa.: Pennsylvania State University Press, 1993); David M. Robinson, *Emerson and the Conduct of Life: Pragmatism and Ethical Purpose in the Later Work* (Cambridge: Cambridge University Press, 1993); Richard Poirier, *Poetry and Pragmatism* (Cambridge, Mass.: Harvard University Press, 1992); George J. Stack, *Nietzsche and Emerson: An Elective Affinity* (Athens: Ohio University Press, 1992).

CHAPTER 1: SUBLIME SCIENCE

1. For recent compelling discussions of Emerson and power, see Michael Lopez, *Emerson and Power: Creative Antagonism in the Nineteenth-Century* (Dekalb: Northern Illinois University Press, 1996) and Lee Rust Brown, *The Emerson Museum: Practical Romanticism and the Pursuit of the Whole* (Cambridge, Mass., and London: Harvard University Press, 1997).
2. For example, Rob Wilson (*American Sublime: The Genealogy of a Poetic Genre* (Madison: University of Wisconsin Press, 1991)) observes that the American sublime in the Romantic dispensations of Emerson and Whitman is an 'immense nature and force' or representations of it in technologies or texts, the poet becoming a voice 'representing, challenging, if not instantiating those emerging powers' (5). Joanne Feit Diehl ('In the Twilight of the Gods: Woman Poets and the American Sublime', *The American Sublime*, ed. Mary Arensberg [Albany: State University of New York Press, 1986], 173–214) seconds this reading, describing Emerson's sublime as a moment when the 'new man', transformed by the universe flowing through him', 'experiences [an] apotheosis... one with the world, he assumes its authority, his speech achieving the clarity of cosmic law' (174). Both are correct in their assessment of the effect of the sublime moment: poetic creativity. Their views are complemented by B.L. Packer in *Emerson's Fall: A New Interpretation of the Major Essays* (New York: Continuum, 1982), 56, and by Julie Ellison in *Emerson's Romantic Style* (Princeton, NJ: Princeton University Press, 1984), 7.
3. Isaac Newton, *Opticks*, in *Great Books of the Western World*, ed. Robert Maynard Hutchins et al. (Chicago: Encyclopedia Britannica), 541–2.
4. Immanuel Kant, *Critik der reinen Vernunft* (Riga, 1781), 214, 204; quoted in L. Pearce Williams, *Michael Faraday: A Biography* (New York: Basic Books, 1965), 61.
5. Kant, *Metaphysiche Anfangsgrunde der Naturwissenschaft* (Riga, 1786), 33; quoted in Williams, *Michael Faraday*, 62.
6. Kant, *Critique of Judgment*, trans. James Creed Meredith (Oxford: Clarendon, 1952), 90–2. For Kant on the sublime, see Rudolph A. Makkreel, *Imagination and Interpretation in Kant: The Hermeneutical Import of the Critique of Judgment* (Chicago: University of Chicago Press, 1990), 78–87; Andrew Bowie, *Aesthetics and Subjectivity from Kant to Nietzsche*

(Manchester: Manchester University Press, 1990), 15–40; Mary A. McKloskey, *Kant's Aesthetics* (Albany: State University of New York Press, 1987), 94–104.

7. A. Wolf, *A History of Science, Technology, and Philosophy in the 18th Century*, rev. D. Mckie, vol. 1 (New York: Harper, 1961), 101.

8. Quoted in Ernst Mayr, *The Growth of Biological Thought: Diversity, Evolution, and Inheritance* (Cambridge, Mass., and London: Belknap Press of Harvard University Press, 1982), 314.

9. Quoted in Michael A. Hoskins, *William Herschel and the Construction of the Heavens* (New York: Norton, 1963), 115. See also Angus Armitage, *William Herschel* (Garden City, NJ: Doubleday, 1963), 117–120; and Wolf, *A History of Science*, vol. 1, 117–120.

10. Quoted in Wolf, *A History of Science*, vol. 1, 405–7. See also Edward Battersby Bailey, *James Hutton: The Founder of Modern Geology* (New York, Amsterdam, London: Elsevier, 1967), 91–128.

11. Marilyn Gaull, 'Coleridge and the Kingdoms of the Worlds', *Wordsworth Circle*, 22:1 (Winter 1991): 47.

12. Whitehead, *Science and the Modern World* (New York and Toronto: Mentor, 1925), 90–105.

13. Here I follow Williams, *Michael Faraday*, 64–5.

14. For Coleridge's idea of the sublime, see Raimonda Modiano's *Coleridge and the Concept of Nature* (London: Macmillan, 1985). Modiano's reading of Coleridge's sublime clearly supports the empirical sublime being discussed here: '[F]or Coleridge, the essential qualities which occasion the sublime are boundlessness and indefiniteness. Yet Coleridge's emphasis is not so much on infinite extension as on the quality of perceptual indistinctness which allows certain objects to lose their individual form and blend with one another into a whole, though not one that can be grasped fully' (115). For a different take on the Romantic sublime that will become pertinent in Chapter 4, see Thomas Weiskel's *The Romantic Sublime: Studies in the Structure and Psychology of Transcendence* (Baltimore, Md. and London: Johns Hopkins University Press, 1976).

15. For Coleridge's merging of Plato and Bacon, see John Smith, *Fact and Feeling: Baconian Science and Nineteenth-Century Literary Imagination* (Madison: University of Wisconsin Press, 1994), 72–7.

16. William Wordsworth, *Selected Poems and Prose of William Wordsworth*, ed. Jack Stillinger (Boston: Houghton Mifflin, 1965), 110.

17. Wordsworth, *The Prose Works of William Wordsworth*, eds W.J.B. Owen and Jane Worthington Smyser, 3 vols (Oxford: Clarendon, 1974), 1:141.

18. Whitehead, *Science and the Modern World*, 80.

19. The following paragraph is drawn from Smith, *Fact and Feeling*, 54–5.

20. Wordsworth, *The Prose Works*, 1:118–19; 1:123, 140; 1:123; 1:123; 1:140; quoted in Smith, *Fact and Feeling*, 54–5.

21. For a compelling discussion of Emerson's return to America after his first trip to Europe, see Brown, *The Emerson Museum*.

22. Robert D. Richardson, Jr, *Emerson: Mind on Fire* (Berkeley: University of California Press, 1995), 29. For more on the presence of Common

Sense Philosophy and Bacon in nineteenth-century American thought, see George H. Daniels, *American Science in the Age of Jackson* (New York and London: Columbia University Press, 1968), 63–101; Theodore Dwight Bozeman, *Protestants in an Age of Science: The Baconian Ideal and Antebellum Religious Thought* (Chapel Hill: University of North Carolina Press, 1977), 3–43; Herbert Hovenkamp, *Science and Religion in America* (Philadelphia: University of Pennsylvania Press, 1978), 3–78; Laura Dassow Walls, *Seeing New Worlds: Henry David Thoreau and Nineteenth-Century Natural Science* (Madison: University of Wisconsin Press, 1995), 15–24.

23. Thomas Reid, *An Inquiry into the Human Mind*, ed. Timothy Duggan (Chicago and London: University of Chicago Press, 1970), 4; 84; 84–5; 261; 268–9.

24. Dugald Stewart, *Elements of the Philosophy of the Human Mind*, 2nd. edn (London: Jun. and Davies, 1802), 5–6; 6, 8.

25. Bozeman, *Protestants in an Age of Science*, 3.

26. Edward Everett, 'Character of Lord Bacon', *North American Review*, 16 (1823): 300; quoted in Bozeman, 3.

27. Albert Barnes, 'The Works of Lord Bacon', *Quarterly Christian Spectator*, 4 (1832): 539; quoted in Hovenkamp, *Science and Religion*, 24; Samuel Tyler, 'Influence of the Baconian Philosophy', *Biblical Repertory and Princeton Review*, 15 (1843): 505; quoted in Hovenkamp, 26.

28. See Daniels, *American Science*, 63–86. I mostly follow his discussion of Bacon in the following paragraph.

29. George B. Emerson, 'Notice of De Candolle', *American Journal of Science and Arts*, 42 (1842): 217; quoted in Daniels, *American Science*, 72.

30. Samuel Tyler, 'The Connection Between Philosophy and Revelation', *Princeton Review*, 17 (July 1845): 402–3; quoted in Daniels, 81; Tyler, 'Influence of the Baconian Philosophy', 493; quoted in Hovenkamp, *Science and Religion*, 25–6.

31. William Paley, *Natural Theology: or, Evidences of the Existence and Attributes of the Deity, Collected from the Appearances of Nature* (London: Faulder, 1802), 81.

32. Francis Bowen, *Lowell Lectures on the Application of Metaphysical and Ethical Science to the Evidences of Religion* (Boston: Little, Brown, 1849), 6; quoted in Hovenkamp, *Science and Religion*, 38.

33. Bowen, 'Emerson's Nature', *The Christian Examiner*, 21 (January 1837), in Perry Miller, *The Transcendentalists: An Anthology* (Cambridge, Mass., and London: Harvard University Press, 1978), 175.

34. John F.W. Herschel, *A Preliminary Discourse on the Study of Natural Philosophy* (Chicago and London: University of Chicago Press, 1987), 4; 4–5.

35. See James Hutton, *Theory of the Earth* (New York: Hafner Press, 1973); John Playfair, *Illustrations of the Huttonian Theory of the Earth* (New York: Dover, 1956); Georges Cuvier, *A Discourse on the Revolutions of the Surface of the Globe* (Philadelphia, 1831).

36. For Emerson and Lyell, see Stephen Whicher, *Freedom and Fate: An Inner Life of Ralph Waldo Emerson* (Philadelphia: University of Pennsylvania Press, 1953), 50–5.

37. Playfair, *Illustrations*, 8–11; 42–56.
38. See Bert A. Bender, 'Let There Be (Electric) Light! The Image of Electricity in American Writing', *Arizona Quarterly*, 34:1 (Spring 1978), 56; and Gaull, 'Coleridge and the Kingdoms of the World', 48.
39. For a recent compelling account of Emerson's 'poetic' methodology, see Laura Dassow Walls, 'The Anatomy of Truth: Emerson's Poetic Science', *Configurations*, 5:3 (1997): 425–62. For work on Emerson's epistemology, see David Van Leer, *Emerson's Epistemology: The Argument of the Essays* (Cambridge: Cambridge University Press, 1986) and John Michael, *Emerson and Skepticism: The Cipher of the World* (Baltimore, Md. and London: Johns Hopkins University Press, 1988).
40. See Titus Burckhardt, *Alchemy: Science of the Cosmos, Science of the Soul*, trans. William Stoddart (London: Stuart & Watkins, 1967).
41. Sir Karl Popper, 'The Rationality of Scientific Revolutions', in *Scientific Revolutions*, ed. Ian Hacking (Oxford: Oxford University Press, 1981), 101.
42. Trevor H. Levere, *Poetry Realized in Nature: Samuel Taylor Coleridge and Early Nineteenth-Century Science* (Cambridge: Cambridge University Press, 1981), 63.
43. L. Pearce Williams, *Michael Faraday*, 4. There have been numerous biographies of Faraday. Williams's book is important for our purposes for its attention to Faraday's education as a philosopher. Joseph Agassi also reads Faraday as a natural philosopher in *Faraday as Natural Philosopher* (Chicago and London: University of Chicago Press, 1971).
44. William Blake, 'Auguries of Innocence', *William Blake: The Complete Poems*, ed. Alicia Ostriker (New York: Penguin, 1977), 506.
45. Plotinus, *The Enneads*, trans. Stephen MacKenna, intro. John Dillon (New York: Penguin, 1991), 5.8.4.
46. Blaise Pascal, *Pensées*, trans. W.F. Trotter, *Great Books of the Western World*, vol. 33, ed.-in-chief Robert Maynard Hutchins (Chicago: Encyclopedia Britannica, 1952), 2.72.

CHAPTER 2:   THE HERMETIC CURRENT

1. Leon Chai, *The Romantic Foundations of the American Renaissance* (Ithaca, NY and London: Cornell University Press, 1987), quotes this passage in his discussion of Davy and Emerson, 141–55.
2. Samuel Taylor Coleridge, *The Collected Letters of Samuel Taylor Coleridge*, ed. E.L. Griggs, vol. 5 (Oxford: Clarendon Press, 1956–71), 309.
3. Andrew Weeks, *Boehme: An Intellectual Biography of the Seventeenth-Century Philosopher and Mystic* (Albany: State University of New York Press, 1991), 48.
4. Ernest Lee Tuveson, *The Avatars of Thrice Great Hermes: An Approach to Romanticism* (Lewisburg, Pa: Bucknell University Press, 1982), 4.
5. See note 12 to the introduction for works that emphasize the importance of science in thinking about Romanticism.

6. M.A. Atwood, *Hermetic Philosophy and Alchemy: A Suggestive Inquiry into 'THE HERMETIC MYSTERY' with a Dissertation on the More Celebrated of the Alchemical Philosophers*, intro. Walter Leslie Wilmhurst (New York: Julian Press, 1960), 7.

7. Quoted in Atwood, *Hermetic Philosophy*, 7–8. Frances Yates in her magisterial study of hermetic thought, *Giordano Bruno and the Hermetic Tradition* (Chicago and London: University of Chicago Press, 1964), writes that '[t]he Hermetic science *par excellence* is alchemy; the famous Emerald Table, the bible of the alchemists, is attributed to Hermes Trismegistus and gives in a mysteriously compact form the philosophy of the All and the One' (150). For an elaboration of the hermetic core of this table, see *Hermetica: The Ancient Greek and Latin Writings which Contain Religious or Philosophical Teachings Ascribed to Hermes Trismegistus*, ed. and trans. Walter Scott (Boston: Shambhala, 1993), especially 'The Poimandres', 115–33.

8. Tuveson, *Avatars*, 34.

9. Yates, *Giordano Bruno*, 2–3.

10. John L. Brooke, *The Refiner's Fire: The Making of Mormon Cosmology, 1644–1844* (Cambridge: Cambridge University Press, 1994), 8–13.

11. Brooke, *Refiner's Fire*, 10.

12. For the impact of hermetic thought on Renaissance thought, see Yates, *Giordano Bruno*; *John Dee, The Rosicrucian Enlightenment* (New York: Barnes & Noble, 1972); Tuveson, *Avatars*, 1–105; B.J.T. Dobbs, *The Foundations of Newton's Alchemy: or, The Hunting of the Greene Lyon* (Cambridge: Cambridge University Press, 1975).

13. Tuveson, *Avatars*, x.

14. Brooke, *Refiner's Fire*, 10.

15. Yates in *Giordano Bruno* locates a counter-tradition in hermeticism, the pessimistic, dualistic, Gnostic one, which held that matter was separate from spirit and evil (22). For Gnosticism, see Hans Jonas, *The Gnostic Religion: The Message of the Alien God and the Beginnings of Christianity*, 2nd edn (Boston: Beacon Press, 1958).

16. Brooke, *Refiner's Fire*, 8.

17. Evelyn Underwood, *Mysticism: A Study in the Nature and Development of Man's Spiritual Consciousness* (Cleveland, Ohio and New York: Meridian Books, 1955), 144–6.

18. Burckhardt, *Alchemy: Science of the Cosmos, Science of the Soul*, trans. William Stoddart (London: Stuart & Watkins, 1967), 25; 103–6.

19. Tuveson, *Avatars*, xii.

20. Toulmin and Goodfield, *The Architecture of Matter*, 25. See also William H. Brock, *The Norton History of Chemistry* (New York, Norton: 1992), 1–40.

21. Burckhardt, *Alchemy*, 123, 130–1; 136–7.

22. James B. Twitchell, *Romantic Horizons: Aspects of the Sublime in English Poetry and Painting, 1770–1850* (Columbia: University of Missouri Press, 1983), 1–2.

23. Eduard Farber, *The Evolution of Chemistry: A History of Its Ideas, Methods, and Materials* (New York: Roland Press, 1952), 34.

24. Allison Coudert, *Alchemy: The Philosopher's Stone* (Boulder, Colo.: Shambhala Press, 1980), 44–7.

25. See Yates, *Giordano Bruno*. Also see Paul Henri Michel, *The Cosmology of Giordano Bruno*, trans. R.E.W. Maddison (Ithaca, NY: Cornell University Press, 1973); Sidney Greenberg, *The Infinite in Giordano Bruno, with a Translation of his Dialogue Concerning the Cause, the Principle, and the One* (New York: King's Crown Press of Columbia University Press, 1950), 3–78; and Alexandre Koyre, *From the Closed World to the Infinite Universe* (Baltimore, Md. and London: Johns Hopkins University Press, 1957), 35–57.

26. Giordano Bruno, *Concerning the Cause, the Infinite, the Principle, and the One*, in Sidney Greenberg, trans., *The Infinite in Giordano Bruno*, 81–2; 88–9; 116.

27. Bruno, 160–1; 161.

28. Bruno, 171; 171–2.

29. Bruno, 172.

30. Jacob Boehme, *The Aurora: The Root or Mother of PHILOSOPHY, ASTROLOGY, and THEOLOGY from the True Ground*, trans. John Sparrow, eds D.S. Herner and C.J. Barker (London: Watkins & Clarke, 1960), 3.

31. Boehme, 41; 39, 40.

32. Boehme, 67–81; 82.

33. Ronald D. Gray, *Goethe the Alchemist: A Study of Alchemical Symbolism in Goethe's Literary and Scientific Works* (Cambridge: Cambridge University Press, 1952), 39–40.

34. Boehme, *Aurora*, 56–9. See also Boehme, *The Signature of All Things, With Other Writings* (London and Toronto: J.M. Dent, 1912; reissued Cambridge and London: James Clarke, 1969).

35. I should here note that Swedenborg was not the only scientifically trained hermeticist in whom Emerson took a great interest. There was also Newton, whose alchemical leanings have been amply displayed by B.J.T. Dobbs in *The Foundations of Newton's Alchemy: or, The Hunting of the Greene Lyon* and in *The Janus Face of Genius: The Role of Alchemy in Newton's Thought* (Cambridge: Cambridge University Press, 1991).

36. Robert D. Richardson, Jr, *Emerson: Mind on Fire* (Berkeley: University of California Press, 1995), 198.

37. E.A. Hitchcock, *Swedenborg: A Hermetic Philosopher* (New York: Appleton Press, 1858).

38. Swedenborg, *Arcana Coelestia*, 2888, in Sigg Synnestvedt, ed., *The Essential Swedenborg: Basic Teachings of Emanuel Swedenborg, Scientist, Philosopher, and Theologian* (New York: Swedenborg Foundation, 1972), 126; *Arcana Coelestia*, 2990–1, in Synnestvedt, 142; Swedenborg, *Heaven and Hell*, trans. George F. Dole (West Chester, Pa.: Swedenborg Foundation, 1976), 94.

39. Gray, *Goethe the Alchemist*, 97; Joseph L. Esposito, *Schelling's Idealism and Philosophy of Nature* (Lewisburg, W. Va.: Bucknell University Press, 1977), 133.

40. Gray, 3–70; Esposito, 21, 154–6.

41. Tuveson, *Avatars*, 33.

42. Gray, *Goethe the Alchemist*, 54–100; Peter Salm, *Poem as Plant: A Biological View of Goethe's* Faust (Cleveland, Ohio: Press of Case Western Reserve University, 1971), 23–5. See also Dennis L. Sepper, *Goethe Contra Newton: Polemics and the Project for a New Science of Color* (Cambridge, Mass.: Cambridge University Press, 1988) and Frederick Burwick, *The Damnation of Newton: Goethe's Color Theory and Romantic Perception* (Berlin and New York: Walter de Gruyer, 1986).

43. There has been no detailed work done on the relationship between Emerson's and Goethe's ideas of science. For work on Goethe and Emerson, see Gustaaf van Cromphout, *Emerson's Modernity and the Example of Goethe* (Columbus and London: University of Missouri Press, 1990) and Frederick B. Wahr, *Emerson and Goethe* (New York: Folcroft Library).

44. Goethe, *Italian Journey*, trans. W.H. Auden and Elizabeth Mayer (New York: Penguin, 1970), 311; 366; 368.

45. Goethe, *On Morphology*, quoted in Ernst Mayr, *The Growth of Biological Thought: Diversity, Evolution, Inheritance* (Cambridge, Mass.: Belknap Press of Harvard University Press, 1982), 457. Goethe develops his discovery of the primal plant in his essay 'The Metamorphosis of Plants', *Scientific Studies, Goethe: The Collected Works*, vol. 12 (Princeton, NJ: Princeton University Press, 1988), 76–97, and he extends the concept of the *Urbild* to anatomy in 'An Intermaxillary Bone Is Present in the Upper Jaw of Man As Well As in Animals', *Scientific Studies*, 111–16.

46. Goethe, 'The Influence of Modern Philosophy', *Scientific Studies*, 29.

47. Goethe, *On Morphology, Scientific Studies*, 43.

48. Goethe, 'The Spiral Tendency in Vegetation', *Scientific Studies*, 105–6.

49. Goethe, 'Polarity', *Scientific Studies*, 156.

50. Goethe, 'The Influence of Modern Philosophy', *Scientific Studies*, 29.

51. Goethe, *Maxims and Reflections*, quoted in Max L. Baeumer, 'The Criteria of Modern Criticism on Goethe as Critic,' *Goethe as a Critic of Literature*, eds. Karl J. Fink and Max L. Baeumer (New York and London: University Press of America, 1984), 10. For the relationship between Goethe's science and literary art, see Salm, *Poem as Plant*.

52. F.W.J. Schelling, *Ideas for a Philosophy of Nature*, trans. Errol E. Harris and Peter Heath, intro. Robert Stern (Cambridge: Cambridge University Press, 1988), 44; 47; 47; 49.

53. Schelling, *Ideas for a Philosophy of Nature*, 44–5; 83; 17–18.

54. Schelling, *On the Relation of the Plastic Arts to Nature, Critical Theory Since Plato*, ed. Hazard Adams (New York: Harcourt, Brace, Jovanovich, 1971), 446–58.

55. Schelling, *System of Transcendental Idealism*, trans. Peter Heath, intro. Michael Vater (Charlottesville: University Press of Virginia, 1978).

56. Levere, *Poetry Realized in Nature: Samuel Taylor Coleridge and Early Nineteenth-Century Science* (Cambridge: Cambridge University Press, 1981), 38.

57. Coleridge, *The Letters of Samuel Taylor Coleridge*, 4:767.

58. From a young age, Coleridge was deep in hermetic thought. As his famous autobiographical correspondence to John Thelwall of 19 November 1796 reads, he began his hermetic studies early, perusing the Egyptian mysteries of Thoth (another name for Hermes) and Taylor's histories of hermeticism: 'I am *deep* in all out of the way books.... Metaphysics and poetry and "facts of the mind", that is, accounts of all strange phantasms that ever possessed "your philosophy"; dreamers, from Thoth the Egyptian to Taylor the English pagan, are my darling studies' (*Letters* 1:260). For Coleridge and hermeticism, see John Livingstone Lowes, *The Road to Xanadu: A Study in the Ways of Imagination* (Princeton, NJ: Princeton University Press, 1986), 209–13.

59. Tuveson, *Avatars*, 194. For hermeticism in America, see Brooke, *Refiner's Fire*.

60. Goethe, *On Morphology, Scientific Studies*, 43.

61. Richardson, *Emerson*, 171.

62. Cavell, *Conditions Handsome and Unhandsome: The Constitution of Emersonian Perfectionism* (Chicago: University of Chicago Press, 1990), 36.

CHAPTER 3: ELECTRIC COSMOS

1. Ernest Lee Tuveson, *The Avatars of Thrice Great Hermes: An Approach to Romanticism* (Lewisburg, Pa: Bucknell University Press, 1982), 17–18.

2. F. Sherwood Taylor, *The Alchemists* (New York: Arno, 1974), 191.

3. Davy wrote this in a 10 April 1799 letter to Davies Gilbert, a friend and patron. Its is quoted in L. Pearce Williams, *Michael Faraday* (New York: Basic Books, 1965), 67. For the influence of Kant on *Naturphilosophie* and electromagnetism, see Barbara Giusti Doran, 'Origins and Consolidation of Field Theory in 19th Century Britain: From Mechanical to Electromagnetic View of Nature', *Historical Studies in the Physical Sciences*, vol. 6, ed. Russell McCormmach (Princeton, NJ: Princeton University Press, 1975), 133–260; Mary B. Hesse, *Forces and Fields: The Concept of Action at a Distance in the History of Physics* (London: Thomas Nelson & Sons, 1961), 157–205; Williams, *Michael Faraday*, 53–94.

4. William H. Brock, *The Norton History of Chemistry* (New York: Norton, 1992), 150; Rene Taton, ed., *A History of Science: Science in the Nineteenth Century*, trans. A.J. Pomerans (New York: Basic Books, 1964–66), 274.

5. Brock, *The Norton History of Chemistry*, 135–7; 135.

6. Oliver Sacks, 'The Poet of Chemistry', *New York Review of Books*, 45: 18 (November 1993), 51n.

7. H.A.M. Snelders, 'Oersted's Discovery of Electromagnetism', *Romanticism and the Sciences*, eds. Andrew Cunningham and Nicholas Jardine (Cambridge: Cambridge University Press, 1990), 223.

8. Snelders, 231–2.

9. Snelders, 235–8; Williams, *Michael Faraday*, 137–44.

10. H.C. Oersted, 'Die Reihe der Sauren und Basen', *Gehlen's Journal fur die Chemie und Physik*, 2 (1806), 509, quoted in Williams, *Michael*

Faraday, 138; Oersted, *Recherches sur l'identité des forces chimiques et électriques*, trans. Marcel de Serres (Paris, 1813), 243, quoted in Williams, 138; Williams, 139.

11. Taton, ed., *History of Science*, 185.
12. Williams, *Michael Faraday*, 143–6; Taton, ed., *History of Science*, 187–91.
13. Davy, *Four Lectures*, quoted in Williams, *Michael Faraday*, 125.
14. Williams, *Michael Faraday*, 24–9.
15. Williams, 153–7.
16. Hesse, *Forces and Fields*, 218.
17. Williams, *Michael Faraday*, 183; Taton, ed., *History of Science*, 194–7.
18. Williams, *Michael Faraday*, 198–226.
19. Doran, 'Origins', 134.
20. Michael Faraday, 'A Speculation Touching Electrical Conduction and the Nature of Matter', *Great Books of the Western World*, vol. 45, ed.-in-chief Robert Maynard Hutchins (Chicago: Encyclopedia Britannica, 1952), 855.
21. For Hooke, see Brock, *The Norton History of Chemistry*, 71–4; for Boscovich, see Williams, *Michael Faraday*, 73–80.
22. John F.W. Herschel, *A Preliminary Discourse on the Study of Natural Philosophy* (Chicago and London: University of Chicago Press, 1987), 246–9; 248; 313–15.
23. Herschel, 324; 340; 329–39.
24. Herbert A. Myer, *A History of Electricity and Magnetism*, fore. Bern Dibner (Cambridge, Mass. and London: MIT Press, 1971), 59.
25. As Sherman Paul observes in *Emerson's Angle of Vision: Man and Nature in the American Experience* (Cambridge, Mass.: Harvard University Press, 1952), Emerson was attracted to electromagnetism even earlier. In 1827, he described an experiment very similar to the one Faraday conducted to demonstrate lines of force: 'I have seen a skilful experimenter lay a magnet among filings of steel, and the force of that subtle fluid, entering each fragment, arranged them all in mathematical lines, and each metallic atom became in its turn a magnet communicating all the force it received of a loadstone' (JMN 3:95; quoted in Paul, 142–3). Though Emerson still described magnetic force in Ampère's liquid terms, he understood that the force occurs in lines, a fact that Faraday discovered for himself in the early 1830s. When Faraday placed iron filings on a sheet of paper near a magnet, he noticed that the filings formed a pattern of lines stretching from north to south, along the poles of the magnet. Faraday concluded that the lines of force were present even if the filings were not, and that the magnet produced a field of force, just as electrically charged objects did (ER 3070–5). Appropriately, Emerson was still intrigued by electricity and magnetism at the end of his career, writing in the 1870s that magnetism is 'a primary phenomenon' (JMN 16:286).
26. Ernst Mayr, *The Growth of Biological Thought: Diversity, Evolution, and Inheritance* (Cambridge, Mass. and London: Belknap Press of Harvard University Press, 1982), 457–8.
27. For more on the polarization of light, see Taton, ed., *A History of Science*, 159–60; 310–12.

28. Taton, 163.
29. Paul makes this point in *Emerson's Angle of Vision*, 143.
30. Gay Wilson Allen, *Waldo Emerson: A Biography* (New York: Viking, 1981), 576–7; Werner Heisenberg, *Physics and Philosophy* (New York: Harper Torchbooks, 1971), 95; Albert Einstein and Leopold Infeld, *The Evolution of Physics: The Growth of Ideas from Early Concepts to Relativity and Quanta* (New York: Simon & Schuster, 1961), 125.
31. Allen, *Waldo Emerson*, 576.

CHAPTER 4: ELECTRIC WORDS

1. Byron, George Gordon, 'Childe Harold's Pilgrimage', *Byron: Poetical Works*, ed. Frederick Page (New York and Oxford: Oxford University Press, 1970), 4:23; 4:24.
2. Richardson, *Emerson: Mind on Fire* (Berkeley: University of California Press, 1995), 101.
3. Francis Bowen, 'Emerson's Nature', *The Christian Examiner*, 21 (January 1837), 371–85, in Perry Miller, ed., *The Transcendentalists: An Anthology* (Cambridge, Mass. and London: Harvard University Press, 1978), 174.
4. R.F. Jones 'Science and English Prose Style in the Third Quarter of the Seventeenth Century', *Seventeenth Century Prose*, ed. Stanley Fish (New York: Oxford University Press, 1971), 55; Jones, 'Science and Language in England of the Mid-Seventeenth Century', *Seventeenth Century Prose*, 100; Jones, 'Science and Language', 103.
5. Robert Adolph, *The Rise of Modern Prose Style* (Cambridge, Mass.: MIT Press, 1968), 20.
6. John Locke, *An Essay Concerning Human Understanding*, ed. Peter H. Nidditch (Oxford: Clarendon Press, 1975), 3.2.1; 3.2.1; 3.9.6; 3.10.22; 3.10.14; 3.10.34.
7. Dugald Stewart, *Elements of the Philosophy of the Human Mind* (London: Cavell & Davies, 1802), 198–200.
8. Andrews Norton, *A Statement of Reasons for Not Believing in the Doctrines of Trinitarians*, 7th edn (Boston: American Unitarian Association, 1859), 16, 20, quoted in Philip Gura, *The Wisdom of Words: Language, Theology, and Literature in Renaissance New England* (Middletown, Conn.: Wesleyan University Press, 1981), 28; Norton, 138, quoted in Gura 29; Norton 48–9, quoted in Gura, 29. Gura's *Wisdom of Words* is an excellent account of the various language theories, German and otherwise, in New England during the first half of the nineteenth century. For a more recent account of German hermeneutical traditions and the New England renaissance, see Richard A. Grusin, *Transcendental Hermeneutics: Institutional Authority and the Higher Criticism of the Bible* (Durham, NC and London: Duke University Press, 1991).
9. Sampson Reed, 'Oration on Genius', *Aesthetic Papers* (1849), 59–65, in Miller, *The Transcendentalists*, 51.

10. Reed, *Observations on the Growth of the Mind*, in Miller, *The Transcendentalists*, 56–7.

11. Coleridge, *The Collected Letters of Samuel Taylor Coleridge*, ed. E.L. Griggs (Oxford: Clarendon Press, 1956–71), 1:626; Mary Bushnell Cheney, *Life and Letters of Horace Bushnell* (New York: Charles Scribner's Sons, 1880), 209, quoted in Gura, *The Wisdom of Words*, 53.

12. Goethe, *Maxims and Reflections*, quoted in Max L. Baeumer, 'The Criteria of Modern Criticism on Goethe as Critic', *Goethe as a Critic of Literature*, eds Karl J. Fink and Max L. Baeumer (New York and London: University Press of America, 1984), 10.

13. For Romantic literary theorists, eighteenth-century aesthetics was grounded on mere imitation, not creation. This sort of mimicry is memorably espoused by Pope in his *Essay on Criticism*, 'Nature to all things fixed the limits fit,/ And wisely curbed man's pretending wit' (51–2) (*Pope: Complete Poetical Works*, ed. Herbert Davis [Oxford and New York: Oxford University Press, 1966]). Poetry becomes a form of limitation, a mirror, not an expression, of nature, which is itself static, resilient to dynamic evolution: 'First follow nature, and your judgment frame/ By her just standard, which is still the same' (68–9). The 'business of the poet', as Samuel Johnson sums up eighteenth-century sensibility through his character Imlac in *The History of Rasselas, Prince of Abissinia*, ed. J.P. Hardy (Oxford and New York: Oxford University Press, 1988), is to discover the general properties in nature and copy them: he is 'to examine, not the individual, but the species; to remark general properties and large appearances: he does not number the streaks of the tulip, or describe the different shades in the verdure of the forest' (27). The overly imaginative poet will leave the models of nature behind; his works will be insane (104).

14. M.H. Abrams, *The Mirror and the Lamp: Romantic Theory and the Critical Traditions* (Oxford: Oxford University Press, 1953), 30–69.

15. Coleridge spearheaded the Romantic revolt against neoclassical taste. For Coleridge, treatises on poetics during the eighteenth century propounded the faculty of the fancy at the expense of the imagination. The fancy 'has no other counters to play with, but fixities and definites.' It is a 'mode of Memory emancipated from the order of time and space; and it is blended with, and modified by that empirical phenomenon of the will, which we express by the word CHOICE' (CC 7.1:305). The fancy rearranges the impressions it passively receives; it is comprised of nothing more than the associative laws of the mind, which distinguish or unite the ideas provided by and limited to sense impressions. The imagination, on the other hand, is creative, not limited to impressions. It has two aspects, primary and secondary. The primary imagination is 'the living power and prime Agent of all human Perception, and as a repetition in the finite mind of the eternal act of creation in the infinite I AM' while the secondary, an echo of the primary, 'dissolves, diffuses, dissipates, in order to recreate' (305). The poet, Coleridge writes, 'must imitate that which is within the thing; active thro' From and Figure as by symbols [?discoursing/discovering/discerning] *Natur-geist...*' (CC 5.2:223).

Coleridge here rephrases Schelling, who maintains in *On the Relation of the Plastic Arts to Nature, Critical Theory Since Plato*, ed. Hazard Adams (New York: Harcourt, Brace, Jovanovich, 1971), that the artist, like a god, creates patterns that reveal the creative spirit immanent in the universe. The poet gives form to spirit, body to soul (447–8).

16. Some of Emerson's close readers have noticed this electrical quality of the prose. John Burroughs, writing of Emerson's style in 1877, claims that it is 'akin to that elusive but potent something we call electricity' (*Birds and Poets, with Other Papers* [Boston: Houghton Mifflin, 1895], 192). William James, one of Emerson's most sensitive readers, said in 1903 that Emerson's greatest achievement was as an 'Artist' because his 'matchless eloquence' 'electrified and emancipated his generation' ('Address at the Emerson Centenary in Concord', *Emerson: A Collection of Critical Essays*, eds Milton R. Konvitz and Stephen E. Whicher [Englewood Cliffs, NJ: Prentice Hall, 1962], 20). More recently, B.L. Packer has observed that he constructed essays characterized by 'ambiguities, lacunae, paradoxes, and understatements' so 'generously' placed that the sentences in his essays are 'charged terminals' that the reader must take the risk of connecting', the reward being 'a certain electric tingle' (*Emerson's Fall: A New Interpretation of the Major Essays* [New York: Continuum, 1982], 6). The 'multiplicity of... conflicting statements' that Matthiessen locates in Emerson, the 'volatility' that Eric Cheyfitz finds, are Emerson's deliberate attempts to write the perpetual forces of a charged, agitated, protean universe that cannot be corralled by static language (*American Renaissance: Art and Expression in the Age of Emerson and Whitman* [New York and Oxford: Oxford University Press, 1941], 3; *The Trans-Parent: Sexual Politics in the Language of Emerson* [Baltimore, Md.: Johns Hopkins University Press, 1981], xii). His sentences, Alan Hodder writes, are like atoms, jewels, or plants (*Emerson's Rhetoric of Revelation: Nature, the Readers, and the Apocalypse Within* [University Park, Pa. and London: Pennsylvania State University Press, 1989], 121). Lawrence Buell correctly characterizes Emerson's style as exhibiting 'unpredictable, vigorous fecundity' (*Literary Transcendentalism: Style and Vision in the American Renaissance* [Ithaca, NY and London: Cornell University Press, 1973], 161).

17. Three of Emerson's strongest readers have discussed the dynamic, unsettling, shocking nature of his tropes. Stanley Cavell proposes that Emerson's troping is the vehicle of his 'onward thinking', of the battle of his thinking to stay fresh and alive, to avert itself from conformity or static conclusion, 'to remain in conversation to itself' (*The Senses of Walden*, expanded edn [Chicago: University of Chicago Press, 1981], 134). Harold Bloom has theorized that Emerson's tropes are 'life-enhancing' defenses that 'burn away context', or the anxiety of oppressive influence, and generate 'a pragmatic fresh center', an impulse to create, to act, an attempt to shun influence and be original (*Kabbalah and Criticism* [New York: Seabury Press, 1975], 118, 120). Richard Poirier calls Emerson's tropes vehicles for 'life, transition, and the energizing spirit', that 'turn' his readers

to activity and reflection (*The Renewal of Literature: Emersonian Reflections* [New Haven, Conn. and London: Yale University Press, 1987], 16–17).

18. Several critics have noticed Emerson's conflation of poetry and prose. As Matthiessen has observed: 'In declaring that the best prose becomes poetic, that the sublimest speech is a poem, Emerson was voicing the special desire of the transcendentalists to break through all restricting divisions' (*American Renaissance*, 22). As David Porter notes, Emerson's essays are 'consciously crafted and as attentive to form as poetry' (*Emerson and Literary Change* [Cambridge: Harvard University Press, 1978], 3). This assessment follows one of the first evaluations of *Nature* in an anonymous piece written in *The Democratic Review* in February 1838: *Nature* is a 'prose poem', asking us to rejoice that 'such a poem as 'Nature' is written' (quoted in Merton M. Sealts and Alfred R. Ferguson, eds, *Emerson's Nature: Origin, Growth, Meaning* [New York and Toronto: Dodd, Mead, 1969], 91). In 1871, James Russell Lowell expressed the same sentiment: 'though [Emerson] writes in prose, he is essentially a poet', as one cannot 'paraphrase what he says, or...reduce it to words of one syllable for infant minds' (quoted in Konvitz and Whicher, eds, *Emerson: A Collection of Critical Essays*, 44). John Jay Chapman championed this view of Emerson's prose in *Nature* in 1897 when he wrote in the *Atlantic Monthly* that the essay is a 'supersensuous, lyrical, sincere rhapsody' (quoted in Sealts and Ferguson, *Emerson's Nature*, 123).

19. Cavell, *This New Yet Unapproachable America* (Albuquerque, NM: Living Branch Press, 1989), 81–2.

20. This definition of metaphor is drawn, of course, from I.A. Richards. See his *Philosophy of Rhetoric* (Oxford and New York: Oxford University Press, 1936), 89–138.

21. The formal elements in *Nature* point to the future, toward the modernist poetic theories of Pound. Hugh Kenner has shown that the ideogrammatic basis for Pound's vorticist poetics was Emerson, indirectly via the sinologist Ernest Fenollosa. Pound's poetics are best detailed, as Kenner explains, by the figure of the knot, a patterned energy. Invoking Buckminster Fuller, Kenner asks us to think of an invisible rope looped into a simple overhand knot. If we pull on the rope, no matter how hard, the knot will not disappear; it is a 'self-interfering pattern.' In sliding the knot along the rope, we are really sliding the rope through the knot; if we have several different sorts of ropes – hemp, cotton, nylon – we can slide all of them through the knot and it will retain its pattern. The knot is not any of these ropes; it is a 'patterned integrity' that the rope renders visible. Like the rope passing through and manifesting the knot, so 'the metabolic flow passes through a man and is not the man: some hundred tons of solids, liquids, and gases serving to render a single man corporeal through seventy years he persists, a patterned integrity, a knot through which pass the swift strands of simultaneous ecological cycles, recycling transformations of solar energy' (*The Pound Era* [Ber-

keley and Los Angeles: University of California Press, 1971], 45–6; 157–8). This view of nature in process, things as knots, underlies Pound's definition of the poetic image: '...a radiant node or cluster;...a VORTEX, from which, through which, and into which, ideas are constantly rushing' (quoted in Kenner, 146; Pound, *Gaudier-Brzeska: A Memoir* [New York: New Directions, 1970], 92). A vortex, like a knot, like a human, like a word, is not the energy generating it but a pattern made visible by and revealing the energy.

The electromagnetic Emerson shares this vision of nature as an interchange of pattern and flux in his description of man: 'A man is the whole encyclopedia of facts...As the air I breathe is drawn from the great repositories of nature, as the light on my book is yielded by a star a hundred millions of mile distant, as the poise of my body depends on the equilibrium of centrifugal and centripetal forces, so the hours should be instructed by the ages, the ages by the hours' (CW 2:3–4). Poetic words, taking on the qualities of nature, share in this process: 'The etymologist finds the deadest word to have been once a brilliant picture. Language is fossil poetry. As the limestone of the continent consists of infinite masses of the shells of animacules, so language is made up of images, or tropes, which now, in their secondary use, have long ceased to remind us of their poetic origins' (CW 3:13). Emerson's own passages in *Nature* bear these qualities, gathering into dynamic, multilayered patterns the flows of nature.

22. Hugh C. Holman and William Harmon, *A Handbook to Literature*, 5th edn (New York and London: Macmillan, 1986).

23. John Hollander, *The Figure of Echo: A Mode of Allusion in Milton and After* (Berkeley, Los Angeles, and London: University of California Press, 1981), 133.

24. Hollander, 113–15.

25. Angus Fletcher, *Allegory: The Theory of a Symbolic Mode* (Ithaca NY: Cornell University Press, 1964), 240–3.

26. Hollander, *Figure of Echo*, 130.

27. Hollander, 114; Fletcher, *Allegory*, 241n.; Hollander, 133–4.

28. Hollander, 117–120.

29. Hollander, 147.

30. Bloom, *Poetry and Repression: Revisionism from Blake to Stevens* (New Haven, Conn. and London: Yale University Press, 1973), 20. See also 'Transumption: Towards a Diachronic Rhetoric (Blanks, Leaves, Cries)', *The Breaking of the Vessels* (Chicago and London: University of Chicago Press, 1982).

31. Quintilian, *Institutes of Oratory*, trans. H.E. Butler (Cambridge, Mass., and London: Loeb Classics, Harvard University Press, 1953), 3.6.37–9, quoted in Hollander, *Figure of Echo*, 135.

32. Hollander, 135–8. Hollander, it should be observed, notes the synchronic aspect of metalepsis only in passing. A 'synchronic treatment of metalepsis – of a trope of a trope, as it were – might *merely* be a *catachresis*, or thoroughly mixed metaphor' (114 – first italics mine). Indeed, one reason that metalepsis was largely viewed as a minor

trope in the classical and medieval rhetorics is because it often leads, as Holman and Harmon (*Handbook*) note, to such 'extreme compression that the literal sense of the statement is eclipsed or reduced to anomaly or nonsense.' In comparing the trope to catachresis, which means 'misuse' in Greek, Hollander points to this tradition. However, though catachresis, like synchronic metalepsis, can be, to quote Quintilian, a 'necessary misuse (*abusio*) of words', the effects of its 'misuse' can be powerful. *The New Princeton Encyclopedia of Poetry and Poetics*, eds Alex Preminger and T.V.F. Brogan (Princeton, NJ: Princeton University Press, 1993) tellingly notes that Milton's 'blind mouths' is an example of catachresis (Hollander, remember, used the words as an example of metalepsis). Another example of catachresis in the *Princeton* comes from Shakespeare's *Timon of Athens*: 'Tis deepest winter in Lord Timon's purse' (3.4.15). In both examples, there is a mixing of metaphors, an inconsistency of modes. The metaphoric association of 'deep winter' and an empty purse strikes us with its ostensible incongruity (as does the association of 'blind' and 'mouth.'). Likewise, the line metaleptically mixes tropes; 'deepest' metaphorically operates on the metonymic 'winter' (associated with empty, bare, cold). Moreover, the comparison between vast winter and a small purse constitutes the figure of hyperbole, which packs the line with further connotation.

33. Fletcher, *Allegory*, 21n.
34. M.H. Abrams, *Natural Supernaturalism: Tradition and Revolution in Romantic Literature* (New York and London: Norton, 1971), 512–13.
35. Thomas Weiskel, *The Romantic Sublime: Studies in the Structure and Psychology of the Transcendent* (Baltimore, Md.: Johns Hopkins University Press, 1976), 23; 24; 24.
36. Weiskel, 28; 29.
37. Weiskel, 29; 29; 31–3. In the most famous passage in which Emerson beholds the sublime, the 'transparent eye-ball' passage, he, like Wordsworth, enacts simultaneously the poet's and reader's sublime. Walking across the common, he is in a normal, habitual relationship to nature, in which snow puddles, field, and sky are distinct. His detailed, almost scientific attention to physical events leads to phase two. While feeling the contradictory sublime feelings of fear and joy, his relationship to the landscape becomes indeterminate, overwhelming. At the point where 'all mean egotism vanishes', he is in phase two, consumed by the infinite. His observations of the physical have led to an insight of the metaphysical. In the midst of indeterminacy, he immediately tropes his way to phase three, a new relationship to the inscrutable, metaphorically substituting a 'transparent eye-ball' for his ego, relating himself to Universal Being. Simultaneously, he metonymically displaces the force of Universal Being into a circulatory force of which he is but a part. His scientific observations have produced a conclusion about the relationship between spirit and matter, energy and its patterns.

38. Angus Fletcher remarks in *Allegory* (245n.) that Paul Goodman's descriptions of uncanny literature (on which more in Chapter 6) aptly detail metaleptic passages. Metalepsis renders a sequence that 'is unifiable on an indefinite number of interpretations but the higher meaning of this plurality is not to be grasped by any act of imagination, feeling, or thought'. For example, the ambiguous messages of the Delphic Oracle or theological mysteries, or a symbol like Nathaniel Hawthorne's black veil in 'The Minister's Black Veil' disseminate meanings that force us 'to think and feel beyond what is presented' (Goodman, *The Structure of Literature* [Chicago: University of Chicago Press, 1954], 253–4). Emerson's sublime passages, like those of Hawthorne, analyze – break down – the faculties, forcing readers to synthesize – piece together – new formations of thought and language.

39. His style converts readers into figurative interpreters just as Puritan sermons transformed auditors to the possibility of being graced. Ann Kibbey has reminded us of how the Puritan sermon treated figures of speech not only as manipulations of the meanings of words, but as palpable figures that would affect hearers on a bodily level. She shows how John Cotton used paronomasia to craft subtle, subliminal meanings that reinforced his overt message by 'getting under the skin', as it were, of his listeners. Cotton defines paronomasia primarily as 'the repetition of like sounds, yet somewhat differing' (Kibbey, *The Interpretation of Material Shapes in Puritanism* [Cambridge: Cambridge University Press, 1986] 13). For him, paronomasia includes repetitions not only of complete words, but also of letters and syllables. He delivered sermons in which phonic patternings reinforced semantic meanings. Emerson clearly places himself in this tradition, though he wishes to convert his hearers not into Congregational saints, but into creative interpreters.

40. Joel Porte, *Representative Man: Ralph Waldo Emerson in His Time* (New York: Oxford University Press, 1987), 153.

41. Clearly, Emerson's hermeneutical theories predict the 'reader response' criticism of the last third of our century. Indeed, both Packer, *Emerson's Fall*, and Hodder, *Emerson's Rhetoric*, have successfully invoked reader response criticism in their discussions of Emerson's style. For the key reader response text, see Wolfgang Iser, *The Act of Reading: A Theory of Aesthetic Response* (Baltimore, Md. and London: Johns Hopkins University Press, 1978).

42. Packer, *Emerson's Fall*, 6; 6; 7; 6.

43. Hodder, *Emerson's Rhetoric*, 131; 131; 133; 138.

44. Burke, 'I, Eye, Ay – Emerson's Early Essay "Nature": Thoughts on the Machinery of Transcendence', in *Emerson's Nature: Origin, Growth, Meaning*, eds Merton M. Sealts, Jr. and Alfred R. Ferguson (New York and Toronto: Dodd, Mead, 1969), 150–63.

45. Quoted in Bishop, *Emerson on the Soul* (Cambridge, Mass.: Harvard University Press, 1964), 145–6.

46. John Jay Chapman, quoted in Milton R. Konvitz, ed., *The Recognition of Ralph Waldo Emerson: Selected Criticism since 1837* (Ann Arbor: University of Michigan Press, 1972), 108.

CHAPTER 5: THE ELECTRIC FIELD OF *NATURE*

1. Abrams, *Natural Supernaturalism: Tradition and Revolution in Romantic Literature* (New York and London: Norton, 1971), 13.
2. Hodder, *Emerson's Rhetoric of Revelation: Nature, the Readers, and the Apocalypse Within* (University Park, Pa. and London: Pennsylvania State University Press, 1989), 7. Hodder goes on to claim that 'No American writer since Jonathan Edwards is more thoroughly steeped in the Christian Bible than Ralph Waldo Emerson' (7).
3. Abrams, *Natural Supernaturalism*, 344. Abrams uses this to describe Shelley's 'Apocalypse by Imagination'; Joel Porte rightly quotes Abrams's language to explain Emerson's idea of apocalypse in *Representative Man: Ralph Waldo Emerson in His Time* (New York: Columbia University Press, 1986), 86.
4. Joel Porte's work on Emerson's visionary strain points to the critical tradition relating back to Carlyle and Oliver Wendell Holmes that reads *Nature* in the apocalyptic tradition. In his first letter to Emerson after the publication of *Nature*, Carlyle wrote, 'Your little azure colored book Nature gave me true satisfaction.... It is the true Apocalypse this when the "open secret" becomes revealed to a man.' Holmes praised *Nature* similarly: 'Nature is the book of Revelation of our Saint Radulphus' [a conflation of 'Ralph Waldo'] (*Representative Man*, 79–102). See also B.L. Packer, *Emerson's Fall: A New Interpretation of the Major Essays* (New York: Continuum, 1982), 22–84; Hodder, *Emerson's Rhetoric*; Sacvan Bercovitch, 'Emerson the Prophet: Romanticism, Puritanism, and Auto-American Biography', in *Emerson: Prophecy, Metamorphosis, and Influence*, ed. David Levin (New York and London: Columbia University Press, 1975), 1–12; and Harold Bloom, *Poetry and Repression: Revisionism from Blake to Stevens* (New Haven, Conn. and London: Yale University Press, 1973).
5. Joseph Wittreich observes that Revelation is thoroughly revisionary: it 'draws upon previous prophecy, inverting its patterns, correcting and amplifying its visions... Though a new prophecy, Revelation serves as a commentary on older ones; it invokes contexts that it interprets and projects a vision requiring interpretation similar to that which it provides for previous prophecy' (*Angel of the Apocalypse: Blake's Idea of Milton* [Madison: University of Wisconsin Press, 1975], 191). While John reverses the patterns of previous prophecy through overt allusion, Emerson, through covert, elliptical allusion echoes and revises the Bible, including Revelation.
6. Austin Farrar, *A Rebirth of Images: The Making of St. John's Apocalypse* (Gloucester, Mass.: Peter Smith, 1970), 19; 20.
7. Richard Poirier observes this relationship between writing and building in Emerson (and other American writers) in *A World Elsewhere: The Place of Style in American Literature* (Madison: University of Wisconsin Press, 1985), xix–xxii; 63–70.
8. Porte, *Representative Man*, 91.
9. Porte, 91.

10. Friedrich Nietzsche, *Thus Spoke Zarathustra, The Portable Nietzsche*, trans. and ed. Walter Kaufmann (New York: Viking, 1982), 137–9.
11. Hodder notes the sexual imagery present in this sentence (*Emerson's Rhetoric*, 28).
12. Hodder, 28.
13. Hodder, 28.
14. Hodder, 28; 30.
15. Abrams, *Natural Supernaturalism*, 41–6.
16. Abrams, 1–42.
17. Packer brilliantly discusses the importance of the 'axis of vision' in Emerson's oeuvre (*Emerson's Fall*, 73–8).
18. Edward P.J. Corbett, *Classical Rhetoric for the Modern Student*, 3rd edn (New York: Oxford University Press, 1990), 435.
19. Bloom, *Agon: Towards a Theory of Revisionism* (New York: Oxford University Press, 1982), 157. This extraordinary passage, hailed by Jonathan Bishop as the microcosm of 'everything Emerson publicly said thereafter' (*Emerson on the Soul* [Cambridge, Mass.: Harvard University Press, 1964], 15), has drawn diverse comment. While the passage was caricatured by Emerson's Transcendentalist friend Christopher Pearse Cranch (see Sealts and Ferguson, eds, *Emerson's Nature: Origin, Growth, Meaning* [New York and Toronto: Dodd, Mead, 1969], 9) and while parts of it were disparaged by one of his most celebratory critics, Bishop himself, as 'innocently absurd at best' (*Emerson on the Soul*, 15), Bloom calls it 'extraordinary', an instance of the sublime (*Agon*, 158) and Poirier deems it an 'evidence of Emerson's metaphoric power exerting itself to authenticate an incredible moment of self-transformation' (*World Elsewhere*, 66).
20. Burroughs, *Of Birds and Poets, with Other Papers* (Boston: Houghton, Mifflin, 1895), 192.
21. For Bloom, the passage is a a crossing to the primal abyss, an example of 'the mode of negation through which the knower again could stand in the Abyss, the place of original fullness, before the Creation' (*Agon*, 158). The image of the transparent eye-ball emblematizes, Bloom argues, Emerson's attempt to avoid influence by returning to the primal waters, the void of Genesis, before God created the earth.
22. Packer, *Emerson's Fall*, 72; Burke, 'I, Eye, Ay – Emerson's Early Essay "Nature": Thoughts on the Machinery of Transcendence', *Emerson's Nature: Origin, Growth, Meaning*, eds Merton M. Sealts, Jr and Alfred R. Ferguson (New York and Toronto: Dodd, Mead, 1969), 157–8.
23. *The New Princeton Encyclopedia of Poetry and Poetics*, eds Alex Preminger and T.V.F. Brogan (Princeton, NJ: Princeton University Press, 1993).
24. As Philip Kuberski suggests in his study of Joyce, puns are sometimes instances of chiasmus in that they are sites where opposing meanings 'cross' (*Chaosmos: Literature, Science, and Theory* [Albany: State University of New York Press, 1994], 71–2).
25. For a discussion of the parallel between eating and prophecy in Emerson, see Porte, *Representative Man*, 94, and Ralph C. LaRosa, 'Invention and Imitation in Emerson's Early Lectures', *American Literature*, 44:1 (1972): 29.

26. Abrams, *Natural Supernaturalism*, 42–3.
27. Bloom has indeed termed this passage a 'triumph of the Negative Way', as the Visionary empties himself of selfhood to become one with the primal abyss (*Agon*, 159).
28. Fletcher, 'Positive Negation: Threshold, Sequence, and Personification in Coleridge', *New Perspectives on Coleridge and Wordsworth: Selected Papers from the English Institute*, ed. Geoffrey Hartman (New York: Columbia University Press, 1972), 135.
29. Burke, 'I, Eye, Ay'.
30. Corbett, *Classical Rhetoric*, 433.
31. Longinus, *Longinus on the Sublime*, trans. W. Rhys Roberts (Cambridge: Cambridge University Press, 1907), 101.

CHAPTER 6: SCIENTIFIC MEDITATION

1. Sigmund Freud, 'The Uncanny', *Standard Edition*, vol. 18 (London: Hogarth, 1959), 226. Stanley Cavell's designation of Emerson's thinking and writing as 'abandonment' provides a clue for considering the uncanny in Emerson. In *In Quest of the Ordinary: Lines of Skepticism and Romanticism* (Chicago: University of Chicago Press, 1988), he describes Emerson's onward thinking and writing as an 'abandonment of and to language and the world', which is a way of thinking about skepticism and of keeping philosophy fresh, alive, in conversation with itself (175). In simultaneously leaving and relinquishing himself to the ordinary – the everyday – Emerson makes it the locus for his thinking, for his acceptance and rejection of skepticism. Cavell makes these remarks in an essay called 'The Ordinariness of the Uncanny', in which he primarily draws on Freud's use of the uncanny to analyze ordinary language philosophy. While the focus of this essay is not Emerson and while it finds Heidegger's use of the uncanny unsuitable for glossing ordinary language, its placement of Emerson, Heidegger, and the uncanny in close proximity is apt, as a close look at Heidegger's development of the *unheimlich*, the uncanny, in *Being and Time* reveals that it illuminates Emerson's abandonment.
2. Martin Heidegger, *Being and Time*, trans. John Macquerie and Edward Robinson (New York: Harper & Row, 1962), 189.
3. Harold Bloom, *Agon: Towards a Theory of Revisionism* (New York: Oxford University Press, 1982), 102.
4. Fletcher, *Allegory: The Theory of a Symbolic Mode* (Ithaca, NY and London: Cornell University Press, 1964), 241n.
5. *The New Princeton Encyclopedia of Poetry and Poetics*, eds. Alex Preminger and T.V.F. Brogan (Princeton, NJ: Princeton University Press, 1993).
6. Richard Poirier, *Renewal of Literature: Emersonian Reflections* (New Haven, Conn. and London: Yale University Press, 1987), 130; 131.
7. Poirier, *Renewal of Literature*, 131; 131.

8. Stanley Cavell, *The Senses of Walden*, expanded edn (Chicago: University of Chicago Press, 1981), 138.
9. B.L. Packer, *Emerson's Fall: A New Interpretation of the Major Essays* (New York: Continuum, 1982), 27.
10. Alan Hodder, *Emerson's Rhetoric of Revelation: Nature, the Readers, and the Apocalypse Within* (University Park, Pa. and London: Pennsylvania State University Press, 1989), 109–21.
11. Burke, 'I, Eye, Ay – Emerson's Early Essay "Nature": Thoughts on the Machinery of Transcendence', *Emerson's Nature: Origin, Growth, Meaning*, eds Merton M. Sealts, Jr and Alfred R. Ferguson (New York and Toronto: Dodd, Mead, 1969), 150.
12. Bloom, *Kabbalah and Criticism* (New York: Seabury Press, 1975), 120.
13. Cavell, *Senses of Walden*, 130.
14. Richard Rorty, *Philosophy and the Mirror of Nature* (Princeton, NJ: Princeton University Press, 1979), 12; 360.
15. Cavell, *Senses of Walden*, 134.
16. Rorty, *Philosophy and the Mirror*, 378.
17. Friedrich Nietzsche, *Ecce Homo, Basic Writings of Nietzsche*, trans. and ed. Walter Kaufmann (New York: Modern Library, 1968), 749. For recent, important work on Emerson and Nietzsche, see Michael Lopez, *Emerson and Power: Creative Antagonism in the Nineteenth Century* (Dekalb: Northern Illinois University Press, 1996); George Kateb, *Emerson and Self-Reliance* (Thousand Oaks, London and New Delhi: Sage, 1995); Irena S.M. Makarushka, *Religious Imagination and Language in Emerson and Nietzsche* (New York: St. Martin's Press, 1994); and George J. Stack, *Nietzsche and Emerson: An Elective Affinity* (Athens: Ohio University Press, 1992).
18. Nietzsche, *The Gay Science, The Portable Nietzsche*, trans. and ed. Walter Kaufmann (New York: Penguin, 1982), 97, 93.
19. Nietzsche, *Ecce Homo*, 755, 755, 714.
20. James S. Hans, *The Play of the World* (Amherst: University of Massachusetts Press, 1981), 7–9.
21. Nietzsche, *Ecce Homo*, 761, 762.

CONCLUSION: INNOCENCE AND EXPERIENCE

1. Wordsworth, 'Ode: Intimations of Immortality from Recollections of Early Childhood', *The Poetical Works of William Wordsworth*, 5 vols, eds Ernest de Selincourt and Helen Darbishire (Oxford: Clarendon, 1940–9), 56–7; 180–1.
2. Coleridge, 'Dejection: An Ode', *The Complete Poetical Works of Samuel Taylor Coleridge*, 2 vols, ed. Ernest Hartley Coleridge (Oxford: Clarendon, 1912), 47–8.

Index